D1277442

STUDIES ON SUCCESSFUL MIDLIFE DEVELOPMENT
*The John D. and Catherine T. MacArthur Foundation Series
on Mental Health and Development*

Other titles in the series
SEXUALITY ACROSS THE LIFE COURSE
Edited by Alice S. Rossi

THE PARENTAL EXPERIENCE IN MIDLIFE
Edited by Carol D. Ryff and Marsha Mailick Seltzer

MULTIPLE PATHS OF MIDLIFE DEVELOPMENT
Edited by Margie E. Lachman and Jacquelyn Boone James

WELCOME TO MIDDLE AGE!
(And Other Cultural Fictions)

Edited by

Richard A. Shweder

The University of Chicago Press
Chicago and London

Richard A. Shweder is professor and chairman of the Committee on Human Development at the University of Chicago. He is the author of *Thinking through Cultures: Expeditions in Cultural Psychology* and the editor of several books.

The University of Chicago Press, Chicago 60637
The University of Chicago Press, Ltd., London

© 1998 by The University of Chicago
All rights reserved. Published 1998
Printed in the United States of America

07 06 05 04 03 02 01 00 99 98   1 2 3 4 5
ISBN: 0-226-75607-6 (cloth)
ISBN: 0-226-75608-4 (paper)

The University of Chicago Press gratefully acknowledges a subvention from the John D. and Catherine T. MacArthur Foundation in partial support of the costs of production of this volume.

Library of Congress Cataloging-in-Publication Data

Welcome to middle age! : (And other cultural fictions) / edited by
Richard A. Shweder.
    p. cm. — (The John D. and Catherine T. MacArthur Foundation
series on mental health and development. Studies on successful
midlife development)
    Includes bibliographical references and index.
    ISBN 0-226-75607-6 (cloth : alk. paper). — ISBN 0-226-75608-4
(pbk. : alk. paper)
    1. Middle age—Cross-cultural studies. I. Shweder, Richard A.
II. Series.
HQ1059.4.W45   1998
305.244—dc21   97-45115
                                           CIP

CONTENTS

Welcome to Middle Age! (And Other Cultural Fictions) is a book about diversity in cultural representations of the life course. The eight essays in the collection give special attention to those years—roughly ages 30–70—represented as "middle age" or "midlife" in the cultural discourse of contemporary middle-class European-Americans. Although the current European-American representation of mature adulthood as midlife or middle age is not the only way to lend meaning and significance to the stages of life, the idea of middle age as conceived, manufactured, and advertised in the "Western world" is rapidly diffusing around the globe and has begun to take hold of the imaginations of cosmopolitan elites in Tokyo, New Delhi, and other capitals of the "non-Western world." The aim of the essays in this book is to examine the emergence and diffusion of a cosmopolitan midlife discourse and to describe some of the alternative ways in which members of different cultural traditions have categorized, organized, institutionalized, and found meaning in the temporal dimension (or "span") of a life. The essays examine representations of the life course in alternative cultural contexts, in Japan, India, Samoa, Kenya, and among African-Americans in the United States, where it seems fair to say that midlife or middle age literally does not exist and where the experience of mature adulthood is imagined, produced, and understood in somewhat different terms.

The contributors to this volume are anthropologists, psychologists, psychiatrists, and historians. All are contributors to the field of cultural studies and have examined representations of the life course in one or more cultural regions of the world (Japan, India, Polynesia, East Africa) or among diverse populations in the United States (African-Americans in Harlem, urban middle-class European-Americans, white members of 1960s countercultural groups in California).

Until recently the study of representations of the life course, especially the study of adult life stages, has not been center stage in cultural studies or in the social sciences more broadly. Over the last ten years however adult development studies have burgeoned in the social sciences and there has been a rapidly growing interest in the cultural construction of mature adulthood. *Welcome to Middle Age! (And Other Cultural Fictions)* is the publication of a series of pioneering papers designed to promote innovative research in this emerging field.

Welcome to Middle Age! owes it existence to many people. Not only did the very idea of the project emerge from the brow of Orville Gilbert (Bert) Brim, but the production of the book would not have been possible without the colleagueship and the generous support of the Mac-Arthur Foundation Research Network on Successful Midlife Development (MIDMAC), of which Bert Brim is the chair and I am a member. Thank you, Bert, not only for your leadership, sustenance, and intellectual taste, but also for giving us all such a very good time.

A meeting of the authors collected here, arranged to overlap with the biannual meeting of the Society for Psychological Anthropology, was held 4–5 October 1995 in San Juan, Puerto Rico, to critique chapter drafts, provide a substantive basis for final chapter revisions, and to discuss the organization and main messages of the book. The meeting turned out to be the best of seminars. It was an exhilarating intellectual experience for everyone concerned. Those in attendance left convinced that the field of cultural studies of individual development is ready to burst forth on the academic scene.

The completion of *Welcome to Middle Age! (And Other Cultural Fictions)* was greatly facilitated by the Center for Advanced Study in the Behavioral Sciences (CASBS) in Stanford, California, where, in a bucolic setting on a "magic mountain" conducive to interdisciplinary conversation and basic research, I was privileged to be a fellow and cochair (with Hazel Markus and Paul Rozin) of a special project entitled "Culture, Mind and Biology" during the 1995–96 academic year, with generous support from the Health Program of the John D. and Catherine T. MacArthur Foundation. Special thanks to Bob Rose, Idy Gitelson, Neil Smelser and Bob Scott for making it all happen. I am also greatly in the debt of Katia Mitova, my talented polymath research assistant, who provided much help with both the organization of the author's conference and the production of this manuscript at every stage of their development.

Richard A. Shweder

Welcome to Middle Age!

Richard A. Shweder

GENERAL THEMES

"Welcome to middle age!" I was thirty-three years old at the time, and I had just injured my lower back on a squash court. "Welcome to middle age!" my squash partner remarked as he observed me unable to stand up straight. It was the very first time I had been invited to think of myself as middle aged and I did not welcome the comment. I did not believe I was middle aged. I did not want to be middle aged. Two decades later I still vividly remember that seemingly casual yet culturally significant remark: "Welcome to middle age!"

That night, still hobbled, I attended the fortieth birthday party of a University of Chicago political theorist and close friend. My friend had a certain peculiarity. For several years proceeding his fortieth birthday party he had exhibited an exaggerated love, indeed an obsession of sorts, for the writings of Ludwig Wittgenstein, and he had cultivated a conversational style by means of which he managed to find Wittgensteinian implications in anything (and I mean anything) anyone said. That night, during his postprandial remarks, he delighted his friends by confessing that as he approached and contemplated the age of forty he had experienced a major "midlife crisis," which he resolved by having a passionate affair with the fabled Austrian philosopher.

I learned something else at the party. Most of the (circa) forty-year-old men I spoke with that evening had already been "welcomed" to middle age, often by lower-back pains or some other early warning sign of physical decline. As I told them about my life-stage transition on the squash court that afternoon they shared with me their remedies for countering, or at least slowing, the drift into middle age. Welcoming each other to middle age, denying it, coping with it, grumbling about it but acknowledging it all the same are real and familiar events and experiences in some cultural worlds. Yet those events and experiences are fabricated as well, and they do not exist in every cultural world.

My experiences of that day twenty years ago, when I was welcomed into middle age, were personally significant. Yet they were also culturally patterned. Indeed, a central theme of *Welcome to Middle Age! (And Other Cultural Fictions)* is that there exists a dominant representation of mature adulthood as "middle age" or "midlife" that characterizes life-span discourse and practice in the middle-class European-American cultural region. This European-American construction of mature adulthood (as "middle age" or "midlife") renders the meanings of mature adulthood primarily in chronological, biological, and medical terms. It emphasizes the marking of birthdays, including the ritualized celebration of decade transitions at ages 30, 40, and 50. It places a stress on issues of physical and mental decline. Until recently the European-American way of thinking about mature adulthood as midlife or middle age, a powerful cultural "fiction" in its own right, has been the exception rather than the rule on a worldwide scale. These days, however, along with Cable News Network, Coca-Cola, and Visa credit cards comes the European-American idea of middle age, which is being rapidly exported to all territories in the contemporary world system. Thus people around the world are increasingly being invited to change the way they think about mature adulthood and to adopt the European-American idea of "middle age."

Welcome to Middle Age! then is about both the European-American cultural fiction known as middle age and the alternative fictions that lend a sense of reality to life course positions in other cultural worlds where mature adulthood is produced and manufactured in different ways, without the ritual celebration of a fortieth birthday party, without a life-stage transition ("Welcome to middle age!") defined in terms of biological or medical criteria (back pains, estrogen decline, hair loss, waning sexual desire), and without the ready use of the idea of a "midlife crisis" to lend meaning to the motives of mature adults.

CULTURAL "FICTIONS"

Given the reality of cultural things, I wish to emphasize that the word "fiction" in the title of the book is used in an affirmative postmodern sense and is definitely not meant to suggest "unreal." Things that are fictions are fabricated, manufactured, invented, or designed but they are not necessarily false. This is especially true of cultural things such as "the Christmas season," a "home run in baseball," the people who count as "uncles" or as "kin" or as "members of the family," and that stage of life between birth and death constructed as "midlife" or "middle age" in the middle-class European-American cultural world. Middle age or the Christmas season are real and palpably manifest in some local cultural worlds, yet they are fictions in the sense that their reality or palpable existence is dependent on the way the human imagination has chosen to inhabit and build a way of life around some optional or selective point of view. The word "fiction," as in *Welcome to Middle Age! (And Other Cultural Fictions)*, is simply meant to suggest the presence of something imaginative that goes beyond logic per se and implicates some form of partiality or discretion, some "native point of view" (see Clifford Geertz's *The Interpretation of Cultures* [Basic Books: New York, 1973]).

Not everything real is something from no point of view, and this is especially true of the cultural "fiction" known as "middle age" or "midlife." There are alternative ways of representing the temporal dimension of life without relying on the idea of middle age. For example, in some cultural worlds described in this book, the stages of life (including mature adulthood) are represented in terms of a social history of role transitions within the context of a residential kinship group. Within such cultural worlds there is no manifestation of a point of view that emphasizes a chronology of years or the biology of aging. Within such cultural worlds one reckons and manages one's life not by reference to age per se (e.g., there may be no annual public recognition of the day of birth of mature adults) and not by reference to biological aging (back pains, menopause) per se, but rather by reference to family position and associated social responsibilities. Within such cultural worlds, changes in behavior are marked and regulated by transitions in family status, including transitions in the status of one's children.

For example, in extended joint family households in some parts of rural India a husband and wife stop having sexual relations when the firstborn son gets married and brings his wife home to the extended family compound. It is thought to be polluting and undignified for two generations to copulate under the same roof. It is a cultural thing. And within such a cultural world, chronological age and signs of biological decline are not, in themselves, relied upon as indices of life stage. Within such a cultural world, the discourse of mature adulthood is not a midlife discourse or a discourse about middle age. It is a discourse about social standing in the family and in the broader community and about the types of responsibilities and activities with which one is, or is not, engaged. Thus, while some essays in this collection describe the European-American cultural fiction known as midlife or middle age, other essays take us into other cultural worlds. They reveal the way the human imagination has been able to adopt one or more different points of view for producing and fashioning a mature adulthood without middle age. They reveal how the culturally imagined life stage of mature adulthood without middle age has become a fact of experience for members of particular communities, thereby implementing and making real an alternative cultural fiction, such as Oriya *prauda* or Samoan *tagata matua* or Japanese *ichininmae*.

Whatever we know about the life course we know through someone's representation of it. These representations of the life course come in many forms, official and unofficial, formal and informal. There are representations that appear in religious sermons, medical texts, government documents, or in works of art, cinema, or poetry. There are representations that appear in diaries, everyday discourse, or in response to interview questions posed by researchers with an interest in the topic. There are representations that function as moral ideals for a community and representations that function to describe the course of life as it is. There are representations articulated by insiders in a community and representations produced by outsiders to make sense of the unstated representations that are implicit in the way insiders actually live their lives. If it is true that cultural fictions are real things whose palpable existence is dependent upon the sharing of some special point of view, then it is to representations that we must look to understand the idea of midlife or middle age as a fact of experience in the middle-class European-American cultural world. It is to representations that we must look to understand the way that other cultural fictions, other representations of mature adulthood, become facts of experience in other cultural worlds. When we look at these representations what do we find?

THE CHAPTERS

Margaret Gullette's essay (chap. 1) is an overview of what she calls the "ideology of midlife decline" that is so characteristic of middle-class European-American representations of the life course. She argues that "belief in midlife decline is a pandemic peculiar to our era, a set of effects with a discernible twentieth-century history and extremely vigorous and insidious maintenance strategies. The disease of life course nostalgia began to be widely cultivated in England and America at the end of the nineteenth and the beginning of the twentieth centuries, the period in which the new terms—middle age, middle life—began to gain currency. 'Middle age' was invented in this period: the age class, the master narrative of decline, the practices of 'prolonging' youth, the cult of youth, the canonical novels that continue to be read in our educational system and discussed as masterpieces."

Margaret Gullette's chapter is written from a "critical age theory stance" (the essay itself is an act of resistance to the dominant and pervasive European-American dread of midlife aging), and it represents and advances a strong version of social constructivist theory (Gullette argues that "nothing bodily is natural in the sense of being unaffected by culture"). The essay is an especially useful way to begin the book. Gullette spells out many of the features of the European-American idea of middle age that are presupposed by or alluded to in other chapters in this book. Her discussion ought to raise the following types of questions in the mind of any reader who is interested in points of overlap and tension between the perspectives of the various contributors to the book: How natural or inevitable is the narrative of midlife decline? How far can a social constructivist position be pushed? Does feminism provide the best or only discourse for empowering women during mature adulthood? What is the relationship between science and ideology (and cultural fictions) in our picture of life course development and aging? What is the proper place for cultural critique and the stance of justification in anthropology and cultural studies?

In chapter 2, Margaret Lock attends to the contrast between conceptions of mature adulthood in Japan and North America, with special attention to differences in the meanings of reproduction and menopause for Japanese and European-American women. Drawing on the work of Philippe Aries, Norbert Elias, and Michel Foucault, she points out that "an individual's family status rather than chronological age was what determined public recognition of maturity in premodern Europe. In contrast, throughout this century, chronological age, above all else, has come to determine maturation and, at the same time, the life course has been subject to increasing surveillance and control by the state, to which academic research into development and aging have contributed."

On top of this contrast Lock adds another: in Japan "precedence has been given . . . to aging as a social process rather than to transformations in individual biology." Lock reviews a variety of historical and contemporary Japanese representations of the life course (ideas about physical and mental decline, e.g., can be found in some classical seventeenth-century Japanese literary texts). Nevertheless her focus is on the predominance in Japan of a conception of life course development as "advancement through the social hierarchy, accompanied by personal maturation and increasing responsibility," including service in the family, rather than as biological decay and physical dysfunction. She makes use of this distinction to explain why menopause has been relatively devoid of significance for Japanese women (no name for it, no discourse about aging ovaries or declining estrogen or hot flashes) and had not been viewed as a medical issue until recently, as the influence of imported European-American ideas and ideals has taken hold.

In chapter 3, Sudhir Kakar searches for the European-American idea of middle age in India, where he is able to find it only among the Westernized urban elite. He reviews various representations of the life course in ancient Hindu texts and in contemporary popular culture (fiction, film, and poetry). In 1980, 75% of 45–59-year-old Indian adults lived with someone in addition to their spouse, and extended joint family living continues to be the cultural ideal on the Indian subcontinent. One of the great virtues of Kakar's chapter is that it draws our attention to the role of younger generations in defining the life course status of mature adults (e.g., the birth of the son of one's son is a defining moment for many Hindu adults). A second great virtue of the chapter is that it draws our attention to certain culture-specific crises of mature adulthood (e.g., the conflict between renunciation and worldly involvement) that may be far more salient in South Asia than in North America and Western Europe.

In chapter 4, Bradd Shore argues that, in the Samoa of the 1970s (the period during which he first collected data on aging and the life course) there was no explicit cultural category of middle age, no cultural sense of lost youth and declining vitality, no obsessive concern with death and mortality, and a strong tendency to dissociate life stage from chronological age per se. He argues that chronological age (and such associated notions as youth culture, midlife crisis, and generation gap) are not the only ways to think about mature adulthood, although a chronological conception of the life course seems to be making inroads among modernizing Samoans in the contemporary population. Shore characterizes the mature Samoan adult as politically powerful and physically active, as involved and influential in family life and civic affairs, as displaying self-control and responsible judgment, and as the embodiment of both active and passive authority. There is no sense of decline, slippage, or decay associated with this life stage, for in Samoan culture mature adulthood is appreciated as a privileged status.

In chapter 5, Usha Menon and I characterize the life course images and domestic life of Hindu women living in extended joint family households in Orissa, India. In the first part of the essay we describe the five ideal stages of a women's life. Oriya women do not conceive of a middle phase of life (middle age) defined either by chronological age (e.g., 30–70) or by markers of biological aging (e.g., poorer eyesight, loss of muscle strength). Their ideal life course scheme does, however, include a phase called "mature adulthood" (*prauda*), which begins whenever a married women takes over the management of the extended household and ends whenever she relinquishes control and social responsibilities to others. The underlying logic of Oriya women's life stage understandings is based on ideas and ideals of social responsibility, family management, and moral duty. Whatever sense of decline is expressed in Oriya women's conception of the life course is reserved for the phase of life after household responsibilities have been passed on to the next generation. In subsequent parts of the essay we raise doubts about recent feminist representations of the domestic life and moral world of Hindu women and trace some connections between Oriya family life statuses over the life course and an Oriya woman's achievement of personal well-being or happiness. We argue that, in rural India, unlike North America, the domestic realm is a privileged realm and that the North American opposition of work and family is of limited usefulness for understanding the meanings of Hindu family life.

In chapter 6, Robert LeVine and Sarah LeVine bring us into the world of the Gusii people of Western Kenya, a world in which the reproduction and bearing of many children and the perpetuation of a patrilineal kinship line is the high ideal of adulthood and where polygamy is an option for older men (mention is made of one man who has six wives and fifty children). As seems to be true of so many of the peoples studied by anthropologists and historians (some of whom are described in this collection), the Gusii do not partition the life course by chronological age. For the Gusii, decline and obsolescence are not the meanings associated with the increased sense of "seniority" that a Gusii man or woman develops over time. Seniority is associated instead with respect, obedience, prestige, and social esteem.

Of course the Gusii do have culturally fashioned and acknowledged life stages. Circumcision defines a life stage for both males and females, and circumcised youths are considered more mature than uncircumcised youths of the same chronological age. Among the Gusii, a woman may well give birth every two years between the ages of 16 and 40. And the end of a woman's reproductive career (which is not necessarily coincidental with menopause) defines a stage within adulthood. Becoming a patriarch or matriarch is what life is all about, and thus the marriage of one's child marks a change in life stage status. In general, among the Gusii, it is good to get older. While recounting the reproductive ideals of Gusii adults LeVine and LeVine take brief note of the winds of change and wonder whether in our contemporary world system representations of mature adulthood less focused on fertility will eventually dominate and supersede the more traditional Gusii worldview.

In chapter 7, we return with Thomas Weisner and Lucinda Bernheimer to the European-American culture world, albeit with attention to a rather special population. Since 1974 the Family Life Styles Project at the University of California, Los Angeles, has been conducting longitudinal research on the practices, developmental trajectories, socialization patterns, and values of two hundred white, European-American families in California who had once displayed a high level of commitment to the countercultural movement of the 1960s.

Perhaps more than any other chapter in the book, Weisner and Bernheimer direct our theoretical attention to the way the transitions and meanings of mature adulthood are linked to transitions in the sexuality, schooling, and family formation of one's adolescent children. While acknowledging cultural variation in life course representations and practices, Weisner and Bernheimer argue that the European-American term "midlife" encodes at least one feature of mature adulthood that is likely to be universal: "Midlife is a relational stage of life experienced through one's children as well as a cultural life stage and personal transition. At midlife, parents try to assist and resist their teen's generational change. . . . Midlife and the teenage transitions that go with it are jointly predictable perturbations in the development of the parent-child unit across the life course. . . . Midlife is not a sharply marked life stage; it has very wide malleability in timing and salience in cultures around the world. We suggest that midlife actually is marked by its being yoked with the adolescent developmental transition."

It is fascinating that the feature of midlife that Weisner and Bernheimer single out as universal seems very close to the Japanese, Oriya, Samoan, and Gusii representations of mature adulthood in terms of social criteria (rather than biological or chronological criteria). This may well be an example where seeing the world through the eyes of other cultures may lead us to recognize a universal process, one that Weisner and Bernheimer have formulated as a theory.

In chapter 8, Katherine Newman argues that the meaning of mature adulthood in American society is not the same across social class and ethnicity. She argues that the middle-class European-American representation of mature adulthood as "midlife" or "middle age" is a missing category and is not part of the "life cycle landscape" for poor African-Americans living in inner-city New York. Newman recounts the historical, generational, and personal experiences of her African-American informants in the Jim Crow South, in the Harlem of the 1940s and 1950s (before "the fall"), and after the fall as well. Newman reminds us that any person's representations of his or her life course is a complex mix of generational meanings, broader cultural meanings, and historically situated personal experiences. She concludes that "place (a combination of period and locale) and race matter a great deal in shaping images and experiences of middle age."

Taken together the essays in this collection are bound to highlight certain common themes. For example, note the contrast between biological (or medical) views versus social relationships as the privileged basis for cultural discourse about the life course. Another example is the role of the younger generation (including the sexual and reproductive behavior of one's children) in defining life course status transitions for mature adults.

The essays in this book are bound to draw the careful reader into certain current controversies in the social sciences. These include, for example, the argument between strong and moderate versions of social constructivism; the debates over the cogency of the idea that not everything that is real exists independent of point of view; the dispute between feminist and cultural pluralist approaches to the issue of female empowerment; and the tension between colonizing and anticolonial conceptions of the life course.

So welcome to middle age! And welcome, as well, to various alternative ideas and images about what it means to be a mature adult.

I THE RISE OF A COSMOPOLITAN
MIDLIFE DISCOURSE

Midlife Discourses in the Twentieth-Century United States: An Essay on the Sexuality, Ideology, and Politics of "Middle-Ageism"

Margaret Morganroth Gullette

> A structure of feeling as deep as this enacts a world, as well as interpreting it, so that we learn it from experience as well as from ideology.
>
> (Raymond Williams)

THE MIDLIFE AGE CLASS AND THE MIDLIFE MUDDLE

Looking over the vast explosion of midlife discourse, both popular and scholarly, that has become such a feature of seventies', eighties', and nineties' common sense in the United States, a cultural inquirer cannot help but observe that the boom has created as well as targeted an audience for the messages.[1] At first glance, it is a group that the mainstream press now regularly labels the "aging baby boomers," referring to persons born in the decades between 1946 and 1964. But in fact the audience now also includes people over fifty and even under thirty who are overhearing the same discourses. There is a vast *age class* being constructed to pay attention to midlife discourse,[2] which is available at practically any level of literacy or of verbal or visual impressionability.

An age class is a culturally constructed unit whose unity is proposed or posited as, precisely, not depending upon any category other than "age." It is different from a cohort or generation as previously known (cf. the Lost Generation or the Depression babies). What the members of the new midlife age class are said to have in common is certainly not a fixed birth date, nor is it a single crucial event in the past. It is a group's supposedly common motion through the life course, called "aging." Insofar as people identify with the construction, the overriding fact of their entire age identity becomes their current—moving—location in an otherwise abstract and universalized life course. Discourse about an age class takes for granted, as well as often explicitly asserting, a commonality that is supposed to override gender, class, race, sexual orientation, national origin, personal psychology, politics, and so on.[3] This notion of an age class, however incoherent and implausible, is reinforced by every discourse addressed to the members of the class (whether describing characteristics supposed to be universal or distinguishing among subgroups in the class).

Since the seventies, the midlife has become an industry within the American publishing industry. Even scholarly "midlife studies"—including my own contribution, which begins by deconstructing the idea of the age class—slightly supports the idea by implication: every reference to "the midlife" or "middle age" supports an effect of "reality." We reify even as we disrupt. To disrupt naive midlife discursiveness, a critic needs first to underline the age class as an effect of the discourses, perhaps its most obvious and therefore unnoticed effect.

Once the age class exists within the orderly sequence of all the other named age classes, it becomes preposterous for anyone in this audience to deny that she or he belongs in it or will move into it eventually (after a certain age, which each person is supposed to decide on, presumably after much agonizing). Consequences flow from simply accepting the category as natural and real. The audience is of course targeted to buy products sooner or later (the title of one pamphlet is *Midlife and Beyond: The 800 Billion Over-Fifty Market* [CRC 1985]).[4] But the niche market is also being persuaded to buy an ideology of the life course similar to those that operate on gender and race, the other body-based systems of ascription that claim to be based on "the natural."[5] In the cultural system that North Americans are exposed to, age ideology focuses on providing meanings about an already-existing phenomenon of the life course: aging-into-the-middle-years-of-life, or midlife aging. It represents midlife aging primarily as a decline and throughout the century has been teaching Americans to "experience" decline at midlife. In what follows, I single out more of the powerful mechanisms that convey and reproduce the ideology of midlife decline, which I call *middle-ageism*.[6]

I am pursuing a radical social constructionist principle, that even here, with age, which I consider the most unabashed of all the allegedly body-based categories, we should look first and hardest for the constructions produced by discourses, institutions, and practices—for the ways in which human subjects are aged by culture.[7] This approach—I call it "critical age studies"—starts with the assumption that little in midlife aging is bodily and that nothing considered "bodily" is unaffected by culture.[8] Taking this strong social constructionist approach alerts us to view age at *any* point in the life course as another arena of power and difference, hierarchy and resistance, interlocking systems and discourses that possess histories and current strategies; it permits us to apply the resources of history and theory to the underanalyzed category of age.[9] In this essay I treat "the midlife" in the United States as just such a case. By highlighting crucial aspects of cultural construction as well as focusing on some of the forces that resist midlife decline ideology, I present a picture of midlife aging as a construct in contest, not inexorably fixed, but subject to demystification and—with great effort—transformation. (Eliminating the category of "middle life," however, is probably no longer possible.) I argue that age analysis when performed on U.S. culture should be critical; that it would fail at every level if it were not critical, and that a critical age studies should be useful theoretically, personally, and politically. Since so many cultural phenomena originating in the United States are wholesaled abroad, critical age studies should also be useful cross-culturally.

***

Propelled into further generalization by the existence of this universalized age class, I was at first puzzled by my impression that the dominant "message" the group is receiving about aging-into-the-middle was so muddled. On the one hand, there is a barrage of discourses produced by writers who seem to be merely, and often unwarily, "reporting" on people—often themselves—who experience aging into the middle years as an unavoidable decline, like a curse. On the other, there are assertions about or by (presumably) other people who are seeking and experiencing midlife "growth" or "change," assertions produced by writers and insitutions whose apparent ideological intention is to do us all good. A 1990 survey by the American Board of Family Practice, for example, told us that most Americans believe they are getting better with age—more compassionate, better able to cope with problems, more sensitive to others. An article in the *Atlantic Monthly* underlined midlife adaptability, competence, pleasures, wisdom (Gallagher 1993). The new name writers currently use, the "midlife" rather than "middle age," also expresses a politics of optimism and recuperation.[10] "I feel fine" can translate into "There's no crisis," or even "There's no problem."

Nevertheless, we also hear—much more frequently and intensely and in unmarked ways—that the dread of aging is widespread and that somewhere in the midlife is the allegedly logical and unavoidable time to stumble into it. "There seems to be a remarkable consensus of opinion among researchers and adult development theorists that entrance into middle age is frequently stormy and stressful" (Sherman 1987,

16).[11] Experts might differ about this "consensus." But as I see it, an invisible cultural combat is being waged around these issues. It is presented uncritically as a dispute about "experience." There are two versions of what people supposedly cannot help but feel or believe about the long middle of the road of life.

In a numbers game about "what people believe," a cultural critic shies off. But if it is a question of the tactics and narrative structures and relative dominance of the conflicting "messages" that are sent, I can hazard a few observations. Look at the nineties boom in menopause discourse, the prostate scare, the heart-disease news for women, the reemergence of the word "testosterone" in contexts of male sexual decline, the explosion of allusions to midlife memory loss, over and above the anecdotes and narratives (in the popular press, best-sellers, films, sitcoms, cartoons) so influential in constructing the ages of life. I see the midlife medicalized and made into a set of problems and always reified as a time of life. (Words such as "crisis" and "stage" are no longer trendy, but the concepts they fixed endure.) Underlying the discourse is the downsizing of people in their middle years, even in the professional and managerial classes, even white males (see Gullette 1995b, 1997).

Aging-into-the-middle is represented as a set of "natural" emotional responses to "facts" presented as inevitable: dour sensations, glances averted from mirrors (much mirror imagery), epiphanies of horrified discovery of one's "entrance" in the age class, expressions of nostalgic pangs (evoked by "oldies but goodies" and other well-rehearsed cues), and so on. Epiphanies, anecdotes, scenes of dread are ubiquitous in print and visual culture—parts of a whole that cumulatively reinforce the belief that decline is ahistorical, inevitable, prior to culture. In short, there's an ideology of "decline" raining over us.[12]

The age class is saturated not only with discrete decline messages but with a totalizing or master narrative to which they adhere. The members of the age class are represented to themselves as passive experiencers of decline and spontaneous tellers of the master narrative. No complete inventory of decline's discursive manipulations currently exists, but a summary of the tone and assumptions of the master narrative of midlife aging may serve to suggest the work that needs to be done (see also "From the Master Narrative of the Life Course: The Entry into Midlife Aging" [Gullette 1997, chap. 9]). The anecdotes selected for print circulation compete on criteria like intensity and self-degradation, which creates an ongoing escalation. Anecdotes bear witness to the emotional power of the "experience" described, thus reinforcing its reality. The references to bad news about midlife aging in newspapers and magazines and novels are often either casual whateverybody-knows or stern never-again-deny-this-truth. Much of decline comes to us unframed: its authors state no intention in regard to us and thus appear innocent of intention. Although their modes are literary and allied to fiction, they appear artless. Decline ideology remains invisible to both its authors and its readers. Taking "the truth about aging" as its domain, decline discourse relegates other assertions to the subordinate and defensive realm of counterdiscourse. Fragments of decline narrative appear "everywhere," as truth suppressed is supposed to do. The counterdiscourses accept that they are less well disseminated, that they evoke incredulity and must therefore laboriously label accepted truths as "myths" and provide statistical support for their "side." Moreover, counterdiscourses come not from everywhere, but from motley, local, and special sources: self-help feel-good guides, the women's movement, and certain restricted "fields" of academe (life course development, sociology, gerontology, midlife studies). Decline, more advantageously, appears to be spontaneous, "experiential," and full of emotion, irrepressible. (Think, e.g., of "the midlife crisis.") The counterdiscourse, insofar as it defines itself as academic, rarely relies on testimony or passionate conviction. It relies on authority. "There's no crisis," meanwhile, blunts critical awareness of middle-ageism and obscures the various struggles individuals may be undergoing to maintain the sense of self at midlife. All discourse that is not critical reifies the midlife—by using "midlife" without comment and by asserting that *its* truths about the middle years are truer—thus reinforcing decline's discursive necessities: that the midlife exist and can have truth said about it.

What are we to make of this confusing cultural war, after having duly noted that the midlife is a field of contestation in which the contestants appear to be grotesquely unequal, and that this war, unlike other cultural wars, goes on completely unacknowledged? In the first place, we should notice the extent to which the muddle in itself constitutes a "message." Before I offer further clarifications, it is important to understand that this message is a subliminal one and that the entire age class is exposed to it. Survey data and reports from the therapeutic community, anthropologists, and sociologists will probably confirm, as the work of Katherine Newman and Thomas Weisner in this collection suggests, that there are important differences in the ways in which subgroups and individuals receive and respond to midlife messages (and I will have more to say about resistance in the last section of the essay), and that these differences are produced by psychological disposition intersecting with cohort, gender, class, race/ethnicity, political formation, and the like. And there may be some people for whom life course optimism or pessimism is a solid and relatively unshakable given, so that they infallibly pick out only those elements of the available discourses that support their chosen worldview. Bracketing those folk, I consider the rest of us potentially vulnerable—in ways most of us probably cannot yet specify—to the subtle and invasive effects of middle-ageism. Whether late-twentieth-century Americans "deny" or "accept" their "being" in "the midlife" (a binary that needs to be theorized in all its parts), many probably fall willy-nilly into some of the emotional and cognitive oscillations generated by the muddle.

One effect of the muddle is to create an unhappy awareness of midlife decline, by producing cognitive confusion, a state of anxiously shifting assessment, elation, and misery in turn. What we know about the harmful internalizations of ageism—and racism and sexism—makes me hypothesize similar internalizations of middle-ageism. Critical age studies asks for more age consciousness to examine its mechanisms and effects.

I believe that for many people aging-into-the-middle has been made into an unavoidable topic of introspection (see "Vulnerability and Resistance" [Gullette 1997, chap. 1]).[13] We write our own scenes of age anxiety: personalized scripts in which we apply decline ideas to the self or deny that they are applicable. Or we go back and forth. Even oscillations of anxiety and reassurance may cut deep into the sources of self-worth. The scenes can take place in the absence of illness, in the presence of material well-being, in lives marked by achievement, in periods otherwise uneventful, in a century in which at forty many people have lived less than half their adult lives. Who could be exempt? is the implicit question decline ideology asks. Although each of us feels isolated when having such feelings and thoughts, midlife decline discourse with its convincing repetitiousness leads us to one conclusion: This "natural" midlife transition, or event, must be as inevitable as biological aging—indeed, indistinguishable from biological aging. This is the view that needs disruption.

Positivism explains midlife anxiety about decline on the grounds that as humans we *are* all "aging," that is, declining. But an age-wise cultural critique requires us to notice that "explanations" necessarily reify the construct being explained. Basically, decline is naturalized by the twin beliefs that the body "fails" at midlife and that this bodily failure matters more than anything else. Belief in "midlife crisis" naturalizes related effects: age grading, the cult of youth, a psychological and even a cognitive side to programmed decline.[14] Discussion about "how few" adults suffer a midlife crisis may try to fight the idea that decline is universal, but ignores, in naive social science fashion, cultural causes: diagnoses, mininarratives of etiology, canceled alternative interpretations, prescribed feelings. (Such causes, when not recognized, cannot be revealed through surveys or interviews.) Additionally, the smaller the percentage alleged to suffer from crisis, the more having a crisis becomes stigmatized.

Those who dislike crisis terminology spawned by stage theory or who refuse the narratives of crisis-and-fall or crisis-and-cure can explain midlife oscillations due to the muddle as "ambivalence," a philosophical necessity or sign of "wisdom" that allegedly knows no age grading. Ambivalence, although apparently a neutral or even-handed concept, is allied with a powerful literary/philosophical view that believes that optimism is torn out of us by life. This is a narrative of aging, and in it experience is always already only subtractive and dread can be embraced as a source of ennobling stoicism.[15]

Such modes of making meaning about aging may be useful to some people. But a radical social-constructionist position opts to argue that everything that underlies the construct "midlife decline" is learned. Not just beliefs, explanations, and narratives, but our very feelings themselves depend on culture.[16] Dread of midlife aging, confusion about what we feel about aging, acceptance of "decline," refusal of anger, are certainly learned. Beliefs are tied to feelings, and feelings come with beliefs attached. Human beings, by dint of living in discursive communities, learn both together: we lack a single term for this compound of emotional/cognitive learning, but the process has a name. Through *age socialization* we learn age categories and their attributes as well as the rule that we must apply them to the self ("my" gender assignment and "my" race are joined by "my" age class). Socialization-into-age-decline is a long process that begins quite early in the life course. I told my first decline story when I was eight. By the middle years we have been readied to believe that certain (bad) things are likely to happen to us and that these are correctly coded as aging. Meanwhile the positive aspects of maturity (competency, compassion, etc.) are not coded as age associated, so that they do not come into direct competition with the decline narrative when words like "aging" or "middle age," or codes like "forty," "fifty," and "menopause," are in play.

This is the first, discursive part of the true midlife crisis of our time: Americans exposed to dominant culture are positioned so that a self-defined "entrance" into "aging" (even as early as the midlife) involves listening to decline messages and perhaps beginning, whether rebelliously or obediently, to apply them to oneself.[17] As long as this culture can reproduce decline as the dominant plot of midlife narrative, without being openly and aggressively and consistently critiqued for doing so, midlife subjects will be positioned so that the best they feel they can do for themselves is to stave off the appearances said to mark decline. Under capitalism, this effort consists mainly of consumption activities. By mimicking youth at great expense, some middle- and upper-class subjects have tried to postpone this crisis—from forty to fifty or beyond.[18] This "success" has been treated by magazine writers as a miracle of cultural manipulation (and the subjects might call it, in some uncertain way, resistance). But it seems unlikely to change much in the internal state of the successful. Does their anxiety start later in life, decrease in degree, or end, as a result? What the better-off do ameliorates nothing in decline discourse; it only exacerbates economic distinctions within the age class.

Everyone "knows" that they will be aged by nature. But a social constructionist approach asks how much is likely to be left of this "knowledge" after a thoroughgoing examination of the learning that constructs the "aging" midlife body, brain, and psyche. As this critical work goes on, some will ask why we should let ourselves be aged by culture in harmful ways. Moving into the interrogative mode, a growing interdisciplinary coalition of forces could unite under the rubric of age studies. Working on its own many age cultures, past and present, armed with cross-cultural contrasts, tenaciously producing critical age theory, age studies in the United States could foreground the midlife to illustrate the concept "aged by culture." There are good historical reasons why "the middle years" was invented first in England and America and why other regions and cultures even in the so-called First World do not (yet) need the term.

Even while being sensitive to many current needs to adhere to decline narratives, age studies could promulgate a concept of resistance to decline ideology. In time, the concept of resistance to age ideology will itself be fully theorized, I hope. Age theorists put resistance into practice every time we disaggregate the midlife by gender, race, class, and so on; every time we apply to "age" the language of "learning" and "construction," every time we locate the intertextual sources of what is called "experience." We resist when we name the material conditions and institutions that produce other decline feelings that can be confused with aging—especially financial decline. We resist when we widen the gaps between the "message" that is sent and the agent who may reject it, every time we break the automatic equivalences between the body in itself and the array of representations assigned to it at various ages. Of course, those who ignore cultural constructions are also, but unwittingly, taking a stance toward midlife decline ideology: they are supporting it.

To understand age ideology in this culture, I think we need to focus on the normative "self" as a compulsory hearer of the cacophony of discourseland, reduced to passivity, reproducing and circulating compulsory age "knowledge." But in addition, we need to assert the self as potentially a conscious arbiter of cultural wars, a magisterial rejecter, meaning maker, namer of subjective reality even in the mystified arena of age identity.[19] For many, this acknowledgment and assertion would require a tremendous revision in thinking—about culture, the self, aging, and the relations between them. People influenced by age studies might want to begin a crucial personal project: an autobiographical practice, in which they disaggregate learned dread of aging as much as possible from whatever economic or affective or bodily changes, if any, they are experiencing.[20] Through age autobiography they would figure out what they personally have been taught to read and speak about as the signs of their own midlife "aging." And they would want to describe their own developing personal strategies for undoing this socialization. The development of age consciousness would change biography/ethnography too—by adding and refining questions that concern life course narrative, cultural cues and scripts for being aged by culture, and other decline forces.

These resistances, once articulated, could become collective strategies. The formation of a collective might not be easy, since so little attention is paid to theorizing age,[21] and since so numbly have people who interrogate everything else accepted midlife aging/dread of aging as natural. Not easy because middle-ageism is shored up by many systems and because there is no antiageist movement explicitly focusing on the midlife. In general, most Americans probably internalize age ideology at the end of the twentieth century far more unwittingly than race or gender or class ideology, because "age" has not been enough estranged by theory or magnified by political activism.

SOCIALIZATION INTO MIDLIFE AGING: EXPOSURE

In the United States in the twentieth-century, aging-as-midlife-decline has next to nothing to do with "old" people, except insofar as it implicitly defines them as those no longer in doubt about being in decline. Midlife decline accelerates the otherwise long span of adulthood, shoving "the end" forward in the life course. "Aging" has become a quintessentially *midlife* problem.[22]

If aging is no longer synonymous with old age, when does it actually begin, in the representations of the media and culture at large? Let us put birth aside as an unacceptable pseudoscientific or pseudophilosophical evasion of the role of culture. The contemporary answer seems to be, "Not long after puberty." In various ways, the still-very-young are bombarded with signals that getting biologically older is going to be a disaster. A physical fitness expert noted as early as 1973 that "the trouble begins at fourteen . . . the physiological threshold of middle age for many."[23] The fitness promoter got something right: adolescence has now come to be the *psychological* threshold of socialization into midlife aging. This is currently the age when the young (presumably, girls first) absorb the cult of youth for the first time, pick up the technologies of youthfulness, learn how to notice "aging" in others and be disgusted by it, and thus lay the groundwork for fearing decline and watching for it not much later on in their own life course.

Certain youngsters seem to be more sensitive to these signals; they get the earliest symptoms of dread. Flushed into the glare of publicity like a celebrity, a very young person may begin to feel physically obsolescent. Michael Jackson took the most extreme weight of the cult of youth and played out in public widespread fantasies of exemption from biological fate. Early on he obtained a magic glove to ward off the inevitable slide and endured surgeries that have made him look more like a frail adolescent than he did when he *was* an adolescent. For Humbert Humbert, Nabokov's apotheosizer of the prepubescent in *Lolita* (1955), fourteen (for girls) was over the hill. The allegedly pathological Humbert has since been joined in this opinion by thousands of anorexic and bulimic girls and now, boys, and by those in the culture who, over the decades, have made serial cults out of Baby Doll, Twiggy, Verushka, and Kate Moss. The anorexic female young act as if having

a mature female body at all attracted the unforgiving spotlight's glare—
as if having less of it would help; they have absorbed the idea that
menarche signals the end. But in a sense all possessors of young bodies
now live in that public glare, feeling as if the censorious *age gaze* were
upon them. By college age, more young women than young men are
unhappy with their body image, as we might expect. But a full one-
third of the men, like 60% of the women, are unhappy. Ten years later,
when they are over thirty, more men will be unhappy.[24]

The "double standard of aging" described by feminists in the 1970s
(see Sontag 1979) is eroding as the commerce in aging targets men
more intensively and everyone at increasingly younger ages. Men now
spend as much as women on items that, when women use them, are
called beauty products. The male products promise to soften a man's
skin and keep him from getting a "tired" look under the eyes—rhetoric
that comes very close to the age-graded blackmail aimed at women.
Men are the fastest growing group of victims for cosmetic surgery.
Quite young men are going in for the silicone implants or liposuc-
tion—"body-sculpting"—that many women are finally eschewing. A
recent newspaper advertisement shows a boy in his very early teens
wearing a shirt saying Life Is Short. Play Hard. That is part of the
speedup of the life course—and the youngest assault on males that I
have seen. By adulthood, the male dollar is also an anxious dollar; men
too feel they are being judged. (Age appears to be overtaking gender
in this system, hard as that may be to believe; see "Men. All Together
Now?" [Gullette 1997, pt. 3].)

Twenty-somethings precociously rehearse for later playing has-
beens. This too is a newly self-conscious age class (known as generation
X-ers, slackers, or baby busters—this last the label that most firmly
locates youth in antagonism to current midlifers). The young display
their age smarts and innocently fetishize (their own) ephemeral youth,
thus learning the need to stave off decline, whatever effort it takes,
through practices supposed to be easy for the young. (Practices internalize meanings; they deepen the feelings *as* they enact the world.)
Thus "normal" kids cultivate the ideal body under the converging
codes of "health" and "fun" and "beauty" in pressurized contexts of
aspiring consumption and aspiring sexuality. There is much controversy about the conformation of the ideal body and the correct motivations for desiring it. Different media validate different images: the teen
or postteen male as engorged sexual athlete, wan androgyne, or post-
graduate sophisticate. But controversy and the proliferation of rival

types serve to keep everyone within the system and many concentrated on the youthist goal. In the mainstream visual imagery we find breast, "virile bulge" (Saul Bellow's creepy term), buttock, pec—these arcs are the distended three-dimensional icons of youth in our contemporary mythology. Later, the young learn, comes flaccidity, the modern equivalent of the Fall. The double chin is our *East of Eden.*[25]

This is a system for producing precocious age-self-consciousness. Young people are all at risk in this system; and if I dare repeat the decline poster slogan, "We're all young once," it is only to underline how universal the risk is. You do not in fact start out young (children are not spoken of as "young"); you fall into "being young"—the sex/age system—at puberty. The stage is set, in our increasingly age-graded and sexualized culture, for "youth" to collect all the conflations. Ah youth! According to the culture, within those brief years come beauty, sexual power, desirability, excitement, intellectual energy, techno-savvy. "Beauty" is a code word for youth, although not all the young are beautiful, as everyone knows while young and then learns to forget. Men in the midlife age class often remember the Kinseyan statistics that their outlets for sex were greatest "somewhere around 16 or 17 years of age. It is not later" (Kinsey et al. 1948, 219).[26] This factoid has had amazing resilience. Some midlifers also remember the alleged statistic that IQ is highest at eighteen and tails down afterward. (That "fact" seems not to have been retained in the system. But some people who do not even believe in IQ believe that their IQ was higher at eighteen or some other early peak.) One way or the other, those years alone have been electrified. The construction of a "peak" moment is crucial. The young may not be dizzied by the hype at the time, but they learn to associate all these values with one short time of life; and as they age, they come to believe they are losing their best chance to get these goods and learn to call this closing down of the future "aging." Although life chances are based on many social givens, such as race, class background, education, social skills, networking, and so on, in representation they often appear to be tightly linked to youth. Given the median age of Americans (the midthirties), for the majority the right age has either passed or is passing.

The effect of constructing a peak is to construct a doom. You have to fall down from it or slide down from it, one. (Both metaphors are available, one for age catastrophists, the other for age gradualists.) The general idea each of us is intended to embody, and enunciate, is that the body fails unless it can be maintained at its peak or ideal moment.

Postpeak, it needs to be improved. But of course we are supposed to know in our "hearts" that maintenance is impossible: that over time, far from improving, and without interference from discourse, the body fails. All we can do is cosmeticize the fact, as morticians do corpses. To make this failure seem a natural fact, improvement over "nature" has to be culturally prescribed beginning at about puberty: shaving, deodorizing, muscle building, or using makeup. All the paraphernalia about the body—the body shaved, plucked, combed, gelled, colored, sweetened, tightened, elevated, uplifted, cut down—is the commercial manipulation of age anxiety. Somewhere between the midteens and the midtwenties, the cult of (bodily) youth has been established in the bulk of each new cohort. The cult has used—created, exaggerated, channeled, conflated—physical narcissism, sexual desire, and rivalry for partners in the sexual and marriage markets, gender division, economic anxiety about aging beyond one's peak, and precocious fear of death.

RESOCIALIZATION INTO MIDLIFE AGING: THE "DISCOVERY"

The fall is some moment that the ideology now leaves men as well as women too twitchy to settle on. Twenty-five? Receding hair? Thirty-something? Being older than the people in the ads? The first laugh lines? Forty? The first grey hair? Noticing that you are the oldest person at the party (concert) (conference)? Fifty, the new magic marker? Should it be an age or a sign? Do the ages matter more than the signs, or are the signs all that matter? As the telltale signs and symbolic ages proliferate, the effect is that each enters the mysterious land of loss separately, unhappily, repeatedly. The culture teaches feelings (e.g., the anxious attitude of anticipating the signs) and lore (what the bad signs are). It prepares us for the process of applying the social learning to our own individual case. It does this most obviously through representations, in one blunt piecemeal way and another more comprehensive and devious way.

The blunt way, found in mainstream magazines and the uncritical social science on which magazines depend, is to tell you directly "how other people feel." One example may suffice. " 'Therapists today estimate that only twenty percent of the western male population' avoid the distressing effects of the male menopause, which is responsible for 'injecting a considerable amount of havoc and unrest into their lives.' "[27] Telling you how other people allegedly feel is a way of "freezing" the world, because it takes for granted that *you will feel the same way.*[28] Trained by a universalizing humanism, I used to react to the topos, "how other people feel," by anxiously trying to edge *my* feelings toward matching the supposedly "normal" response. A cultural critic regards examples of the topos, unless contextualized with great care, as fragments of insinuation, teaching readers of any age or sexual orientation that there is a male menopause and that it is constituted by and discovered through its "distressing effects." A midlife male reader is likely to ask himself how much havoc and unrest he will or does feel. The statistic "twenty percent" baffles rationality. It implies that therapists are the appropriate experts for this situation. In any case, how could therapists, even those who see fifty midlife male clients a week and who network with other therapists to compare notes, know what the entire male population of the First World feels? (If therapists in the 1980s estimated an 80% crisis rate, and current psychologists less, what has changed?) Hostile cultural constructions may of course produce "distressing effects" in anyone who internalizes them. But such effects are not themselves proof of a male menopause.

Bit by bit, if a subject receives them uncritically, reports about the supposed feelings of others appear to add up to a world filled with negative feelings about the midlife. But just in case we miss the point, decline narrative provides the "meaning" of the piecemeal bits. "An understanding of the importance of the precedence of the whole over the parts in all self-conscious experience is crucial" (Medina 1990, 234). If you are hit in the head by a stick, it makes all the difference in the world whether you think it was hurled by an enemy or it dropped from a tree.[29] In the social construction of emotions, Michael Gordon intuits that "the central factor is a person's definition of a situation" (1990, 148) because if you decide the stick was hurled by an enemy, you may be filled with long-term anger; whereas if you decide you somehow are at fault yourself, you will be helpless. Midlife decline narrative names a "natural" enemy—within. Even if some people have good defenses against self-disparagement at midlife, my point is precisely that defensiveness is made necessary.

Once you have accepted the sense of the whole, the bits fall into their expectable places. There is a whole decline narrative, for example, in the before-and-after concept "inappropriately youthful": youth's stylish way, midlife decay. Once you let this concept in, you may read signs of it in other people on the street and in the marketplace, and after you have practiced on others, bring the category home and read the signs on yourself—in the mirror or in the mind. The power of all such concepts is "the extent to which it can provoke what Friedrich Nietzsche called a love of fate among readers who quite literally bring into being the alleged truth of a reflected, patterned world" (Agger 1992, 148). There is a lot of bitterness in love of fate. If you feel compelled to give up a long-customary and favored sexual behavior, hairstyle, walk, type of clothing, esthetic taste, or to adopt a new one, *on the grounds of age,* you may feel sad, coerced and obedient but helpless.[30] "Fate" decreed by culture feels ruthless. If you feel you should give up the behavior but you do not do so, you probably do not feel "resistant" but uncertain or ashamed, maybe even "monstrous."[31] Tones of satire or tragedy, plots of ridicule or disaster—fiction too has its thousand ways of freezing the age norms of the culture. The conversational gambit that John K. Galbraith has called "the Still Syndrome" also supports the category "inappropriately youthful" (Galbraith 1993).[32]

As a scholar of the middle years I am often asked, with some anxiety, when those years begin. The best answer might be, "Whenever you begin to believe that Not-Young, the condition that has been lurking about since late adolescence, finally and undeniably manifests itself." It is whatever you think you cannot postpone. Socialization-into-midlife-aging assures that dread will appear *before* any "signs of aging" appear—long before—to keep us on guard and watchful and behaviorally correct and to encourage us to purchase magical substances that will postpone aging. But viewed from a slightly different angle, dread of aging is what *produces* "signs" of aging. It is that anxious eye that sees and names the first wrinkle or (as in a greeting card in my collection) calls *thirty* the end. As the century has progressed, everyone has been getting older younger.

In the United States in the twentieth century, aging no longer means a geriatric physical process, and it can begin long before marked events like retirement or the last of the children leaving home. Although widely shared, its core is a private emotion: fear of being not-young. In other words, it is a culturally cultivated chronic disease with an adolescent exposure and a no-later-than-midlife onset.

THE INVENTION OF (SEXUAL) NOSTALGIA

Belief in midlife decline is a pandemic peculiar to our era, a set of effects with a discernible twentieth-century history and extremely vigorous and insidious maintenance strategies. The disease of life course nostalgia began to be widely cultivated in England and America at the end of the nineteenth and the beginning of the twentieth centuries, the period in which the new terms—middle age, middle life—began to gain currency. "Middle age" was invented in this period: the age class took on definite attributes; improved health and longevity were countered by the master narrative of decline. Other midlife phenomena we recognize were also invented then: the "empty nest," the practices of "prolonging" youth or "rejuvenation," the cult of youth in general and especially in Hollywood films, the canonical works that continue to be read in our educational system and discussed as masterpieces. My next book project, *Midlife Fictions,* describes aspects of this invention. For my current purposes in this essay, what would be most useful is to take a quick historical sideswipe at nostalgia. Why deconstruct "nostalgia"? First, it is a feeling assumed to be natural. Then, it serves the case for socialization into midlife aging: I can show how the culture began to teach quite young people to look backward in the life course, to past, younger selves, with longing and a sense of unappeasable loss. Looking backward was taught through the material and discursive conditions in which it would be inevitable to *feel* or anticipate loss and then through representations that connected loss to aging into the middle years.

Nostalgia was invented in different ways for men and women. But here I am going to concentrate mainly on how men were taught to look back.[33] For decades various theoretical and activist discourses have been teaching us how to talk about the impositions of ideology, especially about the self-hatred and confusion that sexist, racist, classist, and heterosexist attributions tend to create. Men on the unmarked side of a binary may still believe that they are exempt from other processes of socialization into identity; straight middle-class white men in their middle years, in particular, rack up their exemptions. Feminist men's studies has begun supplying the detail that shows how privilege is constructed.[34] Now, a history of the midlife can show specifically how men also figure in decline narratives, learn age-graded "knowledge" about masculinity, and incorporate it into their age-identity or self-image. And (given the interactive nature of gender relations), women suffer from men's anxiety about aging as well as from their own.

Nostalgia is an old word, a Greek word (*nostos*) about a spatial longing—a longing to return home from a place of exile. In its new temporal or life course sense, the word commemorates an impossibility: if we learn to consider aging as a journey into exile, we learn we never can return (see Gullette 1984). The most solid supports for this life course meaning were being put up around 1900, and its broadest appeal has been since that time. The play *Peter Pan* was one of the innumerable vehicles of the new feeling: it had a huge commercial success in 1904 and became an annual ritual in London and New York. Written by J. M. Barrie while in his forties, it is about a boy who does not want to grow up past six and does not have to. Growing even one year further, as Wendy does, is presented as an exile that girls must suffer because women are responsible for reproduction and nurturing. But during the Victorian era men could fantasize about still being boys and "prolong adolescence well into actual manhood," according to the historian Jeffrey Richards (1987, 105). As the various decline aspects of the midlife consolidated, they made the fantasy of boyhood more necessary—and harder to maintain. As Barrie himself said, about trying to return to the safe haven of childhood, "When we reach the window it is Lock-out Time. The iron bars are up for life." Bernard Shaw noticed that *Peter Pan* was "really a play for grown-up people" (Ormond 1987, 103, 109). More precisely, it was a fantasy intended for midlife men, pressured by many forces in the culture to recognize themselves as aging. What needs explaining most is not the general spread of the term "middle age" (nor the rearrangement of the whole "modernized" life course of which it became a part),[35] but the invention of this belief in *midlife* decline even for men.

Fiction did some of this work. For the first time in the novel, the middle-aged man plays central roles, often, and fewer of these are scripted protectively by patriarchal values. "He" began to get a character—rarely a good one. Narratives about the father written by angry but still terrified adult children, like Samuel Butler's *The Way of All Flesh* (published posthumously in 1903) or Edmund Gosse's *Father and Son* (published anonymously in 1907), saw him as a heavy father. In *Totem and Taboo* (translated into English in 1918 and 1919) Sigmund Freud invented a prehistory for mankind and an allegory of the male generational relations of his own time, in which the boys were forced by patriarchal tyranny to gang up on "dad" (originally a slighting address to older men of low class standing but now a term replacing "father"). In many tones of voice, disciplinary connections, and high/low registers, narratives helped to lower the value of men at midlife. If in one discursive scenario the midlife man deserves death for hoarding women, in others he deserves disgust for being useless, serving the status quo, being incapable of political change, sending his sons off to war to die (World War I, which depended on age-graded enlistment, consolidated this attitude); in others, he's a buffoon lacking midlife authority (James Joyce's *Ulysses,* 1922).

The novel gave the midlife man his own "subjectivity"—it went inside his head and often found there a being who absorbs the lesson that he is a life course loser over the course of a plot that makes him one. Dreiser's *Sister Carrie* (1900, 1912) made the causes of Hurstwood's decline moral and financial, with age just the worsener that the economic system took advantage of. Most midlife novels since, ignoring economic analysis, have produced aging itself as the crucial variable. The professor in Willa Cather's *The Professor's House* (1925) showed how a man could lose interest in his wife, his work, his adult children—suddenly, as an effect of age. The psychiatrist in F. Scott Fitzgerald's *Tender Is the Night* (1934) shows how the most fortunate and privileged midlife man can lose it all—lose his grip, make a fool of himself on water skis needing to prove he is still young, and finally wander off alone into the American provinces, a fate worse than death. Many classics cling to "youth" in an actual boy, as in Thomas Mann's *Death in Venice* (trans. 1924), or to past youthful selves, as in Proust's *A la recherche du temps perdu* (trans. 1922–33) and Waugh's *Brideshead Revisited* (1945). T. S. Eliot's Prufrock moaned, "I grow old, I grow old." Male modernism embraced midlife decline, but so did much popular fiction, native, British, and translated. Ernest Poole, Joseph Hergesheimer, and John Galsworthy spread the bad news to different audiences.

The midlife characters in the works listed above do not conform to a single type, but their fates establish a range of "typical" masculine midlife failures. No matter how else a man read such works, after he had read more than two or three—within the contexts provided for interpreting the middle years—he might have been hard put to evade a sense of the inevitability of midlife decline and knowledge of its symptoms. The fiction writers were inventing the scenes, the tropes, the plots of dispossession, giving reality—depth and pain—to what might have stayed relatively inert in the surrounding nonfictional discourses. They were teaching readers not just what could happen to them, but how to feel about it. No doubt the writers experienced their own aging in decline terms (they were more sensitive to discursive signals; they learned to read certain signs as "symptoms" sooner), and so they enacted it in fiction.

Who would have been the consumers of the new nostalgia? Why was there such a large, increasing, audience of ready consumers of the messages? (As well as a large audience eager to read about good father-ing, happy remarriage, and wisdom and financial success at midlife—the counternarrative of the day.) Nostalgia was fostered by many sources; it would not be fair to blame fiction alone or texts in general (newspapers, magazines, advertisements, psychology, sexology, advice guides; and, by the twenties, silent movies). Anyone who was unhappy about aging for extraliterary reasons would absorb these narratives feel-ingly.

By the standards of 1910, the middle years were a potentially healthy and powerful time of life. Life expectancy had increased and was con-fidently expected to increase further: a man of fifty in the United King-dom could expect to live another 20.2 years (Laslett 1991, 84, table 6.2). His sister could expect two years more. A contemporary American political economist said, "Of 100 persons alive at the age of thirty . . . 48 will not die before 70" (Epstein 1922, 8). As early as 1900, in New England, 9% of the population was over sixty.[36] But after about 1880 there were widespread new causes, operating within the socioeco-nomic, life course, and sexual systems, for men as well as women in the privileged classes to be conscious of regretting their promised ad-vance along the life course. With all that demographic luck, this is ironic. It is also crucial theoretically that beliefs about the emerging middle years had so little to do with health and life expectancy, the bodily measures conventionally assumed to be so central to the midlife.

Anxiety about aging displaces and psychologizes and individualizes and personalizes and makes bodily many other unrelated anxieties. Midlife anxiety about aging is a portable kind of displacement. It can focus on "aging" a vast array of other socially constructed oppressions, from work conditions to racism to gender relations. Pernicious as the belief in midlife decline is to those who hold it, it presents itself as useful insofar as it explains the way the world works. A middle-class, white fifty-year-old woman, who might be tempted to blame her hus-band for infantilizing her or her employer for discriminating against her workplace participation, can instead blame "aging" for "emptying her nest" and leaving her with nothing to do.[37] A thirtyish African-American woman whose husband disappears in the Great Migration can blame her aging body for his absence rather than the systems that forced him to leave town to look for work and that forced her to turn into a sexless granny figure so young.[38] A white midlevel manager who might blame the bosses for coercing him into working longer days learns instead to blame aging or "neurasthenia" for his fatigue or the male "climacteric" for his unwillingness to initiate intercourse.[39] Such transfers have a potentially universal reach, touching people of all political persuasions. Even the man who blames the boss and joins the union may obsess alone about his overwhelming tiredness and reluctant tumescences, find himself more discouraged at the end of the day, and act out his frustrations on those around him.

A good historical case can be made that this kind of displacement of blame onto aging at midlife was particularly useful at the turn of the twentieth century to systems threatened by midlife power and seniority and the ability to organize. We can imagine such powers epitomized by radicals and progressives within the expanding feminist, antiracist, and labor movements of the Progressive Era. Long before old age, indeed rather early in the life course, midlife aging provided the body rather than the body politic or economic as a primary source of concern, creating self-absorption in a locus that could seem amenable to individual control (as opposed to giant powers like conglomerate capitalism, post-Reconstruction racism, and reactive patriarchy). Technologies specifically offered to remedy aging in men became available: corsetry, body building, hormone treatments, and, by the 1920s, diet, fashion, smoking, sex-rejuvenation surgeries, and marrying younger women after divorce. "Control" came to be focused in practices and products sold in the name of health, youth seeking and youth simulation in all their various forms, and other private, age-related "solutions." (These remedies cannot help but be seen to fail, in a culture as quickly primed to be astute about minute variations in physical appearance and functioning.) Midlife decline ideology constructs the situations and the emotions that enclose us in self: doubt, embarrassment, shame, humiliation, despair; it fosters narcissism. By learning to concentrate on an "aging" body, the twentieth-century midlife subject learns how isolated and helpless he (or she) is.

How did the new knowledge of midlife aging get internalized, so that feelings about it could be subsumed mainly under the domain of "psychology"? The twin engines of age anxiety were work and love— or, more specifically, representations of persons as workers and sex performers vulnerable to midlife decline. Although highly overdetermined and complexly interrelated, the disempowering processes would certainly not have been possible without age grading, a newly prestigious way of dividing the human community into groups. Public compulsory education, a late-nineteenth-century reform, immediately became age graded, so that children were segregated by age rather than competence and had to move in lockstep through the school system, youth clubs, and then cohort competition.[40] The general spread of age grading meant that individual differences among people of a particular age or stage were less prominent or even submerged. People could readily be explained or their behavior predicted or their achievements judged not by their temperament (or class, etc.) or what they said about their particular experience but on the basis of being "adolescent" or "young," "forty" or "middle-aged," "empty-nesters" or "menopausal"—or, in time, "baby boomers."

Age competition among men was codified in new ways in their working lives. In the most direct ways, capitalism at the time of the second industrial revolution, between 1880–1929, began to show that it wanted the younger more than the older, whether the young body in the office or factory system, or the young mind in all organizations (Gruman 1978, 359–87). A physician named Osler concluded as early as 1905 that men over forty were "useless," that all good mental work was done between the ages of twenty-five and forty (Cole 1992). At the time, that provoked a storm of rebuttal (Cole 1992, 170–73), but when Randolph Bourne (then twenty-five) extolled youth as the only time of energy and idealism in 1913, and said old men "sit in the saddle and ride mankind," it was simply progressive discourse (Bourne 1913, 12). Men over forty were laid off first from factory work; in the most taxing industries they were wrecks at thirty; technological changes de-skilled older workers or made skilled ones redundant and generally weakened seniority and autonomy.[41] "Workers could anticipate that their income would decline with age even if they did not change occupations" (Ramsom and Sutch 1986, 27–29). In the vastly expanded clerical and sales sectors an employee over forty who lost his job could have a well-founded fear that he would never get another or that the next would provide less income and status. In Elmer Rice's popular allegorical play, *The Adding Machine* (1923), a bookkeeper of forty-five kills his boss when he is fired without warning after twenty-five years.[42]

The work history of midlife men is fragmentary; the emotional history of midlife men is barely thinkable; the history of the narratives produced about midlife aging has yet to be written. But I can propose certain age-conscious historical hypotheses.[43] Looking ahead to midlife, men learned to measure themselves against a new life course conception: the ideal *age-wage profile*—the mental graph a man could draw of his future earnings (and status), first in anticipation, and later in retrospective judgment.[44] In the ideal narrative, a business or professional employee or a skilled/unionized worker anticipates that his earnings will rise as he ages as a reward for age (experience) and in tandem with his family's necessities; and he finds that they do rise.[45]

A man with an increasingly good wage profile in midlife might conceivably ignore the other, cultural, forces that were aging him; he would find himself rewarded for joining the new economic life course system. But the ideal was probably a fantasy for most, as it still is. Actual economic circumstances that threatened or undermined his employment, his status, or his wage security (technological change, monopolistic consolidations after the close of family firms, recessions, strikes lost, unions weakened or busted, increases in living "standards" and other dewaging forces, all of which were powerfully operative by the 1920s) were far likelier to keep him from having a complacent profile: the peak came long before retirement, to be followed at best by a flatness that was now read in the modern way as a decline. In all but the top career categories the mental graph a man drew of his life course income might be a relentless plateau or slide after a short early rise. In the chaos of economically driven age competition, fear of loss, cognitive helplessness, and practical powerlessness, at midlife people themselves reproduced the middle-ageism of the economic system, repeating the bad news about the difference between the generations, the value of being young. How could they not? Looking younger might well appear to provide a slim, local, marginal advantage; if nothing else, a symbolic second chance. When men began to shave, circa 1900, "choosing" to give up their beards symbolized the loss of the "old/wise" connotations and the material advantages of being bearded. Shaving: a hedge against capitalist instability and the age-wage plunge.

If midlife men turned to private life in the family as a refuge from work pressure, age competition, and life course anxiety, they learned to confront their sexual "climacteric"—the loss of some (vaguely defined) past possessions of masculinity, such as desire, sensation, strength, occuring as early as age 45. This midlife male menopause has to be accounted an entirely cultural invention[46]—based on not a shred of change in male physiology. We might be inclined to rank it as the most fearful engine of age anxiety ever produced for men, were it not that we must now consider it in intricate relation to that other fearful engine of age anxiety, the age-wage profile. Although a midlife climacteric has no biological basis,[47] it has served for almost one hundred years as a prime obsession/distraction for those led to believe in it.

On the one hand, men were hearing an urgent, new twentieth-century imperative to be more sexually active in order to affirm their masculinity; on the other, men at midlife confronted the obstacle of age-graded sexual decline based on the alleged decrease in hormonal secretion during the middle years. Carpe diem smashed into endocrinology, with aftershocks we still feel. The have-more-sex imperative was a drastic change from a nineteenth-century economy of restraint (see Gordon 1971; Gullette 1994). In the gerontocratic economy, prudent midlife and older men—unlike boys—were felt to need the least supervision, internal monitoring, and textual warnings; they had the greatest allotment of sexual freedom and admiration for their "restraint." In the sexual sphere, they got the most goods the culture had on offer, for life. "Virility" was based on the production of semen and semen alone; it could last as long as they lived.

This situation of relative privilege for men over twenty-five or thirty and up until old age changed drastically after 1900. Now, as part of what they considered "sexual liberation," sexologists and Freudians and modernists started changing all the metaphors and prescriptions. Before, you were "spent" if you had intercourse; now you were "repressed" if you did not "come" often. Before, you got sick if you overindulged; now it was celibacy that was likely to provoke illness or impotence. In addition to semen, sexual activity now required a newly identified substance, hormonal secretion; but, unlike semen, this was invisible, so attention turned to the outward signs of strength: muscles. On both accounts, sex required youth. Thus young men and midlife men simply changed places in the value hierarchy. "Penis envy," which Freud named but misidentified, became a problem for older men. As the culture moved sexual decline into men's middle years for the first time, it located decline with unlikely exactitude. In 1901 Sylvanus Stall, a minister, wrote a book called *What the Forty-Five-Year-Old Man Needs to Know.* In subsequent years, many followed him in trying to save men from what Stall called "the misapprehension that the procreative vigor of early youth continues until advanced old age." As "vigor" vanished, mental energy was supposed to wane, too. Surgeons invented male sex operations: "monkey gland" or testicular transplants, partial vasectomies (like Yeats's). Popular knowledge of sex surgeries suggests that many men had given up these erstwhile "misapprehensions."

In short, erotic expectations of men were rising at the same time that their midlife endocrinological decay was prophesied; knowledge was spreading about this core deficiency of the midlife male and becoming known to women too. In an additional twist, midlife men were being asked to give up shame about their "male" erotic natures (i.e, give up religious restraint and concern for women and pregnancy), but take on shame about age-related deficiencies. This new "knowledge" proved to be an effective formula for the construction of male self-consciousness, doubt, disesteem, and psychosomatic impotence.[48] Aging, now seen as causing hormonal deficiency, moved up to first place as an explanation for reduced virility. The ages assigned for the onset of hormonal decline ranged around (Stall's) forty-five. Despite the total lack of demographic or medical evidence, forty-five will not seem an arbitrary assignment, when we consider the culture's age grading, its demand for young bodies and brains, and, behind that, industry's speedup of the life course, the specter of the worn-out working man, superannuated at forty-something, and with his income marking his decline.

The novels that locate decline in the middle years of healthy men (characters who do not have syphilis, who are not poor, who do not commit evil deeds) arguably symbolize the curiosity, anguish, or despair that many men came to feel in these general cultural circumstances. Thomas Mann himself, according to sexologist Havelock Ellis, said that *Death in Venice* was about "the pathological climacteric" (1942, 321). Maybe Mann meant to exceptionalize what happens to Aschenbach, but many readers "knew" the normal climacteric could cause strange behavior. All the declines described in fiction indisputably normalize decline.

The multiple factors I gather under the rubric of decline ideology produced other terrible by-products: the elders learned envy of the young; midlife parents, jealousy of their young-adult children. Unaware of being victims of age ideology themselves, men displaced anger against others. Having learned that they age sexually nearly as early as women do, fearing competition from female workers as well as male, having lost the absolute superiority of being sole wage earners, men exacerbated the age/gender superiority that we now refer to as the double standard of aging—discriminating against "older" women in the workplace and in private life.[49] In fiction, good fathers rivaled women as parents and denigrated their same-age wives.[50] Physicians and feminists had been pointing out that, after forty-five, women were healthier than men. Nevertheless, under the sign of the endocrines, female menopause itself came to be represented once again as a disease—now as a (deficiency) disease; psychosomatic problems resulted; a commerce in aging parallel to that for men developed female rejuvenation products and increasingly severe social penalties for failure to buy; a literature of decline featured the female midlife body as grotesque or pathetic in ways that had not been possible before the cult of youth. For men and women both, true midlife crises, although not yet named, were already operational.

Nostalgia is the name of the emotion that was being constructed. I have tried to show how an age-graded economy with a tremendous stake in displacement can produce a wide range of motives and of life course narratives (biomedical/libidinal, novelistic) that make the middle of the life course frightening—at least in anticipation and very likely in reality—and that lead people to look backward with longing. In short, by 1920–35 the midlife body had replaced the young body as the troubling, unwanted one. All this, of course, brings us back to the present.

ALTERNATIVE MIDLIFE NARRATIVES

A close reader of the foregoing miniature history may have concluded, as I do, that on the whole midlife decline—motives for believing in it and representations of it—are still (or again) firmly in place. Our cult of youth is not supported by a holocaust of young men, as was the case after World War I, but it is amply maintained by other forces. Our belief in male hormonal decline no longer leads men to want transplants of young monkey glands, but it propels many into other forms of youth simulation. Postmodern global capitalism more and more threatens every working person (who does not have tenure) with a dipping age-wage curve.[51] A cult of youth that makes youth perishable and irretrievable, an abhorrence of aging that depreciates the middle years and will not decide when they begin—this is still the bodily surface of decline ideology, the bodily binary of its particular power system. This is the peak-and-slide that the dominant culture teaches us to experience as private. Mainstream culture trains us to believe certain ideas, hold certain values, own certain images, practice certain visual discriminations, feel certain emotions. The audience for it maintains and circulates the age knowledge provided by the ideology, repeating as true its claim to be natural and universal, its perverse undecidability at the one crucial point (when decline begins), its reliance on biology, its stoic harshness.

When pressed, people sometimes say to me that the only honest narrative about the life course is a decline and that talking about our "interests" in changing the ideology is illusory language wrongfully borrrowed from discourses that are legitimately political. Alternately, some alpha males, often cushioned by tenure and, whether they know it or not, by the ideal age-wage profile (the one that appears to rise until retirement), deny they are vulnerable to middle-ageism. Even some women assert that the midlife is "a great time of life," as indeed it should be. But thus insulated, they also tend to dispute that they or others are aged by culture; they resist age theory.

But even in the absence of a well-developed age theory, midlife aging may not be a compulsory system. The midlife is now undergoing a tentative late-century revision. There is quite a lot of age refractoriness around, although it is not being seen as in contest against decline ideology. As the well-wishers argue, midlife dread of aging is not universal. In selected and important spheres of life, there is already a range of recognizable resistances.

Let us take one linchpin of male decline ideology, for some men its most emotionally fraught myth. As we saw, men are supposed to believe that their sexual pleasure wanes (will wane, has waned) with age. Has getting men to "learn [this] from experience as well as ideology" (in Raymond Williams's words) worked? A 1984 survey claims to tell us what "the Kinsey generation" is like thirty years later: "What proportion of men and of women experience a decline in sexual functioning after the age of fifty? For men, the answer is *all men*" (Brecher et al. 1984, 17; italics in original). (Age critics can sometimes tell from survey data and its rhetoric what the dominant ideology has succeeded in getting people to believe; surveys reinforce beliefs as they "report.") This report, produced by Consumer's Union, goes on to generalize that men (of this cohort) do envision their sexual lives as a progressive decline "since a peak *in the early twenties or before*" (Brecher et al. 1984, 331; emphasis added). Men who hold this view go by the numbers, as they were taught in their youth. Counting and contrasting, they note that they have sex less often or more slowly, and that this is awful and could not be felt or be understood otherwise. This is biology, it is decline, it is a truth. Some, trying to produce personal evidence of their exemption from the laws of nature, may have recourse to pornography, divorce, and the trophy bride, or to sex practices that objectify and dominate the women or men involved. The consequences of hypostatizing midlife decline and finding it as advertised within your own body radiate far beyond the solitary victim.

The midlife, however, gives other men quite a lot of options for alternative "experience." The Consumers Union study itself suggests this elsewhere, as do several recent studies. These men speak positively. Midlife sex has not changed in quality for them.[52] Or (an even more recent study) it is *better*—even in quantity. "The Janus's research clearly shows that both men and women aged 51–64 have orgasms far more frequently than men aged 18–26."[53] Aside from competing by counting, some men feel that they are artists in bed; the pleasure can be more subtle or more thrilling. They are doing more of the kind of sex they want.[54] They are more considerate to women; they are more competent at giving pleasure. Of course they are still being judged, but they are getting better reviews. This group is on the verge of a counterrhetoric. It is two steps away from saying that young sex was nervous, awkward, embarrassingly out of their control and thus humiliating, self-involved, and foolishly risky about pregnancy. Influenced by the women they love or by feminism or both, these men recognize that they value women's responses and opinions. Some couples may have found a way toward their own versions of the sexual "justice" that John Stoltenberg describes so effectively in *Refusing to Be a Man* (1990); having overcome the trained need to objectify and use women, they have achieved something (sexual, affective, ethical) that both partners might call mutuality.[55] The men in this group have experienced progress and tell a progress story about their sexuality—about "midlife sexuality." Their story is just as credible, and it unseats the decline story—makes it look suspicious. Is decline too boastful about youthful prowess? Possibly macho and antiquated? Certainly it is self-defeating as a man grows older.

As far as male sexuality goes, there is probably an alternative midlife narrative for every mentality. Men in another group will partly agree with the sexy progressivists that young sex was overrated. As for their midlife, they say they have sex less often than before and may enjoy it physiologically a little less; on the other hand, they have intercourse about as often as they want to; having tried the variations they wanted, they use the ones they like. "Sexuality" need not just mean penetration and orgasm; it can include masturbation and what phallocentrism labeled "foreplay." People in this group are still age comparatists: "youth" as they remember or imagine it may still be their reference point. But theirs can also be called a progress story.

These days midlife women, summing up their narrative of sexual pleasure, also tell a wide variety of stories (like much older women as well). Some do concentrate primarily on bodily losses and are devastated by the belief that their beauty/sexuality/mental acuity is vanishing. But my guess would be that fewer women than men operate as biology-based ideologues of decline. When women argue that their sex life is worse than at some earlier time, they tend to refer to the statistical lack of socially appropriate men, AIDS, male preference for younger women, social ostracism of single women, and other obstacles unrelated to their physical capacity for pleasure. Informed by feminist theory, they name sociocultural factors. And some women tell a sexual progress story; again, feminists may have been the ones to spread it. It deals with growing knowledge of one's own body and the means of getting pleasure from it. And it notices that being young and female and heterosexual a generation or more ago often meant being dangerously fertile, unprotected by contraception, and inhibited by sexual conventions; it also meant having sex with those clumsy narcissistic boys. No wonder the midlife can look like an improvement.

Some midlife women, like some midlife men, have discarded the assumption that sexiness refers only to the tactile sensations and emotions of one age group. A big group of both women and men is ready to recognize pleasure connected with the body wherever found along the whole life course. If the point is resistance to the most emotionally fraught parts of the ideology, women will have to shake the myths of menopause too, which became more widely disseminated in the backlash resulting from 1992's "Year of the Woman" (see "Menopause as Magic Marker" [Gullette 1997, chap. 6]).

If we look broadly at examples of existing age resistance in American culture, as suggested in chosen fictions and selected statistics, the popular cure for anxiety about midlife aging seems to be to get older in particular circumstances, which include finding and telling and sharing counterdecline narratives. These include surveys that report that older people make love more often, films and books and songs that show that second times can turn out to be good (too; there's an implied comparison with first times), discourses that do not evoke fears but remind people that older individuals can assimilate new concepts faster, stretch our moral ambitions more, invent new pleasures, control envy and malice better, and that older Americans actually enjoy some aspects of having adult children, bonding with another, and proving we can make our living under late capitalism. But "positive aging" has not sunk into the "common sense" of the tribe, into the jokes, the cartoons, the ads. When it does enter the daily currency of life it often fails to confront the forces constructing decline and may actually obscure them (Gullette 1996).

Countercultural narratives cannot succeed if presented simply as alternative "experience" that happens to be available to men or to the lucky (the rich or the secure, the married, the developmentally able). I have heard people (rightly) resent what they think of as the compulsory optimism of the new midlife story: "Is happiness obligatory?" one man asked me bitterly and revealingly in front of a large audience at a twenty-fifth college reunion. Behind that kind of bitterness might lie a midlife layoff or downward mobility, the counting of orgasms, a bad divorce, unemployed or hopeless or dying children, socioeconomic causes of precocious illness of the kind that kill women and men of color earlier than white women and men and working-class people earlier than those in the middle and upper classes. None of these conditions is usefully attributable to aging. If employers lay off midlife workers because they cost too much or because younger people have been better trained in new technologies, you do not solve such economic problems with wrinkle creams. If you live next to a toxic waste site in a neighborhood overwhelmed with ads for alcohol and cigarettes, have a high-stress job, and develop high blood pressure and heart disease at fifty, do you really want to blame (midlife) aging? Better analysis and techniques for producing age-wise autobiographical narrative would locate the decline elements in one's middle life more accurately. Presumably many more would be correctly attributed to culture—to the politics and economics and representations of the life course—rather than to nature. We would think *middle-ageism* sooner than midlife aging.

Countercultural narratives need to be abetted—framed and explained—by accessible theorizing about middle-ageism as a cultural system. I mean explicit analyses of interpretive and structural elements such as life course narratives, age-wage curves, age hierarchies, the discursive construction of generational conflict, age-related emotions, the subtleties of age ideology, and resistance. As individuals and as producers of culture, subjects in the midlife age class need to learn how to query both of the master narratives of the midlife—both the automatic decline story and the compulsory optimism. Using age theory, we might refuse to perpetuate invidious comparisons—about sexuality or other socially constructed aspects of life. Youth would have many characteristics, good and bad, like the midlife. Only the pressure of age

ideology requires individuals to say, "Better!" or "Worse!" and generalize so much about difference. This attitude defies age grading. It liberates us from the most basic necessity of the ideology of aging, that
there be category differences between youth and the middle years. We
might then retell our life narratives and talk about our revised practices
so that they make sense both as alternative experience *and* as aspects
of an explanatory age theory.

This approach, both analytic about existing feelings and critical of
the culture, could then make more salient the positive powers that can
come only with living into the middle years *and* link these with the
form of temporality called "aging." Youthful death anxiety, for example, could be connected with *under*estimating our power to deal with
the scary parts of adulthood; through aging we discover resilience and
recovery. Some of the treasures of life can become more dear: friendships, for example, and one's children if and as they become friends,
love between the middle generation and the old, appreciation for natural beauty, the power to strive for social justice. By trying to tell a
progress narrative consciously, within an explicitly social-constructionist context, people may learn to "experience" midlife aging differently—recognizing what factors still promote decline.

If midlife women sometimes seem to have access to more of those
autobiographical and critical techniques and affective goods than men,
that is greatly to the credit of American feminism and the narratives
and theories it has inspired. Feminism has been empowering the middle years of women and vice versa. Those who came to feminism young
in the seventies have aged under its benign gaze; many can write a
progress story by comparing where they are economically and/or psychologically with where they were at twenty or where their mothers
were at the same ages. They are the movers and shakers who made the
Year of the Woman live up however weakly to its label; they contribute
to the gender gap in election returns. Women have been helped by a
mass of women's midlife fiction. Starting with Margaret Drabble's
Realms of Gold (1975) and now including Alice Walker's *The Color
Purple* (1982), Doris Lessing's *Diary of a Good Neighbour* (1983), Toni
Morrison's *Beloved* (1987), May Sarton's *Education of Harriet Hatfield*
(1989), and many others, the genre of the "midlife progress novel" has
taken the stigma out of midlife optimism. It has been giving textual
solidity to the proposition that women (despite racism, poverty, or
protective privilege, youthful subordination and lack of self-esteem,

and midlife decline ideology) can use their middle years to either re-cover or grow or both.[56]

Historical study will tell us not only what we believe about midlife aging but how we came to believe it. There is a disempowering politics buried in myths about middle aging. People do not necessarily become more conservative with age (another strategic stereotype of decline or complacency that goes back to the turn of the century). Many women and men from the "sixties generation" participate in collective activities now more than they did then, and more effectively: millions kept us from going to war in Central America in the eighties, support the sur-viving progressive causes, continue to staff the underpaid social service networks of the cities, states, and federal government. People do not necessarily burn out from activism: they get better at it, work the legal institutions more skillfully, write more powerfully, reach bigger audi-ences. There remain objects for desire—amorous, political, and other, all along the life course (one great fear cultivated by romantic decline specialists seems to be that in middle life we will run out of intense wanting and miss it)—and some find in themselves enhanced power to obtain these objects. The decline of the sacralization of marriage, the expansion of the institution of divorce, the improved status of re-marriage, the changing image of the postparental, the expansion of the middle-class with its age-wage curves set later in the life course are all twentieth-century alterations produced by the collective will of people who argued for what they perceived as second chances and thus remade the mainstream midlife. "The midlife" might become a concept partic-ularly well suited to emancipatory practices and theory. I have been attracted by its contemporary ironies and rich historical freighting. Eventually, theorists might be intrigued by the discursive resilience of age ideology and by the possibility that, deconstructed, it might weaken. Before that, however, the whole concept of age needs to be-come troublesome.

In the United States, the current challenge for the baby boom cohort and the entire age class, together, is whether they can rally enough discursive energy, power, and cultural space to counter the devastating effects of middle-ageism that, colonizing far beyond the individual body and its age identity, distort personal narrative and human rela-tions and weaken the possibility of collective action across much of the life course. Critical "midlife studies" can be, at the very least, a valuable resource for an anti-middle-ageist movement. It would be far better, however, for cultural critics of age to lead the way, shucking the pretense of maintaining an impossible neutrality and using their skills to provide histories, anthropologies, and political and economic analyses of midlife ideology, as well as rhetorics that confer reality on a demystified midadulthood in a demystified life course.

NOTES

1. This essay contains sections or material from my work on the midlife in the twentieth century: *Declining to Decline: Cultural Combat and the Politics of the Midlife* (University Press of Virginia, 1997) and *Midlife Fictions*, my name for two works in progress, "The Invention of the Middle Years of Life, 1880–1930" and "The Invention of Male Midlife Sexual Decline." Earlier versions of this essay have been given at the conference, The Art of Aging and Dying, at the Center for the Humanities at the University of California at Santa Barbara (1990) and as the keynote address at the 175th anniversary of the *North American Review* (1990).

2. The midlife age class was in fact constructed for the first time early in the twentieth century (as argued below). Various changes have occurred (e.g., it is now often renamed after the baby boomers), but the category itself is solidly incorporated in the life course. From a historical viewpoint, the age class is being maintained and *re*constructed rather than constructed.

3. Mainstream midlife discourse has come rather far from the view expressed by Karl Mannheim, and still tenable during the Vietnam War, that cohorts would be divided primarily by politics, so that the smaller "*generation-unit* represents a much more concrete bond than the actual generation as such" (Mannheim 1972, 119). In what contexts individuals actually let age override gender, race, and other identities important to them is an open question.

4. Numerous publications for business have hyped the wealth of the age class, although the distribution of wealth within it is, of course, tremendously uneven.

5. One reason for using the term "ideology" here is heuristic. At the present stage of what I call age studies, there is so little description of the discourses that promote differences centered on age that ideology serves for the moment as an alarm and a sign of work to be done. Age ideology could fruitfully be compared to gender or race ideology. See, e.g., Barrett on stereotyping, compensation, collusion, and recuperation (1985, 81–83). But age ideology has techniques appropriate to itself (not shared with the ideologies of gender or race) and these remain to be described. For a defense of the use of the term "ideology," see Eagleton (1991), esp. chaps. 1, 7.

6. I first used this term in "The Wonderful Woman on the Pavement: Middle-Ageism in the Postmodern Economy" (Gullette 1995b).

7. I first used the formulation "aged by culture" in "What, Menopause *Again?*" (Gullette 1993b). See also "Doing Age Theory," (Gullette 1997). Already in the nineteenth century, both antiracism and feminism used social constructionist approaches to understanding race and gender. One locus classicus in the history of the approach is Berger and Luckmann (1966). For the recent proliferation of studies of social "inventions," see Sollors (1989, x–xiii, 237 n. 3).

8. For the first use of the term "age studies" see Gullette (1993a, 45–46) and

Wyatt-Brown (introduction to Wyatt-Brown and Rossen [1993], 5). The University Press of Virginia has started an interdisciplinary book series, Age Studies, edited by Anne M. Wyatt-Brown, Thomas Cole, Margaret Morganroth Gullette, and Kathleen Woodward, among others. The Rockefeller Foundation has funded a program in age studies at the Center for Twentieth Century Studies at the University of Wisconsin—Milwaukee.

9. Philippe Ariès's book about the reconstruction of childhood, *Centuries of Childhood,* should have led to studies of other "ages" of life (besides old age), in other periods, within the discipline of history. Patricia Meyer Spacks's study, *The Adolescent Idea* (1981), should have led to more literary studies than it did. Cultural studies has fixated on youth subcultures without developing the reflexiveness of age studies. To do age studies now, we need to include and relate all stages of the life course, extend Michel Foucault's insights about the "disciplines" of power into the concepts and practices and structures that produce age discourses, and read all texts "for" age as the human sciences have learned to read "for" gender, race, etc.

10. A search of one database revealed that "middle aged" appeared in only one title out of sixty-four items about "the midlife." Although I feel confident in asserting that a kind of antiageist politics produced the written change, I believe it has never been noticed as a result of a politics (compare the overt politics that changed "Negro" into "black" and then "African-American" and "girl" into "woman"). People who would not say "Negro" or call a woman a "girl," use the term "middle aged," quite often about themselves.

11. Notice the untheorized use of the metaphor, "entrance."

12. I first used the term "decline narrative" in *Safe at Last in the Middle Years* (Gullette 1988).

13. On narrativizing the life course, see *Safe at Last in the Middle Years* (Gullette 1988), which posits that ordinary people as well as novelists tell narratives of their life course that fit decline or progress conventions.

14. "Midlife crisis" can also be a semijocular euphemism referring to men in their middle years when they break up their marriages, remarry younger women, buy sports cars, and react to middle-ageism by trying to recapture their youth. Its effect is to exculpate the men and ignore middle-ageism.

15. See "In Defense of Midlife Progress Novels" (Gullette 1988) for a description of some of the high-culture factors that naturalized decline and still elevate it and the metaphors that cluster around it. Since then, I have tried to explain why decline narratives so often locate their characters in their middle years.

16. I draw here on the relatively new study of the history of the emotions, or "emotionology." I am trying to relate "the thinking of individuals" to "the social context of thought" (Billig et al. 1988, 2) and trying to estimate how individuals are affected by ideology, and how much. Emotionology goes beyond "thinking" to relate feelings to social contexts.

17. Newman (in this issue) noticed in her Harlem study that many (especially Spanish) informants did not know the terms "middle years," or "midlife." But subjects may apply ageist decline discourses to themselves in midlife or earlier even without knowing those terms.

18. Higher class status seems to make both men and women *more* vulnerable to the kinds of decline arguments that have purchases built into them: e.g., plastic

surgery, hormone replacement "therapy," objects of fashion. See "Men. All Together Now?" "Menopause as Magic Marker," and "The Other End of the Fashion
Cycle" (Gullette 1997, pt. 3).

19. Such a self is also posited by feminism, antiracism, cultural studies, and
liberation movements. The self cannot help but be affected by ideological attempts
to make its learning "compulsory" early in life and then keep its knowledge un-
changing. "But it does move" [*pur si muove*], Galileo reaffirmed even as he bowed
to state compulsion.

20. See Gullette (1997), which theorizes and practices "age autobiography," esp.
pt. 1, "My Private Midlife."

21. Charles Altieri, along with a few other critics, has noticed how "governing
metaphors for our theorizing . . . privilege space over time" (1990, 2). We could
use more work on why aging (an obvious aspect of temporality) is so neglected a
dimension of theory. Has any theorist of ideology seen age as an ideological system?
Seeing it as such might also freshen the critique of ideology.

22. Even though the word "aging" is often used as a euphemism for old age
or the elderly, it can now refer to people in their middle years and people as young
as the "aging baby boomers."

23. This is quoted with a straight face in a book called *After Forty* (Gorney and
Cox 1973, 77–78) that is supposed to be helpful to women thinking about aging.

24. According to one small study of college students and their parents (Rozin
and Fallon), the gender gap narrowed in the parents' cohort: 59% of the men and
67% of the women were dissatisfied with their body weight. A study of Harvard
and Radcliffe students found that by ten years out of college (1982–92), preoccupation with weight had increased in men (Heatherton [1997] and in conversation).

25. In my collection of age-related visual materials is a 1930 Lucky Strike ad
called "Condemning Shadows." It depicts a drawing in soft pastels of a young
woman in profile; next to her in black silhouette is her profile presumably some
years later wearing a goitrous "double chin." By 1930 flesh under the chin was
apparently considered an effect of overeating, and advertising was already connect-
ing smoking to appetite suppression. Ergo, the motto, "When tempted, reach for
a Lucky instead." The ad continues, "We do not represent that smoking *Lucky Strike*
Cigarettes will bring modern figures or cause the reduction of flesh. We do declare
that when tempted to do yourself too well, if you will 'Reach for a Lucky' instead,
you will thus avoid over-indulgence in things that cause excess weight and by
avoiding over-indulgence maintain a modern, graceful form."

26. Kinsey asked men of all ages for their *memories* of sexual behavoir. From
his data, it is impossible to tell the ages of those remembering teen masturbation,
etc. In other words, a decline narrative already exists; it may affect memory.

27. From a British book, *How to Survive the Male Menopause,* as quoted by
Featherstone and Hepworth (1985, 235). Featherstone and Hepworth took a critical
stance toward these "cultural myths, popular stereotypes, strange rumours and folk
tales" (237), but they believed that the factors that caused them "are major integral
features of all western societies and are now reaching out to influence everyday life
in the Third World" (245). That is, no change is likely, despite critiques like theirs.

28. The metaphor of "freezing" a culture comes from Agger (1992).

29. This is a typical example from the field of the sociology of emotions. I have

lost the citation, unfortunately, but wish to give credit to the unknown author of this most apposite example.

30. On the coerciveness of the practice of "fashion" over time, see "The Other End of the Fashion Cycle: Practicing Loss, Learning Decline" (Gullette 1997, chap. 10).

31. The sociologist Michael Brown, in conversation.

32. What needs to be monitored is the age at which people begin practicing "the still syndrome." Two male college roommates meet five years after graduation: "You still bench-pressing [X number of] pounds?"

33. My work in progress, *Midlife Fictions,* deals with women as well as with men; see also "The Invention of the 'Postmaternal' Woman" (Gullette 1995a).

34. Major figures in the theory of feminist men's studies include R. W. Connell (see Carrigan et al. 1987), Michael Kimmel (1990, 1996), the writers collected in Hearn and Morgan (1990), and John Stoltenberg (1990). Among the historians working in feminist men's studies is E. Anthony Rotundo (1993). Barbara Ehrenreich's *The Hearts of Men* is one of many feminist precursors to the development of feminist men's studies.

Antiracists like David Roediger, in *Towards the Abolition of Whiteness* (1994), are also showing men that they are constructed (as white and of a certain class) in racialized contexts.

35. See Gruman (1978). There is now widespread agreement that the period 1880–1930 saw a basic change in the cultural construction of the elderly and of adolescence. Among the most useful writers on this subject are Cole (1992), Gruman, and Kohli (1986). None of them considers the midlife. Treating the midlife requires focusing the questions differently; it complicates many of the answers already provided and calls for new research and rethinking in a great range of disciplines and across disciplinary boundaries.

36. See Young (1904, 36). Historians interested in the later life course do not use life expectancy at birth to calculate the probable life span, but begin figuring at age 20. Here I am less interested in what a current historian might know about the past than in the beliefs and feelings of those who lived at the time: in short, what an actual adult of that time might reasonably expect. My choice of statistics aims to show that at the age of fifty, a person in 1910 could expect about as much "adulthood" to lie before as behind, and in New England at least would be surrounded by a substantial number of the "old."

In trying to define a new era of longevity, Peter Laslett chose measures that "capture the prospects of persons at the beginning of the Second Age [adulthood, starting at age 25] continuing to live on into the Third Age" [which for him begins between ages 50 and 65] (1991, 85). Even his more precise conditions (10% actually over age 65, a majority of those at twenty-five years of age expecting to reach age 70) had nearly been met *as early as 1910* (see Epstein 1922, 8). Until we give up the received opinion that all great gains in longevity occurred after World War II, we can have no correct sense of what it felt like to be a (healthy, privileged) adult of, say, forty or fifty or sixty in 1910.

37. I am summarizing here material from the letters of Augusta Salik Dublin (Schlesinger Library, Radcliffe College). I learned of these letters through the work of Linda Rosenzweig (1993, chap. 8). On the construction of a postmaternal woman

who is supposed to consider herself "idle, useless, and out of a job," see Gullette (1995a). The metaphor of the empty nest was invented in 1914 by the writer Dorothy Canfield and very quickly moved into mainstream discourse.

38. Although black migrants in the Great Migration usually moved in families, more black men than women moved, leaving a gender imbalance in the remaining population (Johnson and Campbell 1981, 99).

39. See Theodore Dreiser's chapter on the way midlife men were bullied into taking strenuous exercise cures, in *Twelve Men* (1917); see also Tom Lutz (1991). Like aging now, neurasthenia was the cover term for many problems. But neurasthenia had cachet, and midlife aging did not; neurasthenia disappeared when its cachet did, according to Lutz, but "middle age" is unlikely to drop out of the life course.

40. The spread of age grading into many institutional areas is described by Chudacoff (1989).

41. Recent studies of the Homestead strike of 1892 discuss the Victorian industrial conditions that produced precocious aging, illness, and death. *Middletown: A Study in Contemporary American Culture* (Lynd and Lynd 1929) is particularly good on showing the ways in which industry treated midlife men as expendable during the 1920s. Unions fought over issues like seniority and deskilling. See Richard Edwards (1979) and John A. DeBrizzi (1983). Ransom and Sutch provide evidence of "life-cycle deskilling" and "downward occupational mobility" as early as 1875 (1986, 19); they also provide insight on income decline with age (27–29).

42. The white bookkeeper had been expecting to receive a raise for having worked twenty-five years. Gender is related to his story in various ways. His boss tells him that he will be replaced by an adding machine and a girl with a high school education. His emotional state is affected by his fear of having to tell his (nagging, same-age) wife that he has lost his job.

43. In my work in progress, *Midlife Fictions*, I will describe the major factors that produced midlife aging at the turn of the century, for women as well as men. This work might eventually be part of a larger history of the way people in various subject positions in given eras and national situations develop midlife progress or decline narratives. Such histories would want to link the narratives that can be written to economic and cultural as well as to psychological factors.

44. The terms "age-earnings profile," "age-poverty profile," "age-income profile" are used by Stern (1991, 522, 523). For me, the age-wage profile provides a link between "macro perspectives and micro situations and processes" (Marcus 1986, 169 n. 6), and a crucial one: it explains how an economic system can affect a given man psychologically through his actual working life, first in youthful anticipations that get internalized (as personal/class expectations) and then in experiences over the long term. Women's relationships to the age-wage profile are a separate subject, given (to mention only a few factors) midlife female dependency, gender and age discrimination in the workforce, differences in class and education, and the differences between unmarried and married women workers in expectations and working situations. We need far more age-sensitive knowledge of labor history at the turn of the century, and of changes in the age-wage profile in particular, to confirm my speculations here. Unfortunately, data on incomes over time

are very sparse in this period (Claudia Goldin, private communication; see also Goldin 1990).

45. By the turn of the century, the expectation for midlife parents now included, depending on class, either keeping children in high school or sending them on to college. The source for this paragraph on economic changes and their relationship to the idea of the life course is research for the first chapter ("The Origins of Their Despairs") of my work in progress, *Midlife Fictions.*

46. The source for these paragraphs is Gullette (1994) and related research for "The Invention of Male Midlife Sexual Decline," a part of my work in progress, *Midlife Fictions.*

47. John B. McKinlay et al. have titled a paper "The Questionable Physiological and Epidemiologic Basis for a Male Climacteric Syndrome." Conducting met-analyses of clinical studies, over the years McKinlay and his associates have found only the slightest evidence for any decline of testosterone with aging in studies that correct for illness (see, e.g., McKinlay and Feldman 1992).

48. Letters written to Marie Stopes, a medical doctor and popular sex counsellor and author of *Enduring Passion* (1931), show that in the late 1920s and during the 1930s, impotence was a problem for many midlife men who were otherwise healthy and said they loved their wives. Lesley Hall has generously shared with me her notes on Stopes's correspondence with men between the ages of 38 and 70. Hall did not use this as midlife material or consider age in her otherwise fascinating book, *Hidden Anxieties* (1991).

49. Sontag's (1979) "The Double Standard of Aging" needs to be supplemented by accounts of midlife gender relations in American history before and since.

50. This will be explored more fully in two chapters of *Midlife Fictions,* my work in progress: "The Invention of the Necessary Father" and "Deprived of Love and Destined for Divorce."

51. "Women's earnings peak at ages 35–44, while men's earnings peak later in life, at ages 45–54" (Rayman et al. 1993, 140, citing Deborah Figart; see also Gullette 1995b).

52. The Massachusetts Male Aging Study ($N = 1,709$; ages 40–70) found that "the data concerning men's level of satisfaction with their sex life, their partners, and their estimate of their partner's level of satisfaction did not evidence the same age-related changes reported so far for other aspects of sexual activity. . . . Men in their sixties reported levels of satisfaction with their sex life and partners at about the same level as younger men in their forties" (McKinlay and Feldman 1992, 7). Some popular studies also try to prove, or at least assert, how much satisfaction men feel at older ages. See Janus and Janus (1993, 25, 27) and Reinisch and Beasley (1990, 227).

53. *Modern Maturity* (1993, 23). Both the researchers and the reviewer count orgasms and assume that quantity is an important value. Janus and Janus (1993) note "mixed feelings" among their 39–50 year old group and to some extent among men 51–64 as well: "Some respondents still emphasized numbers of conquests and speed of climax" (27).

54. "Contentment with the status quo increased with age, so that nearly a quarter of the men over fifty-five did not desire more experimentation of some sort—three times the number of contented men in their twenties" (Pietropinto and Simenauer 1977, 3). Their sample comprised four thousand men.

55. Such stories also challenge essentialist interpretations of men that see as innate (lifelong) their violence toward women, their need to dominate women, their fear of women, etc.

56. See Gullette *Safe at Last* (1988) and "Midlife Heroines" in *Declining to Decline* (1997) for examples of women writers' progress narratives and theorizing about the genre.

References

ABFP (American Board of Family Practice). 1990. *The Physicians' View of Middle Age.* Report 2, conducted by DYG, Inc. Lexington, Ky.: APFB.

Acton, William. 1875. *The Functions and Disorders of the Reproductive Organs in Childhood, Youth, Adult Age and Advanced Life.* Philadelphia: Lindsay & Blakison.

Agger, Ben. 1992. "Marxism, Feminism, Deconstruction." In *The Politics of Culture and Creativity: A Critique of Civilization,* edited by Christine Ward Gailey. Gainesville: University Press of Florida.

Altieri, Charles. 1990. "Temporality and the Necessity for Dialectic: The Missing Dimension of Contemporary Theory." Paper delivered at the Humanities Center, University of California at Santa Barbara.

Ariès, Philippe. 1962. *Centuries of Childhood: A Social History of Family Life,* translated by Robert Baldick. New York: Vintage Books.

Barrett, Michele. 1985. "Ideology and the Cultural Production of Gender." In *Feminist Criticism and Social Change,* edited by Judith Newton and Deborah Rosenfelt. New York and London: Methuen.

Berger, Peter L., and Thomas Luckmann. 1966. *The Social Construction of Reality: A Treatise in the Sociology of Knowledge.* Garden City, N.Y.: Doubleday Anchor.

Billig, Michael, et al. 1988. *Ideological Dilemmas. A Social Psychology of Everyday Thinking.* London: Sage.

Bourne, Randolph S. 1913. *Youth and Life.* Freeport, N.Y.: Books for Libraries Press.

Brecher, Edward M., et al. 1984. *Love, Sex and Aging: A Consumers Union Report.* Boston: Little Brown.

Carrigan, Tim, Bob Connell, and John Lee. 1987. "Hard and Heavy: Toward a New Sociology of Masculinity." In *Beyond Patriarchy: Essays by Men on Pleasure, Power and Change,* edited by Michael Kaufman. Toronto: Oxford University Press.

Chudacoff, Howard. 1989. *How Old Are You? Age Consciousness in American Culture.* Princeton, N.J.: Princeton University Press.

Cole, Thomas. 1992. *The Journey of Life: A Cultural History of Aging in America.* Cambridge: Cambridge University Press.

CRC (Consumer Research Center). 1985. *Midlife and Beyond: The 800 Billion Over-Fifty Market.* New York: The Conference Board.

DeBrizzi, John A. 1983. *Ideology and the Rise of Labor Theory in America.* Westport, Conn.: Greenwood.

Eagleton, Terry. 1991. *Ideology: An Introduction.* London and New York: Verso.

Edwards, Richard. 1979. *Contested Terrain.* New York: Basic Books.

Ellis, Havelock. 1942. *Psychology of Sex.* New York: Emerson.

Epstein, Abraham. 1922. *Facing Old Age.* New York: Knopf.

Featherstone, Mike, and Mike Hepworth. 1985. "The Male Menopause: Lifestyle and Sexuality." *Maturitas* 7:235–46.

Galbraith, John Kenneth. 1993. "At the Age of 85, a New Cause Fighting the Still Syndrome." *Boston Globe* (October 14), 19.

Gallagher, Winifred. 1993. "Myths of Middle Age." *Atlantic Monthly* (May), 51–68.

Goldin, Claudia. 1990. *Understanding the Gender Gap: An Economic History of American Women.* New York: Oxford University Press.

Gordon, Michael. 1971. "From an Unfortunate Necessity to a Cult of Mutual Orgasm." *Sex in American Marital Education Literature, 1830–1940.* Studies in the Sociology of Sexuality, edited by James Henslin. New York: Appleton-Century-Crofts.

Gordon, Steven. 1990. "Social Structural Effects on Emotions." In *Research Agendas in the Sociology of Emotions,* edited by Theodore D. Kemper. Albany: State University Press of New York.

Gorney, Sandra, and Claire Cox. 1973. *After Forty.* New York: Dial.

Gruman, Gerald J. 1978. "Cultural Origins of Present-Day 'Ageism': The Modernization of the Life Cycle." *Aging and the Elderly: Humanistic Perspectives in Gerontology,* edited by Stuart F. Spicker, Kathleen M. Woodward, and David D. Van Tassel. Atlantic Highlands, N.J.: Humanities Press.

Gullette, Margaret Morganroth. 1984. "The Exile of Adulthood: Pedophilia in the Midlife Novel." *Novel* 17, no. 3 (spring): 215–32.

———. 1988. *Safe at Last in the Middle Years: The Invention of the Midlife Progress Novel.* Berkeley and Los Angeles: University of California Press.

———. 1993a. "Creativity/Gender/Age, a Study of Their Intersections, 1910–1935." In *Aging and Gender in Literature: Studies in Creativity,* edited by Anne M. Wyatt-Brown and Janice Rossen. Charlottesville: University Press of Virginia.

———. 1993b. "What, Menopause *Again?*" *Ms. Magazine* 4, no. 1 (summer): 34–37.

———. 1994. "Male Midlife Sexuality in a Gerontocratic Economy: The Privileged Stage of the Long Midlife in Nineteenth-Century Age-Ideology." *Journal of the History of Sexuality* 5, no. 1 (July): 58–89.

———. 1995a. "The Invention of the 'Postmaternal' Woman: Idle, Useless, and Out of a Job," *Feminist Studies* 21 (2): 221–53.

———. 1995b. "The Wonderful Woman on the Pavement: Middle-Ageism in the Postmodern Economy." *Dissent* 42, no. 4 (fall): 508–14.

———. 1996. "Declining to Decline." *Women's Review of Books* 13, no. 12 (September): 1, 3–4.

————. 1997. *Declining to Decline: Cultural Combat and the Politics of the Midlife.* Charlottesville: University Press of Virginia.

Hall, Lesley. 1991. *Hidden Anxieties: Male Sexuality, 1900–1950.* Cambridge, Mass.: Basil Blackwell.

Hearn, Jeff, and David Morgan, eds. 1990. *Men, Masculinities and Social Theory.* London: Unwin Hyman.

Heatherton, Todd, et al. 1997. "A Ten-Year Longitudinal Study of Body Weight, Dieting, and Eating Disorder Symptoms." *Journal of Abnormal Psychology* 106: 117–25.

Janus, Samuel S., and Cynthia L. Janus. 1993. *The Janus Report on Sexual Behavior.* New York: Wiley.

Johnson, Daniel M., and Rex R. Campbell. 1981. *Black Migration in America: A Social Demographic History.* Durham, N.C.: Duke University Press.

Kimmel, Michael. 1990. "After Fifteen Years: The Impact of the Sociology of Masculinity on the Masculinity of Sociology." In *Men, Masculinities and Social Theory,* edited by Jeff Hearn and David Morgan. London: Unwin Hyman.

————. 1996. *Manhood in America: A Cultural History.* New York: Free Press.

Kinsey, Alfred, et al. 1948. *Sexual Behavior in the Human Male.* Philadelphia: W. B. Saunders.

Kohli, Martin. 1986. "The World We Forgot: A Historical Review of the Life Course." In *Later Life: The Social Psychology of Aging,* edited by Victor W. Marshall. Beverly Hills, Calif.: Sage.

Laslett, Peter. 1991. *A Fresh Map of Life: The Emergence of the Third Age.* Cambridge, Mass.: Harvard University Press.

Lutz, Tom. *American Nervousness 1903: An Anecdotal History.* Ithaca, N.Y.: Cornell University Press.

Lynd, Robert S., and Helen Merrell Lynd. 1929. *Middletown: A Study in Contemporary American Culture.* New York: Harcourt, Brace.

Mannheim, Karl. 1972. "The Problem of Generations." In *The New Pilgrims: Youth Protest in Transition,* edited Philip G. Altbach and Robert S. Laufer, 101–38. New York: David McKay.

Marcus, George. 1986. "Contemporary Problems of Ethnography in the Modern World System." In *Writing Culture: The Poetics and Politics of Ethnography,* edited by James Clifford and George Marcus. Berkeley and Los Angeles: University of California Press.

McKinlay, John B., and Henry A. Feldman. 1992. "Changes in Sexual Activity and Interest in the Normally Aging Male: Results from the Massachusetts Male Aging Study." Invited paper, MacArthur Foundation Research Network on Successful Midlife Development, New England Research Institute, Watertown, Mass., May.

McLeish, John A. B. 1976. *The Ulyssean Adult: Creativity in the Middle and Later Years.* Toronto: McGraw-Hill Ryerson.

Medina, Angel. 1990. Review of David Carr's *Time, Narrative and History*. *Man and World* 23 (1990): 231–37.

Modern Maturity 1993. Review of the Janus Report on Sexual Behavior, *Modern Maturity* (April 28).

Ormond, Leonee. 1987. *J. M. Barrie*. Edinburgh: Scottish Academic Press.

Pietropinto, Antony, and Jacqueline Simenauer. 1977. *Beyond the Male Myth*. New York: New York Times Books.

Ransom, Roger L., and Richard Sutch. 1986. "The Labor of Older Americans: Retirement of Men On and Off the Job, 1870–1937." *Journal of Economic History* 46, no. 1 (March): 1–30.

Rayman, Paula, Kimberly Allshouse, and Jessie Allen. 1993. "Resiliency and Inequality: Older Women Workers in an Aging United States." In *Women on the Front Lines: Meeting the Challenges of an Aging America*, edited by Jessie Allen and Alan Pifer, 133–66. Washington, D.C.: Urban Institute Press.

Reinisch, June Machover, with Ruth Beasley. 1990. *The Kinsey Institute New Report on Sex: What You Must Know to Be Sexually Literate*. New York: St. Martin's Press.

Richards, Jeffrey. 1987. " 'Passing the Love of Women': Manly Love in Victorian Society." In *Manliness and Morality: Middle-Class Masculinity in Britain and America, 1800–1940*, edited by J. A. Mangan and James Walvin. Manchester: Manchester University Press.

Roediger, David. 1994. *Towards the Abolition of Whiteness: Essays on Race, Politics, and Working Class History*. New York: Verso.

Rosenzweig, Linda. 1993. *The Anchor of My Life: Middle Class American Mothers and Daughters, 1880–1920*. New York: New York University Press.

Rotundo, Anthony. 1993. *American Manhood: Transformations in Masculinity from the Revolution to the Modern Era*. New York: Basic Books.

Rozin, Paul, and April Fallon. 1988. "Body Image, Attitudes to Weight, and Misperceptions of Figure Preferences of the Opposite Sex: A Comparison of Men and Women in Two Generations." *Journal of Abnormal Psychology* 97 (3): 342–45.

Sherman, Edmund. 1987. *Meaning in Mid-Life Transitions*. Albany: State University of New York Press.

Sollors, Werner, ed. 1989. *The Invention of Ethnicity*. New York: Oxford University Press.

Sontag, Susan. 1979. "The Double Standard of Aging." In *Psychology of Women: Selected Readings*, edited by Juanita H. Williams. New York: Norton.

Spacks, Patricia Ann Meyer. 1981. *The Adolescent Idea: Myths of Youth and the Adult Imagination*. New York: Basic Books.

Stern, Mark J. 1991. "Poverty and the Life-Cycle, 1940–1960." *Journal of Social History* 24, no. 3 (spring): 521–41.

Stoltenberg, John. 1990. *Refusing to Be a Man: Essays on Sex and Justice*. New York: Penguin.

Stopes, Marie. 1931. *Enduring Passion*. Garden City, N.Y.: Blue Ribbon Books.

Young, Allyn A. 1904. *A Discussion of Age Statistics.* Washington, D.C.: Bureau of the Census.

Williams, Raymond. 1966. *Modern Tragedy.* Stanford, Calif.: Stanford University Press.

Wyatt-Brown, Anne M., and Janice Rossen, eds. 1993. *Aging and Gender in Literature: Studies in Creativity.* Charlottesville: University Press of Virginia.

Deconstructing the Change: Female Maturation in Japan and North America

Margaret Lock

Until the second half of this century, academic explanations about the human life cycle tended to be bifurcated so that the concepts of "development" and "aging" were understood as antithetical. Development was the province of the young and was visualized as a number of age-related changes in body and behavior that culminated in maturation, although these changes were subject to modification, it was believed, as a result of environmental and cultural influences. Human development was intimately associated with the ideas of gain, improvement, and progress, and thus it was, clearly, "a good thing" (Perlmutter and Hall 1992, 14). Aging, on the other hand, was confined to those who no longer "develop"—to adults on the path of decline and deterioration. Senescence was an indicator of irreversible failure, therefore, and was, by definition, a "bad thing." Of the two concepts, *aging*, more so than *development*, has been conceptualized until recently in academic writing as overwhelmingly a biological process, virtually independent of social and cultural influence, and hence uniform through time and space.

From classical times the dominant European conceptualization of the human life span was one of sequential stages punctuated by transitional phases often associated with danger or crises. From the beginning of this century when a scientific approach was applied to the life span, emphasis was placed initially on developmental stages—on infancy, childhood, and adolescence. Then, belatedly, toward the middle of the century as demography changed, the elderly were also made subjects of research. "Middle age" was the last portion of the life span to be "discovered." Until recently this transition has usually been understood as a time of "crisis" in which individuals must face up to what the future holds, including unavoidable physical and social losses culminating in death (Rayner 1979). The end of menstruation, indicat-

Funding for this research was provided by the Social Science and Humanities Research Council of Canada, grant no. 244-77.

ing a loss of reproductive capacity, has often been interpreted as the precipitating crisis for women in middle age (Fink 1980).

Today it is widely recognized that, at the cellular level, death is ever present, even before birth, and, conversely, that aging involves both developmental changes as well as decline. Thus the conceptual opposition between development and aging has been softened and modified, particularly in the hands of those researchers who take a "life-span" perspective rather than focus on particular "stages" of the life cycle. As part of this revision the "normative crisis model" usually applied to middle age (Levinson 1977) has been subjected to questioning and further research.

The usual construction of research questions in connection with the experiences of men and women in middle age reveal some distinctive features that reflect disciplinary interests, gender bias, and fragmentation. Movement through the life cycle involves both biological and social change, but research into the midlife transition has tended to focus, in the case of men, on the trajectory of their work life, while biological aging is essentially ignored. Women's social lives, however, are usually conceptualized as being subordinated to the "biological clock." One result of this gendered distinction is that female middle age has been increasingly subject to medicalization throughout this century in Europe and North America—much more so than that of males—and is generally thought of today as falling within the domain of the gynecologist. The pathological Menopausal Woman takes center stage and, in recent years, has virtually obliterated any other way of understanding female middle age.

In this chapter I will discuss historical and contemporary ideas and practices in connection with female midlife in North America and then turn to Japan in order to show how the meaning of middle age, both as it is politically and ideologically constructed as well as subjectively experienced in everyday life, is significantly different. These differences can largely be attributed to the focus in North America on *individuals* as they age, whereas in Japan attention is given above all to changing *social relationships*. Thus, in contrast to North America, precedence is given in Japan to aging as a social process rather than to transformations in individual biology.

THE FLEXIBLE LIFE COURSE

It remains common for developmental psychologists to discuss "stages of adulthood" and "benchmarks of maturity"; middle age is usually subdivided into early and later developmental stages based on chronological age (Perlmutter and Hall 1992). However, viewing the passage of individuals through the life cycle as an ordered, age-related progression has been criticized as being a retrospective reconstruction—largely a figment of the researcher's imagination (Freeman 1984). Criticisms have also been directed, usually by sociologists and anthropologists, toward developmental psychologists who focus on what is described as decontextualized individual development divorced from social environment, institutions, and local history (Featherstone and Hepworth 1991). It has been pointed out, for example, that both Philippe Ariès (1973) and Norbert Elias (1978) argued that an individual's family status rather than chronological age determined public recognition of maturity in premodern Europe. In contrast, throughout this century chronological age, above all else, has come to determine maturation; at the same time, the life course has been subject to increasing surveillance and control by the state, to which academic research into development and aging have contributed (Foucault 1979). Thus the assessment of what counts as maturity, and the subjective experience of attaining that state, varies through time and space.

Featherstone and Hepworth argue that representation of the life course is presently undergoing reconceptualization. In place of an inflexible, age-based chronology, there is increasing recognition of malleability: the life course is frequently visualized today as a "process . . . which need *not* involve a predetermined series of stages of growth" (1991, 375). Thus, the normative expectations that society may have about passage through the life course are in practice made flexible or even abandoned, a tendency that no doubt has always been present but was formerly masked by the imposition of a powerful analytic scheme suggesting the preponderance of an orderly progression through time. Despite their commitment to flexibility, Featherstone and Hepworth are quick to remind their readers that culture cannot mold nature in any way it chooses and that clear limits are imposed by biology with respect to birth, growth, maturation, and death. However, the development of genetic engineering, new reproductive technologies, and organ transplants, together with other biomedical technologies, are rapidly ensuring that these authors must modify their position somewhat, since, thanks to the artifice of culture, nature is made increasingly malleable and the natural world can no longer be taken for granted (Strathern 1992, 55).

THE PRIME OF LIFE

The human life cycle was conceptualized in Europe from classical times until the end of the nineteenth century as a series of epochs. This doctrine was based upon the magical quality given to certain numbers, of which seven was "ever revered as an especially potent number, the number of perfection" (Sears 1986, 20). Medieval European ideas about middle age were heavily influenced by the writings of early Arab and Greek scholars including Aristotle, who stated that man is in his *akme* (prime) at forty-nine years of age. The number seven multiplied by itself was considered especially significant and was understood as the age of maturity, of "full ripeness"—the perfect age of man. Medieval descriptions of women make it clear that, whereas a mature man was associated with wisdom and perfection, a woman, by contrast, was thought of as "cold" and "dry," "like an old katte" (Dove 1986, 23).

A slightly different but related medieval numerical formulation postulated that "phases" of the life cycle succeeded each other every seven years, so that the seventh, fourteenth, twenty-first, twenty-eighth and so on, until the seventieth year, were all considered to be critical transition periods. The term *climacteric* was used to describe the dangers of any transition or critical period of the life cycle, regardless of age or gender; the grand climacteric came in the sixty-third year and heralded entry into old age and the final portion of the life cycle. By the early nineteenth century the medical profession had appropriated the concept of climacteric and narrowed its meaning to specify that "period of life (usually between the ages of 45 and 60) at which the vital forces begin to decline" (*Oxford English Dictionary*). At least one physician writing at the time stated "I will venture to question, whether [the climacteric] be not, in truth, a *disease* rather than a mere declension of strength and decay of natural powers" (Halford 1813, 317; original emphasis). He went on to observe, in direct contrast to contemporary thinking, that "though this climacteric disease is sometimes equally remarkable in women as in men, yet most certainly I have not noticed it so frequently, nor so well characterized in females" (323) and conjectured in conclusion that it might be the prospect of death that was the underlying cause of distress.

A perusal of nineteenth-century medical literature shows that, concurrently with the consolidation of gynecology as a profession, the concept of the climacteric was reformulated so that its usage was now confined to women. The word *menopause* was invented in the 1820s to describe the end of menstruation, a critical transformation in the larger time span of the climacteric (Lock 1993, 307–9). Although some physicians took it upon themselves to attract middle-aged female patients and treat them for climacteric symptoms, the majority showed no interest in this practice. Both medical and popular literature of the time make it clear, in contrast to medieval conceptions, that for women (of the emerging middle class at least) the "prime of life" might be a rewarding time during which, now past childbearing and rearing, they could take up activities on behalf of the community. Physicians were explicit that women lived longer than men—twenty-five or thirty years past "cessation"—and that although the epoch of forty to fifty-five was often a "perilous passage" for women, afterward a great improvement in health and often in looks was evident. The London physician Edward Tilt asserted that men show more climacteric "decay" than do women (1870, 10). Interested physicians of the time argued among themselves as to whether or not menopause was a significant event and conjectured as to whether the majority of women were disturbed by this transition. Many claimed that menopause was of little importance to most, although it is apparent that women themselves often attributed the end of menstruation with a special importance since they regularly expressed delight that they could no longer become pregnant (Smith-Rosenberg 1985, 195). By the beginning of the twentieth century, however, the tone of certain influential medical literature had shifted.

Charles Reed, president of the American Medical Association in 1901 and 1902, was perhaps to first to state that the "mental condition of the menopause is one marked by depression." He went on:

> A man grows old by merciful and gentle gradations, and so he slides, half willingly, and half unconsciously, into the afternoon of life, with regrets so soft that they can scarce provoke a sigh. But for a woman, man's twenty years of gentle change are compressed into two. . . . It is evolution for him; it is revolution for her. . . She is invited, with cruel abruptness, to be to her husband merely an intellectual companion or a sexless helpmeet, when she had been of late the object of his embraces and the mother of his babes. One third of her adult life is still before her, full of promise of placid enjoyment and great usefulness, but to her, remembering the glory of conquest and surrender,

the future stretches a dreary waste of empty years. (Reed 1904, 741–42)

This passage, and others like it in turn-of-the-century medical writing, indicate that the idea of an epoch has disappeared, replaced by the turbulent event of menopause, limited to women, and negatively associated above all with a loss of femininity and reproductive capacity. This interpretation of female middle age has been elaborated over the course of this century in two directions, formulated on the one hand by psychiatrists and on the other by gynecologists. These differing accounts, although outwardly competitive, paradoxically reinforce each other to produce an exceedingly negative account of female middle age although, significantly, we know very little indeed about how midlife was (and is) subjectively experienced and interpreted by women themselves.

DEPRESSION AND LOSS: PSYCHOANALYSIS AND FEMALE MIDLIFE

Psychoanalytic accounts of female midlife were dominated until about twenty years ago by the idea that every woman would inevitably mourn the loss of reproductive capacity symbolized by the end of menstruation. Helene Deutsch described menopause as a time of "immanent disappointment and mortification" (1945, 460). Her writing influenced Simone de Beauvoir, who described the "sad hours of depression" following menopause, precipitated, she believed, in large part because her "feminine functions" now past, "woman escapes slavery only . . . when she loses all effectiveness" (1952, 550).

Eric Erikson contributed to this gloomy picture when he attempted to portray the "uniqueness" of woman, in particular with respect to her attitudes about space:

> [An] "inner space" is at the center of despair even as it is the very center of potential fulfillment. Emptiness is the female form of perdition. . . . To be left, for her, means to be left empty, to be drained of the blood of the body, the warmth of the heart, the sap of life. How a woman thus can be hurt in depth is a wonder to many a man, and it can arouse both his empathic horror and his refusal to understand. Such hurt can be re-experienced in each menstruation; it is a crying to heaven in the mourning over a

child; and it becomes a permanent scar in the menopause.
(Erikson 1968, 278)

A major contribution that de Beauvoir made in discussing this genre
of literature, with its rhetoric of hurt and loss, was to point out how
women are portrayed in these accounts as "the other, the inessential,
the object" (1952, xvii). In common with Jules Henry (1966) and later
Susan Sontag (1972), de Beauvoir shows how renditions of the experience of aging are gendered. Women's life, it is assumed, has no inherent
meaning aside from sexuality and reproduction, and thus postrepro-
ductive life is quite literally empty. The psychiatric profession has in
recent years self-consciously tried to counter this discourse. A 1989
psychiatric text states, for example, that "the significance of menopause
has changed over time . . . with more social and career options. . . .
Contrary to popular view, this time is not one of depression for women
who have not been depressed before" (Apfel and Mazor 1988, 1337).
Nevertheless, the "double standard of aging" (Sontag 1972) clearly remains pervasive (Greer 1991; Wolf 1990), as does our cultural stereotype that menopause is an exceedingly difficult time (Sheehy 1992).

Un-Natural Body

Although they continue to influence public opinion, psychoanalytic
explanations about the meaning of female middle age have fallen into
disrepute in recent years, at least in their extreme formulation. In contrast, endocrinological explanations have become increasingly pervasive and authoritarian, and are actively promoted by gynecologists as
the "beneficial" way to understanding this part of the life cycle, beneficial, that is, to ongoing health and well-being (Utian and Jacobowitz
1990).

There is explicit concern among physicians, well documented in
the professional literature, about the numbers of "postmenopausal"
women in North America today: "More than 40 million American
women are menopausal; another 3.5 million will be reaching the climacteric age each year for the next 12 years. These women will have
a life expectancy of more than 30 years after menopause" (Sarrel 1988,
25). Many articles then go on to estimate the cost to society of health
care for postmenopausal women (see, e.g., Reid 1988, 25; Lufkin et al.
1989, 205). In addition to drawing attention to the "surplus" of older
women, certain unexamined values are transparently visible in much
of this scientific literature on menopause. For example, female biologi-

cal aging is represented as inherently pathological and the physical condition of young women is taken as the "normal" standard for the bodies of all women, regardless of their age.

Among the many books and articles published for professional audiences and the public, the majority make statements such as the following: "At the turn of the century, a woman could expect to live to the age of forty-seven or -eight" (Sheehy 1991, 227). The inference usually gleaned from such claims is that women rarely lived past what is now understood as middle age until the beginning of this century, and hence the existence of women over fifty years of age is a recent phenomenon and, by implication, not what "nature" intended. Mean life expectancy at the beginning of this century was approximately forty-nine years of age both in North America and northern Europe, but, as Peter McKeown and others have shown, most of the increase in life expectancy in the past one hundred years can be attributed to a marked decrease in infant mortality and, to a lesser degree, to a decrease in the mortality of adolescents, young adults, and women during childbirth. McKeown argues that these changes were due largely to improved nutrition (1976). In recent years medical care has further improved life expectancy rates.

What is all too frequently misunderstood in discussions of female mortality is that mean life expectancy does not indicate the age at which most people died. If they survived infancy, young adulthood, and, in the case of women, pregnancy and childbirth, then, throughout human history, both women and men have had a good chance of living to old age. Nineteenth-century medical texts clearly indicate that physicians understood this to be the case for their patients.

Nevertheless the biologist Roger Gosden states that our "recent mastery of the environment" accounts for the existence of older women, a group ill-suited to life beyond menopause (1985, 2). The gynecologist John Dewhurst describes menopause as "unique" in the animal kingdom and states that, with increasing longevity, modern woman is "different from her forebears as well as from other species in that she can look forward to 20 or 30 years . . . after the menopause" (1981, 592). In these arguments, older women are portrayed as anomalies of nature—cultural artifacts—a state heralded by the end of menstruation, which is conceptualized as a disease-like event. Women, therefore, are inherently prone to pathology in later life.

"Ovarian failure" in middle age was first described at the end of the last century (Oudshoorn 1990), and by 1940 the "failure" of the ovaries to secrete estrogen at menopause was conceptualized as a deficiency and explicitly likened to diabetes or thyroid deficiency disease (Frank 1941, 863). This interpretation was in part facilitated by attention that had been given in European and North American gynecology from the middle of the last century onward to the effects of the "aging" ovary on the entire body (Oudshoorn 1994), and it set in motion a pathological discourse in which emphasis was and continues to be given to the "deterioration," "decline," "decay," and "the inevitable demise" of the ovary at menopause (Haspels and Van Keep 1979). Over the past twenty years these pathological metaphors have increasingly been accepted as "facts," so that menopause is now not merely *likened* to a deficiency disease, but is frequently assumed to be one (Lock 1993; Canadian Society of Obstetricians and Gynaecologists 1994).

Initially medical concern was focused on the menopausal woman and her distress, and estrogen therapy was developed in order to combat symptoms affecting those suffering from this new found disease. However, over the past twenty years, with increasing concerns about the aging population, attention has shifted and "estrogen failure" have been linked in the epidemiological literature to an increased risk for osteoporosis and, of even more significance, to heart disease in later life. It is currently recommended in the medical literature that *all* postmenopausal women take hormone replacement therapy for the remainder of their lives. Nevertheless, these findings are hotly contested among medical professionals and feminists, and by no means established as facts. Research results are confusing and contradictory and, in any case, based on probability samples from which extrapolations cannot readily be made to individual cases. Moreover, hormone replacement therapy has been linked in many studies to an increased risk for cancer (Mack and Ross 1989; Bergkvist et al. 1989). Nevertheless powerful interest groups (drug companies, researchers, physicians) recommend lifelong medication (Maturitas 1988; *Journal of the Society of Obstetricians and Gynecologists of Canada* 1994). Thus female aging is construed as one of accelerating pathology from midlife onward, and menopause—the change of life—is understood as the trigger for an ever-increasing risk of disease, culminating in death.

It is estimated that between 10% and 15% of eligible women take hormone replacement therapy on a regular basis, which suggests that medical discourse has not convinced most women of their potential decrepitude. Initially suggested by the work of Bernice Neugarten more than twenty years ago (1970) and more recently demonstrated by both

Kaufert et al. (1987) and McKinlay et al. (1992), it is clear that the majority of women do not experience a crisis at menopause, which may well contribute to their skepticism about the necessity for medication. Alternatively, the unpleasant side effects many women experience when using hormone replacement therapy may be sufficient to discourage use, or a fear of cancer may lead some women to resist this powerful medication on a long-term basis. To date we have very few narrative accounts about the meaning of middle age for ordinary North American women, but influential feminists, including Germaine Greer (1991) and Betty Friedan (1993) have recently taken critical stands against the discourses of loss and pathology associated with middle age.

The recent furor over what is known as "postmenopausal" or "retirement pregnancy" captures many of the ambiguities evident in most debate about female middle age. Supporters of this procedure, including many women, claim that it is a woman's right to have a baby whatever her age, and that "medical science is finally beginning to erase one of the last and deepest inequities between the sexes" (Wente 1994), that of early female reproductive senescence (in the idiom of the medical literature). Several commentaries claim that men are celebrated for siring progeny in old age, and therefore a double standard operates to criticize women who utilize technological innovations to overcome the limitations of nature. Criticism of this technology has been described by one medical ethicist as exhibiting "paternalism, ageism, sexism and Victorianism" (*Montreal Gazette* 1994). There are other viewpoints, however, including what has been described by Britain's minister of health as the right of the child to have a suitable home, which implies that an elderly mother cannot provide such an environment. The technology is exceedingly expensive and therefore available only to wealthy women, the failure rate is extremely high, together with a demonstrated risk of considerable significance to the health of women undergoing the procedure—points that are not brought up by those who argue for the "rights" of women to bear children until death. Commentaries in support of this new technology, with snappy titles such as "Outsmarting Mother Nature," in common with the dominant discourse about female middle age in general and menopause in particular, assume that young, reproductive women are the ideal, that male body function with its lifelong procreative power is the gold standard, and that women should be assisted in subverting the process of aging at all costs. Not surprisingly, the average life span at the turn of the century is cited to justify postmenopausal pregnancies: "A century ago, the average life span was 46 years for men, 48 for women. Say a woman had a child at the age of 24. She could count on being dead by the time her child was 24. No one assumed that made for an unsuitable home" (*Chicago Tribune* 1994). Once again the spector of the anomalous older woman haunts the rhetoric, but now, thanks to medical science, not only can she remain feminine and menstruating forever (Wilson 1966), she can also give birth at whatever age suits her.

In order to give birth after menstruation has ceased, an egg must be procured from a younger woman. Sometimes a woman has her own eggs frozen for use after menopause; in other cases women become mothers to their own grandchildren after fertilization with eggs taken from their daughters; occasionally older women are made pregnant with eggs taken from aborted fetuses or from eggs donated by unrelated women undergoing in vitro fertilization (many women meet the high cost of in vitro fertilization by agreeing to "donate" several "spare" eggs). To date postmenopausal pregnancies are not routinized, but they have the potential to radically transform the idea of female middle age—to eradicate part of the biological clock that has thus far profoundly shaped our understanding of the life course for women. The potential exists today for malleability in both social and biological aging, making it virtually impossible to discuss a "normative" life course. Below, I turn to Japan, where, despite massive technical, economic, and social transformations, the lives of women are conceptualized primarily in terms of family relations and obligations that take priority over individual aging.

Burnish of Age

Until as recently as ten years ago, 98% of Japanese women married. Today this number has dropped to 88%, and the divorce rate is increasing, but remains low, at 1.45 per thousand, much lower than in North America. Until very recently, virtually all women married in their mid-twenties and produced the required two children within a very narrow time span of five or six years. Families were usually complete by the time the mother became thirty-four years old. Women who remained unmarried at twenty-five were described as *urenoki* (unsold merchandise) or *tô ga tatsu* (overripe fruit). Nevertheless, the average age at marriage has in the past few years increased to twenty-seven, but the basic pattern remains in place. Virtually all children are born to married couples (99% of women who gave birth in 1992 were married or in committed common law arrangements, a figure that has been stable for three decades), and the majority of women stop working once pregnant for the first time (many of them are in effect forced to leave employment since it is believed that women cannot work effectively with young children in the household; see Lock, in press).

Perhaps this remarkable uniformity in the creation of family life is in part a product of a national sensitivity about movement through the life course evident since at least the beginning of this century. A genre of writing existed in Japanese known as *hito no isshô* (people's life span), in which the ideal life course of the people of a village, region, or of the entire nation was set out, indicating that considerable thought was given in early modern Japan as to how individuals should behave as they aged. Japanese society was age graded; in other words, passage through the life cycle was predominantly a social process involving community rituals in which people born in the same year participated together. Rituals associated with early childhood are still widely celebrated in contemporary Japan, although emphasis has shifted away from the community as a locus for these rituals to the family, with the exception of a few rural areas. The marking of birthdays is a recent innovation, and individual biological aging has always been subordinated to social maturation as part of both a family and a community, although the female life cycle has been shaped more by biology than that of males. Middle age—the prime of life (*sônen*)—was understood as a relatively undifferentiated part of the life cycle that commenced with marriage and lasted until ritual entry, at age 60, into old age. Although family celebrations were in order when a young woman reached menarche, as is the case in all other societies as far as we know, the end of menstruation was not noted, either by the family or community.

Similar to medieval European ideas about climacteria, the Japanese marked certain years in the life cycle as "years of calamity" (*yakudoshi*), when people were thought to be at great risk for misfortune or ill health. Today most Japanese think of *yakudoshi* simply as superstition, although individuals may note such years as they themselves encounter the particularly dangerous ones—age 42 for men, 33 for women.

A hanging scroll entitled "The Slope of Age" dates from about the fourteenth century and is the first known depiction of life's course in Japan. It is divided into decades: from age 10 a boy climbs up successive years to reach full maturity at age 50, the highest point on the scroll, after which his path is downhill until, at age 90, he appears old and bent as he sits quietly on a rock, watching a whirlpool at the foot of a waterfall. Seventeenth-century scrolls depict not only the life course of men but also of women, and in at least one rendition of female old age a woman appears bent and leaning on the shoulder of her child. Suzanne Formanek (1992) has shown how in classical literary texts in Japan a theme of regret at both physical and mental decay is evident: crooked backs, tottering gait, wrinkles, whitening and thinning hair, decaying teeth, sleeplessness, snoring, memory loss, and shaky handwriting are deplored and feared by men and women alike from the tenth century on in Japan. However, a counterdiscourse associated with both Confucianism and Buddhism fostered a more positive outlook.

Narrative accounts given by Japanese women who are at present in their fifties make it clear that many of them, both urban and rural residents, spend a good deal of time and energy in cultivating one or more art form.[1] Archery, flower arranging, calligraphy, the tea ceremony, classical poetry, and dance ("traditional" art forms, as opposed to learning a foreign language, taking cookery classes, etc.) are thought of as well-trodden "paths" (*dō*) to self-development and spiritual awareness (Lock 1993). Closely associated with the philosophy of Zen, these paths have long been a means whereby people can remove themselves temporarily from the demands of everyday life while cultivating personal discipline, the objective of which is, in theory, to escape this world of desire. This process commences for many individuals from early socialization, is lifelong, and is based on an ideology that accepts the possibility of human perfectibility over time, a condition that transcends and continues beyond the unavoidable decline of the human body.

From at least the days of Confucius (fourth century B.C.), this "heritage of possibilism" (Plath 1980, 5) has been dominant in East Asia, and its lasting influence in present-day Japan remains evident. Movement through the life cycle (as we will see below, the dominant image in Japan for aging is one of a cycle) is visualized primarily as a process of advancement through the social hierarchy, accompanied by personal maturation and increasing responsibility. For a man, this was formerly accomplished to a large extent in the world outside the household of which he was a part, and for a woman it took place initially in her parents' home and then, after marriage, in the household of her husband's parents. Daily life was, in theory, filled with duty, shaped by mutual obligations until finally, following Confucius, at age 70, individuals could for the first time "follow their hearts' desire" without violating social expectations. Thomas Rohlen has pointed out how in this eventual escape from the heavy demands of a Confucian-ordered world, a life of self-discipline and personal cultivation is transformed in old age into that of the "iconoclastic world of the laughing Zen priest" (1978, 139). The enlightened Zen master attains a freedom based on obliteration of self, of all physical needs and desire, and achieves a merging with the oneness of the universe. Buddhism, particularly in the form of Zen, has served in part throughout Japanese history as a bridge between the decidedly this-worldly demands of Confucianism and what is taken to be an inevitable yearning for escape and for a spirituality that transcends this world. Women were not necessarily excluded from traveling this spiritual path since they could in theory become nuns just as, ideally, an old man could become a priest. Obviously neither peasants nor artisans usually enjoyed the luxury of literally traversing a spiritual path, nor in all likelihood did most aristocrats, but nevertheless a theme of self-discipline culminating in eventual escape from the toil of this world has been dominant throughout Japanese history.

It is against this discursive background that the aging of individuals takes place in Japan, as part of an ethos in which the elderly are in theory at once respected and spoiled; where until recently one was expected, at age 60, to don a bright red childlike kimono for a celebration known as *kanreki oiwai* (which literally means a return back through time), designed to remind participants about the ceaseless repetition of birth and death, and of the continued regeneration of both the household and the great cycles of the cosmos. Traditionally a circle was used to illustrate this cycle of regeneration, half of it being the human life cycle, and the other half the progression of the ancestors toward karmic rebirth. Confucianism encourages respect for the elderly (of course, some fail to heed its advice and senility is feared; see Ehrlich 1992; Plath 1988), a respect that continues into the afterlife with the transformation through ritual of deceased family members into ancestors (Plath 1964; Smith 1974).

In Japan's culture, experience is still valued as fundamental to maturity, age denotes wisdom, authority, and a hard-won freedom to be flexible and creative. Numerous prominent figures are decidedly elderly by Western standards—the reelection of the eighty-year-old mayor of Tokyo in the recent past being one obvious example. Even in that most fickle of industries, the entertainment world, older women are often respected and admired, not only for their artistic skills, but for their beauty. When David Plath talked to mature Japanese about how they had changed with age, many made use of the word *atsuka-mashisa,* best glossed as "boldness" or "nerve." Similarly, women I have interviewed, when asked how they would characterize female midlife, often used the same word, implying that because age brings experience one can afford as one gets older to "let go" and be playful. A good number of women indicated that they were enjoying their new-found freedoms, the fruits of maturity—of "full flowering"—and several went on to state that they were actually looking forward to old age because they would no longer have to "keep a low profile" and display feminine reserve (Lock 1993).

The three-generation household, the *ie,* was for three-quarters of a century—from the formation of the modern Japanese state at the Meiji Restoration until the end of the Second World War—recognized as the official family unit in Japan. In this household are enshrined the ancestors, representatives of moral and spiritual values that are actively instilled into younger generations by the adult woman of the house-hold, herself the core or center of the family. Feudal Japan exhibited an acute sensitivity to class and occupational difference, but with the creation of the early modern state, difference was in theory obliterated, and Japanese women were appealed to for the first time as a unified body in terms of gendered social roles to be carried out within the confines of the household (Nolte and Hastings 1991). Modeled on the samurai system of feudal times, and laced with a little late-nineteenth-century European sentiment, the "good wife and wise mother," as she was popularly known, was formally educated to discipline herself for her role in the family.

Although in feudal Japan women were sometimes described as "borrowed wombs," from the end of the nineteenth century they came to be thought of primarily as nurturers of other family members in addition to economically productive members of the household, tasks that they retained throughout the life cycle, although their specific du-ties changed through time. Obviously reproduction was important, and the bearing of a son particularly so, but the Japanese have through the years been remarkably flexible about the formal adoption into their families of infants, children, and even adults, should a couple not pro-duce offspring or the family be faced with the early death or mental or physical incompetence of an eldest son. The *dominant* image of a woman in Japan for more than one hundred years has been that of nurturer, a quality with which all females are assumed to be endowed by nature (Mitsuda 1985). Emphasis is given in this ideology to dedication to a lifelong gendered role, and actual reproduction is rendered somewhat less important. Japanese feminists have coined the term *boseishugi* (the doctrine of motherhood) to capture the essence of this ideology.

Ideally, women's lives in Japan are expected to become meaningful in terms of what they accomplish for others rather than for themselves (Plath 1980, 139). This was and still is especially true for those who live at the hub of an extended family, a household explicitly recognized as belonging to the husband's lineage. As part of the *ie* a woman reaches the prime of life in her fifties and, in theory, enjoys the acme of her responsibility, which, although it gradually wanes, is never extinguished unless she succumbs to severe senility or some other catastrophe. At this stage of the life cycle, having raised two or more children to adulthood, an individual is recognized as fully mature—as *ichininmae*—a complete adult (Lebra 1984). Some Japanese women still live in these circumstances (approximately over 20% of households are three-generation units), and their days are filled with monitoring the household economy, care and education of grandchildren, and care and nursing of dependent in-laws, added to which many take on part-time work.

Because the social order is understood as being coterminus with the interests of individuals, an ideology of service for others is not intuitively experienced as oppressive. On the contrary, early socialization and maturation are conceptualized as the gradual transformation of individuals into eminently social and moral beings, a process which is thought of very positively and not, as post-Enlightenment Western epistemology might have us believe, as a repression or displacement of individual needs. Moreover, in Japan socialization is not understood as a matter of learning how to maximize one's own interests while reluctantly conforming to the constraints unavoidably imposed by society. Nor does growing up take the form of a search for a "true," autonomous self, but rather is a process in which individuals come to understand themselves first and foremost as social beings, as products of units and forces larger than the individual, and without which they could not exist. With respect to the concept of "self" Plath (1980, 218) has reached the conclusion that "the American archetype . . . seems more attuned to cultivating a self that knows it is unique in the cosmos, the Japanese archetype to a self that can feel human in the company of others."

Plath visualizes maturity in Japan as a "rhetoric of long engagements with intimates" (1980, 226). Ideally, therefore, during the course of maturation the Japanese self is disciplined to merge into the social order, at times to such an extent that in retrospect it is possible to say matter-of-factly, as did one or two women I have talked to, "I have no self," implying that they have devoted their entire adult life to the nurturance of others.

Contemporary Japan is indeed, as has so often been claimed, a land of paradox. It is a society in which technological mastery of the environment is unsurpassed, where the electronic age reigns supreme and unabashed consumerism and materialism have usurped almost all desire for simplicity (a condition that was formerly highly valued as a statement about the futility of worldly desire). In the midst of this massive transformation, people strive to retain a cooperative life in which "self" is busily occupied with the maintenance of harmonious social relations, particularly through shared endeavor or labor. But it is also a society where, especially for mature people, an inner, secret space exists more or less securely sealed off from the onslaught of the daily round. This introverted self strives to live in tune with the changing seasons, to accept the inevitability of the passing of time, and the ephemeral nature of material things; in other words, to be at one with a greater order that eclipses and transcends the banal everyday world— a space of private fantasy and reflection, of secrets and desire. Thus, self is created and recreated in daily life, beyond and within the confines of the physical body, through committed participation in social life and through self-reflection— activities fostered through individual discipline. Paradoxically, the self travels a path to maturity that in classical Buddhist thinking requires its eventual dissolution and other-worldly transcendence, although this may, of course, take many lifetimes to accomplish.

RIDING OVER DISTRESS

In Japan the physiological changes of female midlife aging are constructed in a significantly different way from those in North America. The end of menstruation has been recognized for many hundreds of years in traditional Sino-Japanese medicine as the "seventh" stage in a woman's life, when a quality known as *tenki*, intimately associated with the female reproductive cycle, goes into decline. When the decline in *tenki* is too abrupt it is recognized as the cause of numerous nonspecific symptoms that often last for a few years, including dizziness, palpitations, headaches, chilliness, stiff shoulders, a dry mouth, and so on (Yasui and Hirauma 1991), but no *specific* word was reserved for the time when *tenki* went into decline or for the physical effects of this stage of the life cycle.

Toward the end of the nineteenth century the term *kônenki* was created to convey the European concept of the climacterium. Japanese doctors of the time, more than one hundred of whom went to Germany to study medicine, were fascinated with the newly discovered concept of the "autonomic nervous system." This idea, when it was first clearly articulated in Germany in 1898 caused a stir in medical circles everywhere. In Japan it "fitted" with the holistically oriented physiological approach characteristic of Sino-Japanese medicine. Later, in the 1930s when a close association was postulated between the endocrine system and the autonomic nervous system, Japanese physicians made a connection between *kônenki* and disturbances in the autonomic nervous system, an association that the majority of Japanese physicians and women still accept today (Lock 1986) but which is virtually absent in North American discourse about menopause.

Another factor, which no doubt worked historically in Japan against the construction of a narrowly focused discourse on the aging ovary and declining estrogen levels, was that Japanese doctors, unlike their Western counterparts, had practiced little surgery before the twentieth century, a specialty that was disparaged by the powerful, physiologically oriented herbalists of the traditional medical system. Furthermore, anatomy as it was conceived in Enlightenment medical discourse in Europe had relatively little impact in Japan until the twentieth century, and autopsies and dissection were not widely practiced (Kuriyama 1992). Japanese gynecologists did not have the first-hand experience of removing and dissecting many hundreds of ovaries as was the case for a large number of late-nineteenth-century European and North American gynecologists (Laqueur 1990) and their "gaze" (in Foucault's idiom) remained predominantly physiological rather than anatomically oriented.

This interpretation of the middle-aged female body is not fueled entirely, however, by historical circumstance. Comparative survey research has shown that the pattern of symptoms about which Japanese women complain at *kônenki* (if indeed they complain of anything), is significantly different from that in North America.[2] Hot flashes and night sweats, assumed in the West to be the sine qua non of menopause, occur much more frequently in North American surveys of middle-aged women than in a comparable Japanese survey (Lock et al. 1988), so much so that the cultural construction of menopause and *kônenki* are influenced by what I have termed "local biologies" (Lock 1993). The typical symptoms of *kônenki*—shoulder stiffness, headaches, dizziness, and so on—are not recognized by most North American physicians as having any relation to the end of menstruation, no doubt because people do not believe that the autonomic nervous system is implicated. Thus, *kônenki* and menopause are not the same concept, although in Japanese translations from Western literature it is usually assumed that they are.

In North America, menopause is understood as an event—the end of menstruation has been isolated from the more general process of aging specifically in order to control it through medication. In contrast, *kônenki* is regarded above all as a process, integral to and inseparable from aging, and is therefore commonly associated with graying hair, changes in eyesight, stiffening joints, and so on (Lock 1986). Until recently it was assumed that, with the exception of a minute number of pathological cases, women would simply "ride over" (*norikoeru*) any physical distress which might occur at this stage of the life cycle. I well recall one Japanese gynecologist asking me, with, I thought, more than a touch of chauvinism, "Why do Western women make such a fuss about menopause?"

Although Japanese physicians are well acquainted with North American gynecological literature, they have not so far accepted the idea of the end of menstruation as a disease, nor even as a progressive, irreversible decline in general health. Nor are they overly concerned, as yet, about osteoporosis and heart disease, both of which have a much lower incidence in Japan than in North America. What captures the imagination of the Japanese medical world when they reflect on an aging population are senile, incontinent elders who have suffered a stroke. Furthermore, physicians and patients in Japan are cautious, by North American standards, about the administration of hormone replacement therapy—medication that is regarded as potentially iatrogenic, all the more so because the pill (compounded of essentially the same ingredients as hormone replacements) is not available for contraceptive purposes in Japan despite repeated heated debates on the subject. If a prescription is needed to counter symptoms of *kônenki*, a herbal concoction is likely to be the medication of choice, although, under drug company pressure, this situation is changing somewhat (*Shufu no tomo* 1991).

The end of menstruation has not been a particularly potent signifier for either doctors or women in Japan, in part, no doubt, because the concept of reproduction implies much more than a clearly demarcated biological process. Replication and continuity of the household are first and foremost what reproduction is all about, and assurance of this highly valued process usually transcends any concerns about the biology of individual women. Perhaps it is not so remarkable therefore, that despite fears about iatrogenesis, when interviewed, the majority of a sample of fifty women of reproductive age living in Tokyo agreed that if a postmenopausal woman did not have two children and wished to complete her family, then resort to technology to induce pregnancy would be appropriate (Lock, 1997).

There are signs that in recent years a shift is taking place so that attention is now being paid both to family obligations and to individual biology. This change is not only due to what has been termed the "privatization" of the family, but also to modifications in the clinical practice of gynecology in Japan. Until recently obstetrics and gynecology have not usually been separated from one another, and individual physicians own and run small hospitals where their income is derived largely from deliveries, abortions, and minor surgery. Recently, however, gynecologists find their medical practices less lucrative than was formally the case because most women choose to have their babies in tertiary care facilities, and second, because the abortion rate is somewhat reduced due to a more effective use of contraceptive devices (despite the unavailability of the pill). Thus there is a burgeoning movement to medicalize *kônenki,* due in part to pressure from pharmaceutical companies, but also influenced by the economic pressures under which many gynecologists in private practice now find themselves. Some gynecologists are currently setting up counseling services for middle-aged patients, while others are busy writing books and articles for popular consumption on the subject of *kônenki* (Lock 1993). These changes, together with the additional influences of the English language professional literature and international conferences on menopause, have resulted in a groundswell to make the Japanese medical approach to menopause more "scientific."

Nevertheless, despite these changes, in addition to the presence of an aggressive pharmaceutical industry, so far the situation does not remotely resemble that in North America. Individual aging, although regrettable, is not yet understood as "a bad thing" nor as a disease-like condition, although the numbers of bed-ridden elderly are recognized by everyone as one of the most pressing social problems in Japan today.

THE PATHOLOGY OF MODERNITY

During the course of the past twenty years *kônenki* disorders, along with a range of assorted illnesses,have been recast as "diseases of modernization" (*gendaibyô*) or "civilization" (*bunmeibyô*) (Kyûtoku 1979; Murakami et. al 1979). The plethora of newly "discovered" syndromes and neuroses said to be of recent origin and thought to abound in the urban centers of modern Japan are intimately associated with what is taken to be a loss of traditional values, the rise of the nuclear family, and the embrace of individualism. People identified at high risk for diseases of modernization are inevitably members of what has become known as the New Middle Class, the urban nuclear family. Men, women, and children are all vulnerable to these diseases which have arresting names: "apartment neurosis," "moving day depression," "child rearing neurosis," "the kitchen syndrome," "school refusal syndrome," "adolescent frustration syndrome," "video generation lethargy," "salary man depression," "maladjustment-to-the-job syndrome," "fear of going to work," and the latest and most unnerving of all these problems: "death from overwork." The incidence of this plague of distress is accounted for in government, medical, and many popular accounts through a moralistic rhetoric in which a close relationship is postulated between health and well-being, both physical and mental, and individual behavior. It is frequently suggested that rapid postwar changes in both values and the structure of social relationships, in particular the family, are directly implicated in producing transformations in individual behavioral styles that are not conducive to good health. The painful and sometimes fatal symptoms from which victims of *gendaibyô* suffer are often dismissed out of hand by those in power as, in effect, signs of indolence or willful nonconformity (Monbushô 1983). Alternatively, patients are medicated and monitored by the medical and psychological professions and individual narratives of distress are thus transformed into a medicalized discourse about the sick body, although recently victims and their families have been fighting back at times.

Despite the fact that women are routinely expected to give up work once they become pregnant, there is nevertheless considerable ambivalence about the life of the so-called full-time housewife. Thanks largely to the mechanization and commoditization of housework, housewives have sardonically had their day described as *san shoku hiru ne tsuki* (implying an easy permanent job with three meals and a nap thrown in). The rhetoric associated with housewives implies that, in contrast to other hard-working Japanese, many are selfish, idle, and leisured. They are unsurpassed consumers with endless time to fill, living a life of luxury and ease unknown in Japanese society until this time (Eto 1979). Alternatively, housewives have been accused of becoming excessively fastidious, withdrawn and nervous, overly concerned with tidiness and order. In both scenarios the middle-class housewife has departed from the fully occupied, balanced, and correctly disciplined life of the "good wife and wise mother" of the traditional extended household. In a society driven by the work ethic, this anomalous woman, once she becomes middle aged, is highly vulnerable, it is believed, to a distressful time at *kônenki* and is singled out as a potential victim of "menopausal syndrome." When I asked what kind of woman is most likely to have trouble at *kônenki* a Kobe gynecologist had the following to say:

> Let me see . . . I guess those who are relatively well off, who have few children and lots of free time, and those whose families don't have much "communication" with one another. Also those who are introverted. Those women who go out a lot, or who have lots of hobbies and friends don't have so many symptoms. The ones who have trouble tend to concentrate on their own bodies. (Lock 1993, 276)

An Osaka gynecologist, when asked if he thought that all women experience trouble at *kônenki* answered: "Not necessarily. Women who are busy, who don't have much leisure don't have many complaints. *Kônenki shôgai* is a sort of 'luxury disease' (*zeitakubyô*), it's 'high class.' Women with lots of free time on their hands are the ones who say its so bad."

It is not surprising, therefore, that given the pervasiveness of this moralistic rhetoric, most women confine any physical distress they experience at this stage of the life cycle to the ears of their friends and close relatives (although I remain convinced, based on survey research coupled with intensive interviewing, that rather few women experience the debilitating symptoms that would be described as menopausal in North America). Middle age is conceptualized first and foremost as a social process, a process in which the biological changes associated with aging are one small part. Above all it is close human relationships and reproduction of a healthy family that are of most concern to Japanese women throughout their adult life (although this may change as future generations age in their turn).

In response to the "graying society," the Japanese government has been explicit that care for the majority of the elderly is best performed in their own homes. Although public and private institutions have been constructed throughout Japan, the number of elderly who need care far exceeds the space in these facilities. Income tax credits have been introduced for those who live with dependent elderly relatives, and what is known in government documents as the "Japan welfare society" explicitly encourages the creation of a "new residence system" comprising three generations living as one unit (*Ohira Sôri no Seisaku Kenkyû-kai Hôkokusho* 1980). The government is also explicit about the tasks of middle-aged women in this new living arrangement, namely, that they should provide nursing care for their elderly relatives with very little if any supplementary support from the outside (Kōsei Hakusho 1989). Thus the task of female middle age is still officially understood in Japan as one of family nurturer, in spite of the fact that over 60% of Japanese women are in the workforce, the bulk of them out of economic necessity (Saso 1990).

Public debate among Japanese women about the meaning of female middle age is concerned above all with the way in which their lives continue to be shaped by paternalistic government policies. Debate focuses on the extent to which individuals should actively try to break out of this mold. Few women are prepared to abandon their dependent elderly relatives to face their fate alone, although many of them have experienced or face an intolerable burden of fifteen years or more virtually confined to their houses as caregivers (Lock 1993). Nevertheless, the majority accept that their prime function is to care for their relatives, which may include their grandchildren in addition to the dependent elderly.

Recently discussion about *kônenki* has been taken up in Japan in the media, among women's groups, and in professional journals. Some health care professionals, feminists, and others argue that women should actively foster their own health rather than devoting themselves exclusively to the care of others. If this requires medical assistance, then clearly this is the sensible path to follow, even though this has not been the pattern to date. These activists want the moralistic rhetoric that associates *kônenki* symptoms with indolence and luxury replaced by a more scientific approach toward understanding female aging.

A rhetoric promoting increased individualism is abroad, a rhetoric that usually takes North American discourse about menopause as superior, and is based on two erroneous assumptions: first, that *kônenki* discourse should be replaced by a modern, scientific discourse grounded in the assumption of a universal biology and, second, that knowledge about hormone replacement therapy is scientifically proven. The meaning of middle age is clearly undergoing a transformation in Japan, but the idea of aging as a natural process intimately associated with social maturation remains pervasive, and, for the majority of women, nurturance of the family exemplifies this maturation.

Constructing Middle Age

The life course in both Japan and North America has been conceptualized historically as movement through a series of developmental sequences leading to eventual aging and death. In both settings physical aging is feared, but in Japan a concern about physical decline has been tempered by the idea that maturity and experience bring wisdom and insight, a positive construction not evident in North American discourse. Moreover, individuals in Japan are understood as being immersed in a larger social order whose continuity extends over many generations.

In both cultural settings the idea of a normative ordered life course, a narrative of development and decline, is currently questioned by certain segments of society (much less so in Japan than in North America); moreover, in Japan people are alert to changes in North American thought (the reverse is not, of course, the case). Nevertheless, dominant ideas about female middle age in these two cultural settings have become increasingly divergent during the past several decades. In Japan, marriage and childbirth take place in a remarkably uniform and narrow time frame; individual aging remains subordinated to the idea of social maturation, which in turn is intimately associated with procreation and family relationships. A woman's position as nurturer in the family is naturalized as a biologically determined gendered difference, and care of family members, in theory and usually in practice, takes precedence over individual aging and personal interests.

In contrast, the medicalization of female middle age in North America has ensured that the dominant discourse is one that focuses on individual biology to the detriment of concern about social and economic factors, family relationships and obligations. Because biology is understood as universal, this discourse on aging is assumed to be applicable to all women. The idea of a "normative crisis model" precipitated by the end of menstruation is widely accepted, despite empirical evidence from survey research among women located outside clinical settings indicating that this is not the case (Avis and McKinlay 1991; Kaufert and Lock 1991). This is not to suggest that some women do not experience distressing physical symptoms at the end of menstruation, and medication may be appropriate in such cases. However, an exclusive focus on biological changes and physical discomfort glosses over socioeconomic and ethnic differences among women and renders all women essentially alike. In addition, because the biomedical model is so powerful, biological differences among women are generally ignored and, when noticed, considered anomalous. The dominant approach to female aging throughout the entire life cycle remains unchallenged, namely that female biology is by far the most important variable to be considered; for some researchers biology is assumed to determine a woman's whole life course.

Discourse and rhetoric in both Japan and North America, both professional and popular, is shaped by tacit knowledge—unexamined assumptions about female biology, the significance of aging, and what women's contribution to society should be. A major step toward a new form of inquiry into aging would be to expose ruthlessly such tacit knowledge for what it is—value laden sets of beliefs. Technological advances have made it possible for us to manipulate aging and reproduction in previously unimaginable ways, but to routinize such invasive technologies without first examining widely shared assumptions about female aging would be ill-advised.

One set of assumptions in need of dispassionate examination are certain claims to scientific objectivity made in connection with menopausal research, an arena driven by drug company interests. Very few longitudinal epidemiological studies exist to support often-repeated truth claims. Further, extrapolations are repeatedly made from non-representative populations to society at large, and the medication that study populations receive has been modified during the course of surveys, producing confusing and erroneous results (Kaufert 1994; Lock 1993; McKinlay et al. 1992). Meanwhile, the well-documented evidence that it is poverty and not a lack of estrogen that puts women at greatest risk for chronic disease of all kinds is glossed over, and estrogen (expensive though it is) continues to be touted as a wonder drug that will help prevent everything from tooth loss, to Alzheimer's disease, to coronary heart disease.

Another approach to questioning tacit knowledge would be to attribute more weight to subjective experiences and accounts given by individual women about their encounters with aging. The diversity and flexibility of meanings, together with the contradictions associated with midlife by individual women reveal the way in which dominant ideologies and subjective experience are so often at odds. Finally, comparative work, with all its attendant difficulties of translation across cultures, is a very fruitful way of examining received wisdom about aging that usually slips by unnoticed.

NOTES

1. Interviews lasting between one and one-half and two hours were conducted in the homes of 105 women. Approximately one-third are what is known as "professional housewives" living in Kobe, one-third are factory workers in southern Kyoto, and one-third live and work in farming villages in southern Nagano, a fishing village in Ehime, and a forestry village in Shiga prefectures.

2. In 1984 I conducted a questionnaire survey with over 1,300 Japanese women, ages 45–55 inclusively. Three occupational groups are represented in the survey: farmers, factory workers, and housewives. This survey was designed to be directly comparable with research carried out in Manitoba by Patricia Kaufert with over 2,500 Canadian women and in Massachusetts by Sonja McKinlay and colleagues with over 8,000 women. See Lock (1993) for further details on sampling procedures and a complete data analysis.

REFERENCES

Apfel, Roberta J., and Miriam D. Mazor. 1988. "Psychiatry and Reproductive Medicine." In *Comprehensive Textbook of Psychiatry,* 5th ed. Edited by H. I. Kaplan and B. J. Sadock, 1331–39. Baltimore: Williams & Wilkins.

Ariès, Philippe. 1973. *Centuries of Childhood.* Harmondsworth: Penguin.

Avis, Nancy E., and Sonya M. McKinlay, 1991. "A Longitudinal Analysis of Women's Attitudes toward the Menopause: Results from the Massachusetts Women's Health Study." *Maturitas* 13:65–79.

Bergkvist, Leif, Hans Olav Adanir, Ingemar Persson, Robert Hooves, and Catherine Schairer. 1989. "The Risk of Breast Cancer after Estrogen and Estrogen-Progestin Replacement." *New England Journal of Medicine* 321:293–97.

Canadian Society of Obstetricians and Gynaecologists. 1994. *Report of the Menopause Consensus Committee.* Ottawa.

Chicago Tribune. 1994. "Dads Can Be Old. So Why Can't Mothers?" (31 December).

De Beauvoir, Simone. 1949. *The Second Sex,* translated by H. M. Parshley. New York: Bantam Books.

Deutsch, Helene. 1945. *The Psychology of Women: A Psychoanalytic Interpretation,* 2 vols. New York: Grune & Stratton.

Dewhurst, John. 1981. *Integrated Obstetrics and Gynecology for Postgraduates.* Oxford: Blackwell Scientific Publications.

Dove, Mary. 1986. *The Perfect Age of Man's Life.* Cambridge: Cambridge University Press.

Ehrlich, Linda. 1992. "The Undesired Ones: Images of the Elderly in Japanese Cinema." In *Japanese Biographies: Life Histories, Life Cycles, Life Stages,* edited by S. Formanek and S. Linhart, 271–81. Vienna: Verlag der Österreichischen Akademie der Wissenschaften.

Elias, Norbert. 1978. *The Civilizing Process: The History of Manners.* Oxford: Basil Blackwell.

Erikson, Erik H. 1968. *Identity: Youth and Crisis.* New York: W. W. Norton.

Eto, Jun. 1979. "The Breakdown of Motherhood Is Wrecking Our Children." *Japan Echo* 6:102–9.

Featherstone, Mike, and Mike Hepworth. 1991. "The Mask of Ageing and the Postmodern Life Course." In *The Body: Social Process and Cultural Theory,* edited by M. Featherstone, M. Hepworth, and B. S. Turner, 371–89. London: Sage Publications.

Fink, Paul J. 1980. "The Psychiatric Myths of the Menopause." In *The Menopause: Comprehensive Management,* edited by B. A. Eskin, 111–28. New York: Masson Publishing.

Formanek, Suzanne. 1992. "Normative Perceptions of Old Age in Japanese History: A Study Based on Literary Sources of the Nara and Heian Periods." In *Japanese Biographies: Life Histories, Life Cycles, Life Stages,* edited by S. Formanek and S. Linhart, 241–69. Vienna: Verlag der Österreichischen Akademie der Wissenschaften.

Foucault, Michel. 1979. *Discipline and Punish: The Birth of the Prison.* Harmondsworth: Penguin.

Frank, Robert T. 1941."Treatment of Disorders of the Menopause." *Bulletin of the New York Academy of Medicine* 17:854–63.

Freeman, M. 1984. "History, Narrative and Lifespan Developmental Knowledge." *Human Development* 27:1–19.

Friedan, Betty. 1993. *The Fountain of Age.* New York: Simon & Shuster.

Gosden, Roger R. 1985. *The Biology of Menopause: The Causes and Consequences of Ovarian Aging.* London: Academic Press.

Greer, Germaine. 1991. *The Change: Women, Ageing and the Menopause.* Auckland: Harnish Mailton Publishers.

Halford, Henry. 1813. "On the Climacteric Disease." In *Medical Transitions,* vol. 4. College of Physicians in London. London: Longman.

Haspels, A. A., and P. A. Van Keep. 1979. "Endocrinology and Management of the Peri-Menopause." In *Psychosomatics in Peri-Menopause,* edited by A. A. Haspels and H. Musaph, 57–71. Baltimore: University Park Press.

Henry, Jules. 1966. "Forty-Year-Old Jitters in Married Urban Women." In *The Challenge to Women,* edited S. Farber and R. Wilson, 146–63. New York: Basic Books.

Journal of the Society of Obstetricians and Gynecologists of Canada. 1994. Canadian Menopause Consensus Conference, Special Issue, vol. 15, no. 5.

Kaufert, Patricia. 1994. "A Health and Social Profile of the Menopausal Woman." *Journal of Experimental Gerontology* 29:343–50.

Kaufert, Patricia, Penny Gilbert, and Robert Tate. 1987."Defining Menopausal Status: The Impact of Longitudinal Data." *Maturitas* 9:217–26.

Kaufert, Patricia, and Margaret Lock. 1991." 'What Are Women For?': Cultural Constructions of Menopausal Women in Japan and Canada." In *In Her Prime,* edited by J. K. Brown and V. Kerns, 201–19. Urbana: University of Illinois Press.

Kōsei, Hakusho. 1989. *Arata na kōreishazō to Katsuryoku aru chōju fukushi shakai o mezashite* (Toward a new image of the aged and a vigorous long-lived society with good social welfare). Tokyo: Kōseisho.

Kuriyama, Shigehisa. 1992. "Between Mind and Eye: Japanese Anatomy in the Eighteenth-Century." In *Paths to Asian Medical Knowledge,* edited by C. Leslie and A. Young, 21–43. Berkeley and Los Angeles: University of California Press.

Kyûtoku, Shigemori. 1979. *Bogenbyô* (Illness caused by mother).Tokyo: Sanmaku Shuppan.

Laqueur, Thomas. 1990. *Making Sex: Body and Gender from the Greeks to Freud.* Cambridge, Mass.: Harvard University Press.

Lebra, Takie. 1984. *Japanese Women: Constraint and Fulfillment.* Honolulu: University of Hawaii Press.

Levinson, Daniel. 1977. "The Mid-Life Transition." *Psychiatry* 40:99–112.

Lock, Margaret. 1986. "Ambiguities of Aging: Japanese Experience and Perceptions of Menopause." *Culture, Medicine and Psychiatry* 10:23–46.

———. 1993. *Encounters with Aging: Mythologies of Menopause in Japan and North America.* Berkeley and Los Angeles: University of California Press.

———. 1997. "Perfecting Society: Reproductive Technologies, Genetic Testing, and the Planned Family in Japan." In *Pragmatic Women and Body Politics,* edited by M. Lock, and P. Kaufert. Cambridge: Cambridge University Press.

Lock, Margaret, Patricia Kaufert, and Penny Gilbert. 1988. "Cultural Construction of the Menopausal Syndrome: The Japanese Case." *Maturitas* 10:317–32.

Lufkin, Edward C., and Steven Ory. 1989. "Estrogen Replacement Therapy for the Prevention of Osteoporosis." *American Family Physician* 40:205–12.

Mack, T. M., and R. K. Ross. 1989. "Risks and Benefits of Long-Term Treatment with Estrogens." *Schweizerische Medizinsche Wochenschrift* 119:1811–20.

Maturitas. 1988. Editorial, "Consensus Statement on Progestin use in Postmenopausal Women." 11:175–77.

McKinlay, Sonja, Donald Brambilla, and Jennifer Posner. 1992. "The Normal Menopause Transition." *Human Biology* 4:37–46.

McKeown, Peter. 1976. *The Modern Rise of Populations.* New York: Academic Press.

Mitsuda, Kyôko. 1985. "Kindaiteki Boseikan no Juyô to Kenkei: Kyôiku suru Hahaoya kara Ryôsai Kenbo e" (The importance and transformation of the condition of modern motherhood: From education mother to good wife and wise mother). In *Bosei o tou* (What is motherhood?), edited by H. Wakita, 2:100–129. Kyoto: Jinbunshoin.

Monbushô. 1983. *Tôkôkyohi mondai o chûshin ni: Chûgakko, kôtôgakko ron* (A discussion of junior and senior high schools: Focus on school refusal). Tokyo: Monbushô.

Montreal Gazette. 1994. "Outsmarting Mother Nature" (8 January).

Murakami, Yasusuke, Kumon Shunpei, and Satô Seizaburô. 1979. Bunmei to Shite no ie shakai (Household Society as Civilization). Tokyo: Chûô Kôron Sha.

Neugarten, Bernice. 1970. "Dynamics of Transition of Middle Age to Old Age." *Journal of Geriatric Psychiatry* 4:71–87.

Nisen nen no Nihon (Japan in the year 2000). 1982. Tokyo: Keizai Kikaku Chôhen.

Nolte, Sharon, and Sally Ann Hastings. 1991. "The Meiji State's Policy." In *Recreating Japanese Women, 1600–1945,* edited by Gail Lee Bernstein, 151–74. Berkeley and Los Angeles: University of California Press.

Ohira Sôri no Seisaku Kenkyûkai Hôkokusho 3 (Reports of the Policy Research Bureau of the Ohira cabinet no. 3). 1980. *Katei no kiban no jûjitsu* (Enrichment of the Japanese family base). Tokyo: Ôkurashô Insatsu Kyoku.

Oudshoorn, Nelly. 1990. "On the Making of Sex Hormones: Research Materials and the Production of Knowledge." *Social Studies of Science* 20:5-33.

———. 1994. *Beyond the Natural Body: An Archeology of Sex Hormones.* London and New York: Routledge.

Perlmutter, Marion, and Elizabeth Hall. 1992. *Adult Development and Aging,* 2d ed. New York: John Wiley & Sons.

Plath, David. 1964. "Where the Family of God . . . Is the Family: The Role of the Dead in Japanese Households." *American Anthropologist* 66:300–317.

———. 1980. *Long Engagements.* Palo Alto, Calif.: Stanford University Press.

———. 1988. "The Age of Silver." *The World and I* (March): 505–13.

Rayner, Eric. 1979. *Human Development: An Introduction to the Psychodynamics of Growth, Maturity and Aging.* National Institute Social Services Library. London: George Allan & Urwin.

Reed, Charles Alfred Lee. 1904. *A Textbook of Gynecology.* New York: D. Appleton.

Reid, Robert L. 1988. "Menopause. Part I, Hormonal Replacement." *Bulletin: Society of Obstetricians and Gynecologists* 10:25–34.

Rohlen, Thomas. 1978. "The Promise of Adulthood in Japanese Spiritualism." In *Adulthood,* edited by E. Erikson, 125–43. New York: W. W. Norton.

Sarrel, L. L. 1988. "Estrogen Replacement Therapy." *Obstetrics and Gynecology* 72: S2–S5.

Saso, Mary. 1990. *Women in the Japanese Workplace.* London: Hilary Shipman.

Sears, Elizabeth. 1986. *The Ages of Man: Medieval Interpretations of the Life Cycle.* Princeton, N.J.: Princeton University Press.

Sheehy, Gail. 1992. *The Silent Passage: Menopause.* New York: Random House. (Portion first published in *Vanity Fair* [October 1991]: 222–63.)

Shufu no tomo. 1991. "Josei Horumon no Himitsu o shireba, motto Wakagaeru, motto Utsukushiku naru" (If we know the secrets of female hormones, we can become younger again and more beautiful). *Shufu no tomo* 75:S1–S42.

Smith, Robert. 1974. *Ancestor Worship in Contemporary Japan.* Palo Alto, Calif.: Stanford University Press.

Smith-Rosenberg, Carroll. 1985. *Disorderly Conduct: Visions of Gender in Victorian America.* New York: Alfred A. Knopf.

Sontag, Susan. 1972. "The Double Standard of Aging." *Saturday Review of Society* 55:29–38.

Strathern, Marilyn. 1992. *Reproducing the Future: Anthropology, Kinship and the New Reproductive Technologies.* New York: Routledge.

Tilt, Edward. 1870. *The change of life in health and disease: A practical treatise on the nervous and other affections incidental to women at the decline of life.* London: John Churchill & Sons.

Utian, W. H., and Ruth S. Jacobowitz. 1990. *Managing Your Menopause.* New York: Prentice Hall.

Wente, Margaret. 1994. "If Men Can Do It Why Can't Women?" *Globe and Mail* (1 January).

Wilson, Robert A. 1966. *Feminine Forever.* New York: M. Evans.

Wolf, Naomi. 1990. *The Beauty Myth.* Toronto: Random House.

Yasui, Hiromichi and Hirauma Naokichi. 1991. "Kanpô de kangaeru Kônenki Shogai to wa donna mono deshoka" (When using the thinking associated with herbal medicine, what are menopausal disorders?). *Fujin Gahô* (September): 370–79.

THREE

The Search for Middle Age in India

Sudhir Kakar

For a while I thought I would never find it. I began looking for middle age in diverse settings by asking people what they thought were the various ages of a person. I remember putting this question to a young boatman in Benares as he took me on a leisurely ride down the Ganges, a retired soldier on a bus journey to Bangalore, a well-known woman editor of a daily newspaper in Delhi, an unemployed vegetable seller and his wife and his sister in Hyderabad whom I had just finished interviewing on the subject of social violence between Hindus and Muslims. Middle age did not seem to exist or at least it was never spontaneously mentioned as long as my question and the subsequent conversation were in Hindi. I finally discovered its hiding place when, at a cocktail party in Delhi, I asked the guests (in English, and sounding faintly Shakespearean) what they thought were the various "ages of man." For these upper-middle-class men and women, educated in the English-speaking and Westernized milieu of convent and private schools, familiar with popular American and British writings on the stages of life, and consuming a steady diet in the English-language newspapers and magazines on the middle-age spread and the midlife crisis, the increased risk of coronary disease in middle age, and the problems of menopause, middle age was a familiar concept and a known territory—a Western import that no longer seemed like one.

For their more traditional, Hindi-speaking counterparts, an infinitely larger part of the country's population, there were only three ages of a human being: childhood, youth, and old age. A wit would reduce this number further when she remarked: "All Indians are born old and spend the rest of their lives in getting older." The section on rejuvenation in texts of traditional Indian medicine, Ayurveda, seemed to agree; they recommend beginning this regimen when a person turns thirty years old.

With my Hindi-speaking respondents, I had to probe further and, in fact, even "lead the witness" by asking whether there was not a transition period between youth and old age before some of them caught on to my intent and "remembered" that there was indeed also an *adher-awastha*. The standard dictionary—*Brahat Hindi Kosh*—defined *adher* as "middle age, declining years," while another dictionary was more concrete in defining it as an adjective for a person between the ages of thirty and fifty. There is also another word for middle age— *prorha*, which the dictionary defines as someone who is "older; between thirty and fifty; whose intelligence is fully developed; experienced; deep; in the middle years; in the declining years." In ordinary conversation, though, most would use *prorha* in the sense of a quality of age, namely a wise maturity, rather than employing the word to refer to a particular span of years in the second half of life.

The chronological certainty in the dictionaries on the years that constitute middle age is matched by the Dharmashastras (the semi-sacred books of the Hindus on law and personal codes of conduct), which, proceeding from an ideal life span of one hundred years, arrive at a different chronological construction of middle age. In defining the duties and conduct appropriate to the four stages of life—*brahmacharya* (apprentice), *garhasthya* (householder), *vanaprastha* (forest dweller), and *sanyasa* (renunciant)—middle age could conceivably be considered as equivalent to the *vanaprastha* stage which, the texts assert, lasts from the fiftieth to the seventy-fifth year. Within this wide range, which begins at thirty according to modern Hindi lexical usage, the idea of middle age seems more and more amorphous, at least as far as chronological age is concerned.

The fluidity of the concept of middle age is further underscored by popular sayings that portray the onset of middle age varying according to gender. *Teesi-kheesi*, for instance, is an expression that is used for women. It means that when a woman reaches the age of thirty (*tees*), her face caves in and teeth jut out (*khees*), a sign of old age. A man, on the other hand, is *satha-patha*, signifying that even at sixty (*sath*) he remains a virile youth (*patha*). On the other hand, consistent with the nature of Indian proverbs and popular sayings wherein for almost every pithy assertion there is another one maintaining its opposite, *sathia-jana* (to become senile) is a condition which strikes one at sixty.

The question as to what is regarded as middle age in India also remains unresolved in social science research. Almost all the socioeconomic studies are concerned with the "old" or with "aging in India."[1] Given their urban bias, the "old" are identified as those who have retired from a full-time job, generally government service, where retirement is mandatory for workers at age 58. This rough and ready reckoner for the beginning of old age proper—and thus, implicitly, the end of middle age—does not apply to women or even to 90 percent of Indian men, who do not work in the organized industrial or government sector. Demographers, on the other hand, have age groups based on formal criteria adopted from similar Western studies. This procedure has the virtue of permitting comparisons of demographic statistics across the globe but tells us nothing about what Indians consider the middle years of life or whether they consider this period a well-defined entity at all.[2]

Giving up the quest for a precise chronological definition of middle age in India and following the majority of my respondents in viewing it as the beginning of old age, the first act of the drama of the second half of life, the question arises: When and how does middle age come upon us? In Indian terms, what are the heralds of *burhapa*? The answer to this question is clear and consistent through centuries across varied sources that reflect Hindu life and mores—from ancient texts to modern ethnographic accounts. In the religious-ideal image of the *vanaprastha* stage, the curtain rises: "When a householder sees his skin wrinkled, and his hair white, and the sons of his sons, then he may resort to the forest" (Manusmrti 6.1.23). With characteristic nit-picking, commentators on this pronouncement of Manu, the lawgiver, have argued through the centuries whether these are three separate grounds, each of which is sufficient by itself, or whether all must exist together. The evidence of modern anthropological studies suggests that today the operative part of Manu's dictum on the beginning of the third quarter of life is not the physical signs of aging but the arrival of "sons of sons." In other words, middle age, for both men and women, is marked by changing roles in the life cycle of the family once the son is married, brings his wife home, and begins to produce offspring (see Vatuk 1983, 71; Fernandes 1982). I have a suspicion that it was not much different in ancient times. In the epic of Ramayana, the fateful events of the story are set in motion when King Dashratha sees grey hair on his temples *after* the marriage celebrations of his eldest son, the god-hero of the epic, Rama. In the Hindi version of the epic, King Dashratha, loved and revered throughout the Hindi heartland, "took a mirror in his hand, saw his face in it and adjusted his crown. He saw that the hair above his ears had become white as if old age is saying, 'O King! Make Rama the crown prince and fulfil the purpose of your birth and life'" (Tulsidasa, n.d.; my translation). The rest—the opposition of Dashratha's youngest wife to this proposal, Rama's fourteen-year exile, the war with the demon king Ravana, and so on—is, as they say, *itihas*—the Hindi word for both history and legend.

Although anthropologists corroborate textual evidence that men and women in India associate the beginning of *burhapa* with the birth of "sons of sons," I would be inclined to refine this formulation further. From my clinical experience, it is the marriage of the first child—whether son or daughter—and the confrontation with the procreative activity of one's offspring, a sudden not-to-be-repressed awareness of his or her sustained sexual activity, which heralds the psychological transition of men and women into middle age. For the information of incorrigible almanac makers of the life cycle, this event is likely to occur around an average age of forty-five for a man and forty for a woman in urban areas and, reflecting the demographic patterns of marriage in India, a couple of years earlier in rural settings.

Representations of Middle Age in the Hindu Tradition

If, as we saw above, there are parallels between ancient texts and contemporary accounts of life as lived in the Indian heartland on the markers of middle age, it would be intriguing to search for a similar continuity in the representations of middle age and what constitute the main psychological themes of this stage of the life cycle. Let us begin with the "oughts" of middle age as enumerated by Manu.

> Abandoning all food raised by cultivation, and all his be-longings, he may depart into the forest, either committing his wife to his sons, or accompanied by her.
>
> Let him offer there five great sacrifices according to the rules, let him wear a skin or tattered garment; let him bathe in the evening or in the morning; the hair on his body, his beard, and his nails unclipped. Let him honor those who come to his hermitage with alms. . . .
>
> Let him always be industrious in privately reciting the Veda; let him be patient of hardship, friendly toward all, of collected mind, giver and never receiver of gifts, and compassionate toward all living creatures. (Manusmrti 6.1.3–8).

These verses are followed by others on the importance of restricting diet ("may either eat at night only or in the daytime only") and a list of ascetic practices to be followed, such as exposure to heat in the summer, living under the open sky during the rainy period, and dressing in wet clothes during winter. The ascetic regimen and the study of sacred texts prepares a person for the last stage of life and leads to the religiously desired end of a complete union with the supreme Soul (ibid. 6.1.23.32).

In its religious images, then, middle age constitutes a decisive break in the mode of one's life. It means a withdrawal from family ties and family affairs—the departure for the forest—and a radical renunciation of all worldly concerns and pleasures that were a province of the previous, "householder" stage. It denotes an end to sexual life, since married life is to be continued up to fifty years of age, Manu tells us firmly, and not thereafter. Middle age means an entry into a period of ever-increasing asceticism and an involvement with "ultimate concerns," as the person prepares for the last stage of life and the end of this particular individual life cycle.

We know from other accounts that this religiously desirable radical renunciation was not without conflict, especially for the rich, the mighty, and the powerful, and there were weighty voices in the tradition that opposed this notion of ascetic withdrawal. The fifth century poet-philosopher Bharatrihari is frankly skeptical: "Renunciation of worldly attachment is only talk of scholars, whose mouths are wordy with wisdom./Who can really forsake the hips of beautiful women bound with girdles of ruby jewels?" (Miller 1990, 82).

I would, therefore, suggest that in the ancient Indian cultural universe there was a specific middle age "crisis" of renunciation versus worldly involvement that is compellingly depicted in an episode from the second great epic of the Hindus, the Mahabharata.

Although the Pandavas were victorious in the epic war, Yuddhishtra, the eldest brother, was deeply saddened by the death of so many relatives. In his middle age (after all, his nephews are sexually active), Yuddhishtra announces his intention of retiring to the forest instead of ascending the throne of Hastinapur. He extols the virtues of *vanaprastha*—compassion toward all, control of body and mind, lack of envy, nonviolence, and truth. Abandoning the kingdom and all its satisfactions, Yuddhishtra would lead the ascetic's life in the forest to free himself of the depression gripping him:

> I will neither grieve for anyone nor feel joy. I will regard praise and blame alike. Renouncing hope and affection, I will become free and not gather material possessions. . . .

I will neither laugh at a person nor disparage anyone. I will always present a cheerful face and will control my senses. I will travel down any road and not ask for directions. I will have no wish to go to any specific place or in any particular direction. There will be no purpose to my comings and goings. I will neither look forward nor glance backwards. (Mahabharata, Shantiparva, 9.14–19; my translation)

Yuddhishtra's brothers, spokesmen for the other side, which espouses an increased involvement in life and affairs, try to convert him to their point of view (ibid., secs. 8–18). Arjuna extolls the merit of having wealth since it makes other ends of life—virtue, sensual pleasure, and final liberation—possible. He sees the retirement into the forest as an admission of defeat. It is only someone who cannot look after his sons and grandsons, who cannot satisfy the demands of the gods, sages, and ancestors, who can be content in the forest.

Another brother, Nakula, stresses the heavy responsibility resting on the shoulders of the middle-aged householder for the "maintenance of the world" since all beings depend upon him for their protection, sustenance, and development. Nakula is not against withdrawal, but he does not believe that one needs to take the radical step of retiring into the forest; an inner emigration is enough. Renunciation should be of things that ensnare the mind, not of one's home.

Draupadi, the common wife of the five brothers, seeks to persuade her eldest husband that retirement to the forest is only appropriate for brahmins, not barons. Withdrawal from the world, she avers, is for cowards and the impotent who are unable to enjoy its pleasures. Rationalizing the traditional ideals of middle age as depending upon a person's station in life, she argues that universal compassion, the taking of alms, studying and asceticism, are virtues of a brahmin, not of a king. The highest duty of the king is to wield the rod in punishment of evildoers, to protect the good, and to remain steadfast in battle. You have not obtained this kingdom by listening to readings from holy books, she tells Yuddhishtra. The kingdom was not presented to you as a gift, nor did you get it by convincing others through arguments or through religious rituals and sacrifices. You have obtained it through the force of arms, and it behooves you now to enjoy the fruits of your victory.

Yuddhishtra's middle-age crisis, initiated by the carnage of the epic war, persists: "This earthly kingdom and these various objects of enjoyment do not please my mind today. Sorrow surrounds me from all sides." After long "sessions" with some therapist-sages and even with Lord Krishna himself, Yuddhishtra finally comes out of the crisis, regaining his mental equilibrium, with an enhanced perspective on human life and effort. He understands, for instance, the existential loneliness of a human being: "Just as a traveler acquires companions on his journey, each one of us has the temporary company of brothers and relatives, wife and children" (ibid. 28:39). He understands that there is no Divine Giver who can restore to a person what has been lost. He learns the overwhelming role time plays in human affairs:

> Even an intelligent and learned man cannot fulfill his desires if the time is not ripe, whereas an ignorant fool gets what he wants if the proper time has come. Time makes the wind blow with the force of a gale, time makes the clouds give rain. Time makes the lotuses flower, and time makes the trees grow strong. Night becomes dark or light through time, and it is time which gives the moon its fullness. If the time has not come, trees do not bear flowers or fruits. The current of a river does not become fierce if its time has not come. Birds and snakes and deer and elephants do not come into heat if their time has not come. If the time has not come, women do not conceive. If the time is not ripe, a child is neither born nor dies, nor does it pick up speech. Without its proper time, youth does not come and the sown seed does not sprout. (Ibid., 25:8-11)

Yuddhishtra realizes that sorrow and happiness follow each other and that one does not always suffer sorrow nor always enjoy happiness. Further, "Happiness and misery, prosperity and adversity, gain and loss, death and life, in their turn wait upon all creatures. For this reason, the wise man of tranquil soul should neither be elated by joy nor crushed by sorrow" (ibid. 25:31).

The middle-age crisis of renunciation versus involvement is, then, positively resolved through the acquisition of a specific (to use an Eriksonian expression) "virtue"—*equanimity*. Ideally, the Indian tradition seems to say, the contribution of middle age to human development is a sense of equanimity that is neither a resignation from life nor a withdrawal from human effort and struggle; instead it provides a person with a wider psychological context for his actions. Equanimity implies the acceptance of the transitory nature of all relationships and emotional states. It includes an awareness that human strivings are insufficient to reach desired goals unless the "surround," too, is ripe for the success of these efforts. In more psychological language, middle-age equanimity involves a final renunciation of infantile omnipotence and grandiosity and the Faustian fantasies of youth.

Besides the crisis of involvement versus renunciation and its ideal resolution in equanimity, the second theme that strikes me in Sanskrit texts has to do with middle-age sexuality. More precisely, the crisis of renunciation versus involvement has the sexuality of this stage of life as one of its central issues. Perhaps the oldest mention of this theme occurs in the Rig veda (2500 B.C.E.) where Lopamudra, who has been waiting for a long time for her ascetic husband to sire a child, says, "For many autumns past I have toiled, night and day, and each dawn has brought old age closer, age that distorts the glory of bodies. Virile men should go to their wives" (Doniger O'Flaherty 1981, 250).

The sexual *Torschlusspanik* ("panic before the closing of the door"), which is hinted at in Lopamudra's speech, makes the middle-age man especially vulnerable, at least as far as the texts are concerned. Sanskrit literature is replete with middle-aged men's sexual infatuation with young women and the tragic consequences of such autumn-spring unions. In the Ramayana, Dashratha must banish his beloved eldest son Rama to the forest because of the rash promise he has made to Kaikeyi, his fourth and youngest wife with whom he is completely be-sotted.

In the Mahabharata, the king Santanu, Bhishma's father, becomes infatuated with a fisher's daughter. He goes to the father to ask her hand. The fisherman agrees to the match on condition that the son born to his daughter inherit the kingdom. Santanu cannot consent to this condition. He returns to his palace where he sinks into a depression born of a middle-aged man's unfulfilled passion for a young woman. Bhishma, on coming to know the reason for his father's grief, goes to the fisherman. Bhishma promises both the renunciation of the king-dom and of his sexual life, which could result in progeny that would threaten the rights of the sons born to the fisher's daughter. He then brings her to the capital of Santanu's kingdom and hands her over to a grateful father.

From the viewpoint of an outsider, especially an unsympathetic youthful observer, Dashratha and Santanu cut faintly ridiculous fig-ures. Sanskrit poets, on the other hand, give expression to the personal, subjective side of the middle-aged man's conflict between the ideal of renunciation and the (perhaps inappropriate) demands of his sexual nature. Bharatrihari, who, legend has it, vacillated between renunciation and sensual indulgence, finding them equally attractive and equally deficient, is a privileged witness of the middle-aged man's difficulties "letting go" of sexual life.

> Cut off all envy, examine the matter,
> tell us decisively, you noble men,
> which we ought to attend upon:
> the sloping side of wilderness mountains
> or the buttocks of women abounding in passion?

and

> Why all these words and empty prattle?
> Only two worlds are worth a man's devotion:
> The youth of beautiful women wearied by heavy breasts
> and full of fresh wine's excitement,
> or the forest. (Miller 1990, 61)

Bharatrihari's poems are not the romantic lyrics of a young man nor are they youth's passionate celebration of a woman's beauty. They combine a middle-aged man's clarity of vision in matters of sexual passion together with resentment at his helplessness in the face of such desire.

> Surely the moon does not rise in her face,
> or a pair of lotuses rest in her eyes,
> or gold compose her body's flesh.
> Yet, duped by poets' hyperbole, even a sage,
> a pondering man, worships the body of a woman—
> a mere concoction of skin and flesh and bones. (Ibid., 68)

The seventh-century poet Mayura is even more stark in depicting the dilemmas of middle-aged sexuality. According to the legend, he wrote his *Mayurastaka* out of his passion for his own daughter—in any case, out of a sexual infatuation that cut across generational boundaries—and was cursed with leprosy as a result. Even in the formalized conventions of Sanskrit poetry, Mayura's sexual vulnerability is palpable.

> Before your father was a youth I was a young man, yet I
> went into the forest when I had seen you, to follow and
> find the coupling place of tigers. His feet about the gilded

one and his rod flushing out to crimson were as nothing
to my youth, who am an old man and a King's poet. . . .

Rearing the green flame of his tail, the peacock casts the
hen beneath him in the dust of the King's walk. He covers
her, and we can hardly see her. She cries and he cries; and
the copper moons in the green bonfire of his tail die down;
and I am an old man. (Mathers 1929, 6:108–9)

Besides the desperation of a self-conscious sexuality that he would
both keep and let go, Mayura also expresses self-disgust at the hold
this sexuality has on him.

Old maker of careful stanzas as I am, I am also as the
fishmonger's ass and smell to you in riot. He is insensate
and does not care though the Royal retinue be passing. He
climbs and is not otherwise contented. And he brays aloud.
(Ibid., 110)

The poets, then, take us to the heart of the dilemma of the middle-
aged man as it is represented in ancient Indian literature. Whereas the
Dharmashastras only tell us about the "oughts" of conduct in the third
quarter of life and the epics of all the difficulties that lie in the path
of a desired equanimity, the poets isolate the chief obstacle to man's
quest for renunciation—the forsaking of sensual life.

THE LIFE AND TIMES OF THE MIDDLE-AGED TODAY

In 1980, demographers tell us, three-fourths of the middle aged in
India—defined as persons ages 45-59—lived with others besides their
aging spouses. These "others" could be old parents or close family relatives of the parent's generation as well as married sons and unmarried
children of both sexes (Bhende 1982, 12). This family living pattern
has been changing rapidly in the last fifteen years, especially in the
middle and upper-middle classes of the metropolitan cities. Thus a
1988 study of four hundred students from these classes in Delhi revealed that over 80 percent lived in nuclear families (Gangrade 1988,
24–35). Yet, as a whole, it would be fair to maintain that a majority
of the middle aged in India today spend their lives in family formations
larger than the nuclear family.

The role of the middle aged in the family is somewhat ambiguous.
In a study of the elderly in a semirural community in Delhi, the anthropologist Sylvia Vatuk found that the ancient ideal of *vanaprastha* con-

tinues to exercise a considerable hold on the Indian imagination (Vatuk 1983, 71). With the marriage of the first son, which initiates a new reproductive sequence, it is generally expected—by the middle-age couple and by others in the family and the community—that family responsibilities will be handed over to the next generation. The middle-aged couple, meanwhile, becomes increasingly concerned with spiritual life and religious contemplation. Although culturally valued and rewarded, this ideal is rarely found in practice. Vatuk observes that this transition in roles seems easier for men, who become more and more peripheral to the household's day-to-day activities and shift their interest to the outside world. Most of them are content if they are deferred to by the younger generation, even if the deference is nominal, and as long as they are at least formally consulted in important decisions affecting the family.

Demographic data, which shows a comparatively precipitous decline in childbearing of Indian women in their thirties, suggests that there is a marked reduction in the sexual activity of men at the beginning of middle age. Whether this reduction arises from the Hindu cultural ideal of renunciation of sexuality at this age, or whether, as I have suggested elsewhere, it may be influenced by the ever-increasing representations of the wife as a mother—an inhibitor of a man's sexual interest in marriage—remains to be determined (Kakar 1978).

The middle-aged woman's role is defined by her assumption of the role of the mother-in-law. Relinquishing control over the household to the daughter-in-law often proves to be a difficult task and usually takes place toward the end rather than the beginning of middle age. Proverbs from various parts of the country tell us of the mother-in-law's tenacity and the daughter-in-law's savage wishes as they struggle over household power. A Marathi proverb says, "Sasu gele thik jhale ghardar hati aale" (I am glad the mother-in-law is dead, the household is now in my hands). It has a Hindi counterpart that translated says, "If my mother-in-law dies and my father-in-law lives, I [the daughter-in-law] will rule the household." In Bengali, there is

> Ekla gharer ginni hali bujhi ma;
> Nishwaske bishwas ki—nadche duto pa.

This translates into English as

> On the deathbed of the mother-in-law, the daughter-in-law's mother tells her, "Understand well my daughter, now

you alone will rule this household." The anxious daughter replies, "It is not enough to trust the failing breath, her legs are still moving."

The reluctance of the middle-aged woman to give up her power has partly to do with the vicissitudes of the woman's life cycle in traditional India. As I have elaborated elsewhere, as a daughter a woman is a mere sojourner in her parents' home. As a young bride and daughter-in-law she occupies one of the lowest positions in her new family, where obedience and compliance with the wishes of the elder women of the family, especially those of her mother-in-law, are expected as a matter of course. It is only as she ages and becomes a mother, especially the mother of sons, that power in the family begins to come her way. Seniority holds out enormous rewards not just in status but in actual decision making (Kakar 1978, chap. 3).

In life, as in Hindi movies, the middle-aged woman's giving up of familial power, symbolized by handing over the keys to the household's store of food supplies and linen, occurs after many years of friction, shifting alliances, and—at least in Hindi movies—pleas by various members of the younger generation, "Maji, ab to aap puja path kariye" (Mother, you should now engage yourself in prayer and religious rituals.) In the movies, there is often a scene near the end where the struggle between the mother-in-law and the daughter-in-law is finally resolved by the older woman's admission of the younger woman's sterling qualities of character and disposition—traits about which she had expressed grave misgivings in the beginning. She then hands over the bunch of keys to the daughter-in-law in a ceremonial gesture in front of other assembled family members with the words, "Bahu [daughter-in-law], from now on the household is in your charge. I am off to Kashi"—Kashi or Benares being the feminine counterpart of the "forest" to which men in ancient India withdrew for their retirement.

In actual life, even when they gradually withdraw from direct household responsibilities, middle-aged women (and to a lesser extent, men), try to control the behavior of younger family members by taking over the role of "keepers of the tradition." In this role, ideal for the feelings of moral superiority it engenders in the middle aged and the venomous dislike it produces in the young, the dress, deportment, and social interactions of the younger generation are closely monitored and measured against traditional standards and are, of course, invariably found wanting. An empirical study of two hundred college students in Jaipur,

Rajasthan, reveals that aging men and women are seen by the young as conservatives who dislike any change or interference with the established way of doing things. Young women, perhaps because of their greater contact with the elderly at home and also because their deportment is a special object of the older family members' attention, feel this more strongly than the young men (Sharma and Bhandari 1971).

With the notions of *ruob* (authoritativeness) toward the young and *adab* (respectfulness) toward the old, there is little intergenerational familiarity in India (except, of course, in the upper middle class in the metropolitan centers) as it exists in countries such as in the United States. Men and women seek intimacy with their own age cohorts. For women this intimacy generally takes place within the extended family, while men spend more and more time with other middle-aged men of their village and caste community talking of "serious" matters and abjuring the frivolous pursuits of their youth, such as going to the cinema.

As for the social status of the middle aged and their relationships with the younger generation, the theology of *burhapa* holds that, in traditional Indian society with its extended family system and well-defined hierarchies of power and authority, its age-old channels of respect and obedience, and its socialization that extolls the wisdom of age above the energy of youth, older people are automatically the recipients of deference, respect, and all the support and care they need in their declining years. The anthropology of aging, on the other hand, reveals this is a myth (see, e.g., Vatuk 1983; Dak and Sharma 1987; Kumar and Suryanarayna 1989; Kanu et al. 1987; Anantharaman 1979). These studies support the view that, from a peak at the onset of middle age, power, authority, and prestige decline sharply until in true old age only a husk of deference is left without any real respect. This state of affairs is attributed to the break up of the extended family system as a consequence of modernization. With their traditional skills regarded as obsolete and their experience viewed as irrelevant, the aging are seen by their children and by the larger community as economic and social liabilities. With an increase in geographic and physical mobility among the young, the elderly no longer receive the care and support they presumably commanded in earlier, happier times.

Representations in Contemporary Hindi Literature

Reflecting its relative inconsequentiality, both demographic and in popular consciousness, the literary representations of middle age are few and far between. A less-than-thorough but more-than-cursory search in contemporary Hindi fiction and poetry unearthed only a few short stories where the main protagonist is clearly middle aged. There are also some poems where childhood memories are summoned by a middle-aged mind or where middle-aged eyes rediscover the village where one lived as a child.

Here, I shall take up only one story in some detail—*Silver Wedding* by Manohar Shyam Joshi, an immensely popular writer who has enjoyed considerable acclaim for scripting some of the best-known television serials of the last decade (Joshi 1990).

Yashodar Pant, the "hero" of the story is what Indian intellectuals and the upper classes derisively, and the rest enviously, call a *babu*, a low-ranking government official in the vast bureaucracy of the Indian state. Perhaps in his late forties or early fifties—his exact age is not clear—Yashodar, nearing the end of his undistinguished career, is the head of a small section in the Ministry of Home Affairs. The story opens on the day of his twenty-fifth wedding anniversary, which Yashodar, a man of habit who dislikes any change in his routine, treats like as other day as he prepares to go home at the end of the day's work. Rising from his desk exactly at 5:30 P.M. by his old-fashioned watch (which a younger colleague would have him throw away and replace with a new Japanese digital model), he is asked by his colleagues to order tea and sweets in celebration of his "silver" wedding anniversary. Yashodar refuses since such celebrations are not a part of his tradition and he finds them, in his two favorite English words, "somehow improper."

For the last few years, Yashodar has felt increasingly alienated from his family. His eldest son has a job in an ad agency and is paid a salary that matches that of his father. Yashodar finds such high salaries paid to the young as somehow improper. His second son is preparing for his examinations for the civil service, having refused a perfectly fine job offer into the lower rungs of the bureaucracy the previous year. A third son has gone to the United States to study on a scholarship, while the grownup daughter is refusing all marriage proposals and is threatening to go off to the states for further studies. Yashodar *babu* is a democrat and would never insist that the children follow his advice to the letter. But it is too much when none of them even consult him and do exactly what they want: " 'Granted that your knowledge is greater than mine, child, but there is no substitute for experience! Whether you agree or disagree with me, just go through the pretence of consulting me once.' The children reply, '*Babba*, you are the limit! Why should we ask you about things of which you have no idea?' The children show unmistakable signs that they are going to be of little comfort to him in his old age."[3]

Yashodar's wife too has changed a great deal with middle age. She has become independent and increasingly self-assured. He finds his daughter's wearing of jeans and sleeveless tops somehow improper but his wife is vigorous in the daughter's defence. "I did all that covering of my head with the sari on your say-so but my daughter will do exactly what the rest of the world does," she says. The wife often complains that when she came into his extended family as a bride there were many restrictions placed on her behavior by her mother- and sisters-in-law and that Yashodar never stood up for her. "I was young but lived the life of an old woman," she says. "The children are quite right in not following your old fashioned ways and neither will I." "Why have you become so serious?" she asks. "You saw two movies a week when you were young, cooked meat on Sundays and sang *ghazals* and film songs." Yashodar *babu* accepts that he has changed but feels that with the years a certain kind of age-appropriate maturity (*buzurgiat*) is called for in a man. He tells his wife that the way she has started wearing sleeveless blouses in her *burhapa*, favors high heels and eats outside the kitchen are all somehow improper. "Anyway I am not stopping you from doing all this," he says, "therefore you should also not object to my way of life."

Yashodar's wife and children strongly disapprove of his recently acquired habit of stopping by the Birla temple in the evening on his way home from office. Here he listens to discourses of holy men and does some meditation himself. "*Babba*, you are not so old that you should visit the temple daily and engage in all this religious fasting and rituals," his children complain. Actually, Yashodar *babu* is not very religiously inclined. He is only trying to follow the ideals inculcated in him by his mentor, long since dead, who not only got Yashodar his job but also taught him about life and its meaning. One simply must get more involved in religious and spiritual life as one gets older. Like his mentor before him, Yashodar *babu* too goes to the temple every day, spends time in prayer and the study of religious books. When his mind complains of its disinterest in such activities, Yashodar chides it, "You *should* be interested. Along with the illusory attachment to the world, one has to give God some place in one's life. One should now hand over the kingdom to the younger generation and proceed to the forest."

When Yashodar tries to meditate after his morning and evening prayers, he finds his mind more involved in the family problems than in the Almighty. Yashodar would like to learn the right technique of meditation. He consoles himself with the thought that perhaps the proper time for these practices is after his retirement. They are prescribed for the *vanaprastha* stage and Yashodar *babu* feels he will return to his ancestral village for this stage of his life—"far from the madding crowd, you understand!"

When he reaches home, Yashodar finds that his children have given a silver wedding party to which they have invited their friends. There is cake and whiskey—both of which he finds somehow improper— and Yashodar escapes to his room on the pretext of saying his prayers. His eyes closed, he carries on an imaginary conversation with his dead mentor who, echoing the understanding arrived at by Yuddhishtra in the Mahabharata, says, "In the beginning and at the end you are all alone. You cannot call anyone in this world your own." Yashodar wants to ask his mentor what his attitude should be in face of the difficulties his wife and children are causing him. But the mentor seems bent on talking about the loneliness of this stage of life: "What wife and what children! That is all *maya* [illusion] and this Bhushan [Yashodar's eldest son] who is today jumping all over the place will one day feel as much alone and helpless as you are feeling today." Yashodar *babu* would like to carry on this imaginary conversation when he is interrupted by his wife. The guests are leaving and the presents must be unwrapped. One of them is a woolen dressing gown from his eldest son. "This is for you to wear instead of that torn old sweater when you go to fetch milk in the morning," says the son. Yashodar's eyes moisten. He does not know whether the unshed tears are because his son has not offered to get the morning milk himself or whether he is reminded of his mentor who also used to wear a dressing gown on his morning walks.

Silver Wedding highlights some of the themes we have encountered earlier in other accounts of middle age, both in ancient Sanskrit texts and contemporary social science studies. First, the middle aged are conservers of traditional values. In the conflict between tradition, represented by Yashodar's dead mentor, and modernity, represented by his children, Yashodar is squarely on the side of the Hindu tradition, which views the renunciation of worldly concerns and a turn toward a more inward, spiritual life as the main task of middle age. The task itself is difficult, and more so for women than for men, which is illustrated by the struggles of Yashodar's wife.

Second, in middle age as we look back on our lives there is a resurgence of memories of childhood and youth, of those who have loved us and given us guidance. There is satisfaction afforded by the act of recollection itself rather than in some kind of instrumental "stock taking," which has been posited as a dominant concern of the "midlife crisis" in the West. As Yashodar gradually liberates himself from the constraints imposed by his career, family, and active existence in society in general, his ability to relive the past in his imagination increases. Indeed, as Maurice Halbwachs observes, this greater capacity to redescend into the past may be related to the social function of the elderly as keepers of the society's traditions, preservers of traces of its past, and in the encouragement society gives them to devote their energies to acts of remembering (Halbwachs 1992, 47–50).

Third, this stage of life reveals the glimmerings of man's existential loneliness and triggers the anxiety associated with the glimpses of one's ultimate helplessness. The awareness of this loneliness is inherent in the act of withdrawing from the family and the world, a step recommended by Hindu tradition. The underlying anxiety of this momentous emotional and psychological event is only articulated by the writers, the keepers of a society's wishes and fears.

The well-known Hindi writer Nirmal Verma has made the depressive loneliness of middle age the focus of two stories: "Sookha" (Drought) and "Subah ki Sair" (The morning walk) (Verma 1988, 1983). "Sookha" is narrated from the viewpoint of a young woman in the first days of her new job as a college lecturer. She has been asked to take care of the dreary details of a literary seminar in a provincial town in Rajasthan, which is in the grip of a drought. The star invitee to the seminar is a middle-aged writer from Delhi who has not written anything for a decade. The story is replete with haunting images of the writer's isolation and lack of contact—the "drought," of course, is an inner condition rather than an external event. For a fleeting moment, the woman and the writer come together, a moment of human understanding and sympathy that revives the man, an unexpected shower on a parched inner landscape, before the drought descends again.

"Subah ki Sair" describes the morning walk of a retired army colonel, Nihalchand, who lives alone except for an elderly servant. His wife is dead and his only son—in the Indian middle-class parents' youthful dreams and middle-aged nightmares—lives in the United States. Nihalchand spends his time eating, sleeping, and talking to himself. The highlight of his day is his morning walk, which follows exactly the same route every day and has as its last station a well-preserved, deserted Mughal monument—rather like the colonel himself—in the middle of the jungle. Here the colonel eats a frugal breakfast packed by the servant, lies down, closes his eyes, and lets a reverie that has a strongly, hallucinatory quality unroll on his inner screen. A young girl of fourteen, a dearly beloved playmate of his teens, shyly approaches the colonel's prone form. She talks to him about their common memories and asks questions about his wife and son. Nihalchand is not sure whether he is awake or asleep and where these voices are coming from. "Whose voice was it? Or was it only an illusion, a betrayal? This discordant voice, arising from the jungle of old age, an orphaned, burning voice, knocks at the door. You open the door and there is nothing, only an unending vista of emptiness, no one near or far. No love, no attachment, no pain of infatuation—not even pain. Nothing to be seen, neither the face of his wife nor the remembrance of the son, nothing—only I. Who are you, Nihalchand, what are you?" (73; my translation).

In contemporary Hindi fiction and poetry, middle age does not constitute—as in some of Western rhetoric—the "prime" but rather the decline of life. The prevailing mood is not of optimism and renewed confidence at entering the second half of life but of a barely concealed despair. The desired equanimity of Sanskrit texts has given way to depression; the struggles of ancient poets with middle-aged sexuality are replaced in modern writers by a narcissistic absorption in the minutiae of one's life, past and present.

MOVIES AND MIDDLE AGE

In the last decade, there has been a sea change in the sociological composition of the audience for popular Hindi cinema. Earlier, this cinema catered to the entertainment needs of a predominantly middle class, "family" audience. Today, the largest section of its viewership is lower middle class, male, urban, and young. Of the many changes in the form and content of movies that this shift in audience has brought about, it is the relatively low visibility of middle-aged characters that is of special interest to us. Movies have become focused on youth to an unprecedented degree. There is little development of any other character besides that of the young protagonists. Reflecting solely a youthful perspective, the middle-aged characters of the movies—parents, uncles and aunts, bosses at work, and others in position of authority—are always seen as fulfilling certain functions in relation to the youthful hero and heroine and have no existence or individuality in their own right. However, as compared to the elderly, such as grandparents, who are shown as being invariably kindly disposed toward the young, the middle aged are more variable in their representation. Generally, the middle aged in popular Hindi cinema fit one of several categories.

Supportive of the young.—In these roles, the middle-aged character, often a parent, will show empathy for the hero or the heroine, support his or her aspirations even when these are in opposition to the wishes of the rest of the family. If from outside the family but in a position of authority, the middle-aged person is firm but kind, a dispenser of wise counsel and, often, of more concrete, material assistance.

Supportive of the social order.—Here, the middle-aged person is the representative of a rigid social order and a hidebound morality, most often pertaining to what is and is not a desirable marriage for the youngster. He or she is an unfeeling oppressor of the young who seeks to bind their joys and desires. Traditional and conservative, the middle-aged person is authoritarian and is occupied solely with finding ways to thwart young love.

Laughable.—In these roles, the middle-aged person is caricatured as someone whose eccentricities are a result of some kind of age-related deterioration of the mind. Or, the middle-aged character is laughable because he or she insists on being youthful—that is, has not become reconciled to the loss of youth and the inappropriateness of sexuality. This kind of inappropriate behavior on the middle-aged person's part, which makes him or her an object of derision for the young, is also reflected in popular Hindi sayings. "Seeng kata kar bachda banana" (to become a calf by cutting off one's horns) is used in case of a middle-aged man foolish enough to hanker after youth. Its counterpart for a woman is, "Boodhi ghodi lal lagam; aao logo karo salaam" (The old mare has red reins; come, people, salute her). The laughter at the middle aged—their lack of physical prowess and the gap between their sexual promise and performance, is without any sympathetic undertones and reverberates with sarcasm. For the young, this derisive laughter represents an aggressive release from the stranglehold the middle aged have over their lives.

Beta (Son) is one of the few box office hits in the past couple of years where the middle-aged characters, even if caricatures, are at least drawn with some attention to detail. Raju, the hero of the story, lost his mother at birth and from the age of five has been brought up by his stepmother, Lakshmi. Raju adores Lakshmi with the desperate longings of a motherless boy, although she married his father only to lay her hands on their considerable property. The estate, however, had belonged to Raju's mother, who had willed it to her only son and stipulated that he could not sell or make a gift of it until after his marriage and then, too, only with the consent of his wife. In being nice to the boy and turning him into a mother worshipper, Lakshmi has planned to have the estate signed over to her after Raju grows up. She has kept Raju unlettered, making him work with his sharecroppers in the fields, so that she and her brother, who lives with them, can embezzle large sums of money from the estate. The sister and brother have also conspired to have Raju's father declared insane. He is kept confined in one room of their sprawling mansion.

Raju falls in love with Saraswati, a girl from another village, and marries her. Lakshmi has no objections since she also needs Raju's wife's signature for obtaining the property. She is confident that she can easily manipulate her rustic and presumably naive daughter-in-law. However, to make certain that the couple does not develop any strong intimate bond that might threaten her supremacy in the household, Lakshmi tells Saraswati to desist from conjugal relations since astrologers have predicted that Raju would die if he became sexually active before the age of twenty-five.

Saraswati soon sees through her wily mother-in-law's games and proves to be more than a match for her. After an unwise open confrontation in which Saraswati tries to enlighten her husband on her mother-in-law's real character and where Raju sides with his adored mother and hits Saraswati, the young woman becomes more circumspect in her continuing battle with Lakshmi. She succeeds in having her father-in-law freed from his imprisonment, exposes the financial misdeeds of Lakshmi's brother, and cleverly maneuvers a situation where Lakshmi has no option but to hand over the keys to the stores, and to the safe, to her daughter-in-law. To seal her victory at this dramatic high point of the movie, she reveals that she is pregnant, about to become the mother (she hopes) of the all-important son. The last resort for the mother-in-law in their deathly struggle is to try and poison Saraswati. "In this house only one of us can live," Lakshmi declares to her brother. "She dares to challenge *me*? Does she not realize that I am a female snake, quite capable of devouring my own young, to say nothing of destroying hers?" Saraswati finds out that the milk her husband brings her has been poisoned by her mother-in-law. Raju, however, refuses to believe in his stepmother's villainy and to prove Lakshmi's innocence, drinks the milk himself. As he hovers between life and death, Lakshmi finally undergoes a change of heart and allows a doctor to save his life. Alluding to the Ramayana, she says, "Even Kaikeyi [Rama's stepmother] had Rama exiled only for fourteen years and here I was prepared to take my Rama's very life. If I had done so, no one would have ever believed in maternal love again."

The three middle-aged characters in the movie—Lakshmi, her brother, and Raju's father—are obviously viewed from the perspective of the young. The two men are really minor characters, relegated to the sidelines. Raju's father—passive, weak, and helpless and yet a "good" man is perhaps the most peripheral, an accurate reflection of one major view of the father's role in family life with advancing age. (The other has him a rampaging household tyrant, terrorizing women and children). Lakshmi's brother is portrayed as a laughable buffoon, whose villainy is quite ineffectual and depends on the support of his sister for its success.

The central middle-aged character in the movie is undoubtedly Lakshmi. Cold, scheming, and utterly ruthless, Lakshmi is the witch-like mother-in-law of popular Hindu culture. Whereas between the ages of fifteen and thirty, the woman (or rather, her womb) is the object of much praise in sayings and songs for her potential as a mother, the same woman, when she crosses into middle age (when she becomes a mother-in-law) is now damned in songs and proverbs as a witch, a snake in female form, or as a *churel*, a malevolent female ghost. The reason for this transformation, as I pointed out above, is her supreme authority in matters of the household, an authority cordially resented by the daughters-in-law. Besides the discord of this specific role relationship, it also seems that the entire anger of young women against their socially imposed roles and restrictions becomes channeled in resentment against the mother-in-law. Tamil women ask, "Will my mother-in-law never die, will my sorrows never end?" and the Marathi saying, "Mother-in-law died in summer but tears are shed during the monsoon," has its counterparts in other languages. Thus although a middle-aged woman in India enjoys immense authority, there always lies a shadow on her power, a constant undermining of her authority by that part of the culture that mirrors the anger of young women and their wishes to replace their mothers-in-law.

This image of the middle-aged woman as a powerful oppressor

whose power is under constant sniping is true only for the mother of adult sons. Middle-aged women without children or those with only daughters are tragic figures and, with the death of their husbands, pitiful, since they have no property rights and must often subsist on the charity of others—an image hauntingly captured by the closely cropped heads of widows bent in prayer or reverie in the pilgrimage centers of Mathura or Benares.

CONCLUSION

In this essay, I have attempted to elaborate on Hindu ideas of middle age, in ancient and contemporary India, noting both the continuities and discontinuities from the past to the present. For the past, I took as my sources such texts as the epics of Ramayana and Mahabharata, the Dharmashastras and Sanskrit poetry. For contemporary India, my sources were popular sayings and Hindi fiction and cinema. My findings can be summarized in the following paragraphs.

Although there is a specific word for middle age in contemporary lexical usage, there is no particular awareness of this period as a separate stage of life. Generally, "middle age" is considered the first part of old age and is associated with images of decline rather than a "prime" of life.

There is no particular age explicitly related to the onset of middle age. In both ancient and modern texts, middle age is heralded by a change in the person's role in family life. Specifically, middle age begins with the marriage of the first child, that is, the initiation by the next generation of a reproductive sequence of its own.

The chief psychological requirement, the task of this age, as represented in both older and contemporary texts, is a renunciation of the concerns of family life and of the outside world that had so far dominated in adulthood. In ancient poetry and modern fiction, this culturally desired goal of withdrawal triggers a psychological crisis, especially in men. The Sanskrit poets represent this crisis in terms of the despair associated with a renunciation of sexual life. The old texts see this crisis as one whose successful resolution leads to a specific "virtue" of this stage—a sense of equanimity. In contemporary fictional representations, the crisis is accompanied by a depressive awareness of one's existential loneliness and the frightening images of the helplessness awaiting the person at the end of life.

The culturally desirable goals of renunciation and withdrawal are much more difficult for the middle-aged woman than for the man.

Because of certain vicissitudes of the female life cycle in India, the middle-aged woman clings stubbornly to the authority and power in the household that come her way at this stage of life. An object of resentment for the younger generation, especially her daughters-in-law, who constantly try to undermine her power, the middle-aged woman is generally portrayed as an oppressive witch-like character who is secretly scorned by the young.

NOTES

1. The main collections of these studies are Bose and Gangrade (1988), Desai (1982), Dak and Sharma (1987), Pati and Jena (1989), de Souza and Fernandes (1982).

2. For whatever this information is worth, the middle-aged population of India, according to American demographic criteria, i.e., the 45–59 age group, was 10.33% of the total population in the 1981 census. Currently, this will be about 90 million people. See Bhende (1982).

3. Here and elsewhere through the telling of this tale, quoted lines are my English-language paraphrases and thus do not have corresponding page numbers in the Hindi original.

REFERENCES

Anantharaman, R. N. 1979. "Perception of Old Age by Two Generations." *Journal of Psychological Researches* 23 (3):198–99.

Bhende, A. A. 1982. "Demographic Aspects of Aging in India." In *Aging in India,* edited by K. G. Desai. Bombay: Tata Institute of Social Sciences.

Bose, A. B., and K. D. Gangrade, eds. 1988. *The Aging in India.* New Delhi: Abhinav Publications.

Dak, T. M., and M. L. Sharma, eds. 1987. *Aging in India: Challenge for the Society.* Delhi: Ajanta Publications.

Desai, K. G., ed. 1982. *Aging in India.* Bombay: Tata Institute of Social Sciences.

De Souza, Alfred, and Walter Fernandes, eds. 1982. *Aging in South Asia: Theoretical Issues and Policy Implications.* New Delhi: Indian Social Science Institute.

Doniger O'Flaherty, Wendy, trans. 1981. *The Rig Veda.* London: Penguin.

Fernandes, Walter. 1982. "Aging in South Asia as Marginalization." In *Aging in South Asia: Theoretical Issues and Policy Implications,* edited by A. de Souza and W. Fernandes, 1–23. New Delhi: Indian Social Science Institute.

Gangrade, K. D. 1988. "Crisis of Values: A Sociological Study of the Old and the Young." In *The Aging in India,* edited by A. B. Bose and K. D. Gangrade, 24–35. New Delhi: Abhinav Publications.

Halbwachs, M. 1992. *On Collective Memory,* edited by Lewis Coser, 47–57. Chicago: University of Chicago Press.

Joshi, Manohar Shyam. 1990. "Silver Wedding." In *Mandir ke Ghat ki Paudhian* (The riverfront steps to the temple), 23–40. Delhi: Saroj Prakashan.

Kakar, Sudhir. 1978. *The Inner World: A Psychoanalytical Study of Childhood and Society in India.* New Delhi: Oxford University Press.

Kanu, P., et al. 1987. "Attitude of the Second Generation toward Aging Problems." In *Aging in India: Challenge for the Society,* edited by T. L. Dak and M. L. Sharma. Dehli: Ajanta Publications.

Kumar, V., and Suryanarayna. 1989. "Problems of the Aged in the Rural Sector." In *Aged in India: Socio-Demographic Dimensions,* edited by R. N. Pati and B. Jena. New Delhi: Ashish Publishing House.

Mathers, E. Powys. 1929. *Eastern Love: English Versions.* Vol. 5, *The Loves of Radha and Krishna and Amores.* London: J. Rodker.

Miller, Barbara S., trans. 1990. The Hermit and the Love-Thief. Delhi: Penguin.

Pati, Rabindra Nath, and Basantibala Jena, eds. 1989. *Aged in India: Socio-Demographic Dimensions.* New Delhi: Ashish Publishing House.

Sharma, K. L., and Prabha Bhandari. 1971. "A Study of Students' Stereotypes toward Aging." *Indian Journal of Gerontology* 2 (1):20–27.

Tulsidasa, Goswami. N.d. *Shri Ramacharitamanas.* Gorakhpur: Gita Press.

Vatuk, Sylvia. 1983. "The Family Life of Older People in a Changing Society: India." In *Aging and the Aged in the Third World.* Pt. 2, *Regional and Ethnographic Perspectives.* Edited by J. Sokolovsky. Williamsburg, Va.: College of William and Mary, Department of Anthropology.

Verma, Nirmal. 1983. "Subah ki Sair" in *Kavve aur Kala Pani* (Crows and black water), 65–80. Delhi: Rajkamal Prakashan.

———. 1988. "Sookha." *Hansa* (April), 71–86.

II ALTERNATIVE CULTURAL REPRESENTATIONS OF THE LIFE COURSE: MATURE ADULTHOOD WITHOUT MIDDLE AGE

Status Reversal: The Coming of Aging in Samoa

Bradd Shore

It seems apparent that the modern ethnographic record on Samoa, surely among the most frequently scrutinized of anthropology's favored field sites, begins with the question about the relation between culture and the aging process. Margaret Mead's classic 1928 account of Samoan adolescence, though now notoriously controversial, signaled the coming of age of anthropology as an empirical discipline studying the complex relation between human nature and cultural variability (see Mead 1928a). In addition to Mead's early work on adolescence, Lowell Holmes has studied Samoan "aging" from a gerontological perspective that refers less to the shape of a life course than to the study of the latter stages of Samoan life (Holmes 1983).

If the numerous ethnographies of Samoan social organization provide some idea of the social categories and institutions that shape Samoan childhood, youth, and old age, they tend to be conspicuously silent on the topic of middle age.[1] As our own term "middle age" suggests, this period of life is often understood as an in-between category, bridging other more salient cultural categories by which a life history is measured. This essay will attempt to correct these gaps in Samoan ethnography by providing a social and cultural account of Samoan middle age. It will not explicate the Samoan *cultural category* of middle age since there does not appear to be any such explicit category. Instead, it will concentrate on the cultural construction of the middle years in the context of Samoan cultural models of the life course. Inevi-

The research on which this study is based was carried out in the summer of 1976 in the village of Lalomalava, Savai'i in Western Samoa. The fieldwork was supported by a grant from the Center for Field Research and by two teams of research assistants who accompanied the researchers through Earthwatch Expeditions. Senior researchers on the team included Margaret MacKenzie, Virginia Little, and myself. I wish the thank the chiefs and the Women's Committee of Lalomalava for their help during our stay. Special thanks is due to the Honorable Tofilau Luamanuvae Eti, now prime minister of Western Samoa, whose hospitality we enjoyed during the course of our stay in his village.

tably, then, this analysis of the middle years will entail a more general ethnography of the cultural structuring of aging in Samoa.

Research Methods

The analysis is based on a survey of aging in Samoa I conducted with a research team in 1976 in the village of Lalomalava, on the island of Savai'i. The team collected detailed census data on the village, information on political and social organization, and a large body of more specific information on social, cultural, and medical dimensions of aging. In addition to general information I gained during my four years of residence and research in Samoa, this essay is based on several kinds of data collected in 1976. A series of fifteen intensive interviews with a cross section of male and female villagers of different ages provided basic insights into Samoan age-related concepts and categories.

In addition, researchers went into local schools and collected 187 sets of essays from students ranging from fifteen to eighteen years old. About one-third were in English; the rest were written in Samoan. Students were asked to describe the stages of life they found the most and the least attractive and to explain their answers. These essays were carefully analyzed, and responses were coded by type to generate quantifiable data on young people's attitudes toward different life stages. Answers were analyzed by grade level of respondent as well as by gender.

Using these interviews and these relatively free-form essays, we were able to establish a set of five baseline categories that Samoans appear to use in modeling a life history. These Samoan life-stage categories are *pepe* (baby/infant), *tama'ititi* (child), *tagata talavou* (youth), *tagata matua* (adult), and *toea'ina* or *lo'omatua* (old man or old woman). We did not assign specific ages to these categories. As we shall see, chronological age turns out to be less important for Samoans than other salient markers of life stages.

Using these life-stage categories, I constructed a detailed checklist of possible associations with each of the five life stages. This checklist was distributed to every member of the village over age 14. We collected well over two hundred completed checklists, and these were then analyzed to construct a profile of villagers' attitudes toward different life stages. This profile distinguished respondents both by gender and by age group to provide a sociologically nuanced portrait of attitudes toward aging.

Is "Middle Age" a Viable Cross-Cultural Concept?

In undertaking a cross-cultural analysis of middle age, we need to address the complex issue of the nature of the unit under study. Just what do we mean by "middle age?" Using either cultural and biological indices of age can change radically the way an individual is categorized. Chronological definitions (e.g., individuals between the ages of forty and fifty-five) may be intuitively obvious for the populations of modern industrialized ages. But what constitutes middle age in a population with a radically different life expectancy? For many populations, such as traditional Australian aborigines, for instance, the chronological span we term "middle age" would have to be considered old age. In other words do we define middle age in absolute terms, or in relation to a particular population's age structure? Even more radical is the question of whether chronological age is necessarily the best way to approach the study of middle age.

Middle Age as a Cultural Construct

There is also the problem of cultural and historical variability in how life stages are modeled. Since perceptions of age are always mediated by cultural models of a life course, simple cross-cultural comparisons are difficult. The current American notions of middle age can hardly be dissociated from such historically and culturally rooted concepts as "generation gap," "midlife crisis," and "youth culture." I would suggest that our own notions of middle age are shaped by four important general cultural factors:

1. There is a long Western tradition of organizing the idea of a life history via a narrative that defines the process of aging in terms of a set of predictable "crises" and potential resolutions. The notion that the life course can be modeled in terms of life crises informs a Western literary tradition ranging from King Lear to Holden Caulfield.

This tradition has in part shaped academic theories of aging as developmental "crises" as in the Freudian and Eriksonian models of aging, which conceive of transitions in life stages as developmental and social crises that can have more or less successful outcomes.

2. Middle age conceptualized as a "midlife crisis" is linked to a pervasive Western fear or denial of death. A significant aspect of the modern Western midlife crisis involves a recognition of one's own mortality.

3. Middle age takes on its cultural value in relation to a future-

oriented conception of history. Our linear (rather than cyclical) model of history is associated with generational discontinuities that are, in turn, influenced by notions of technological and social "progress." The presumed inevitability of "generation gaps" is thus more than the belief that the experience of members of different generations will be different because they have lived for different amounts of time and during different time periods. I presume that this sort of gap is more or less universal in human experience. Modern notions of a generation gap are based on notions of increasing obsolescence of the past and presume a continual historical evolution in requisite knowledge and skills; this linear concept then shapes perceptions of elders as obsolete and their experience largely irrelevant for the young. Modern notions of middle age as midlife crisis are inseparable from these cultural conditions.

4. Midlife in contemporary industrial societies is also evaluated against the backdrop of the Protestant work ethic and its correlates. Aging is understood in relation to deeply rooted cultural assumptions about the intrinsic value of work and activity to self-worth and a corresponding devaluation of leisure or passivity.[2] Self-esteem is tied to notions of productive competence and self-control or autonomy so that nonproductivity, relative passivity, and social dependency become experienced largely as negative and regressive attributes.[3]

While it is fair to say that some of these Western assumptions have affected Samoan attitudes toward aging, our 1976 data suggest that, for rural villagers, aging was understood largely in relation to Samoan assumptions about status, activity, energy, bodily movement versus stasis, and death, assumptions that are quite different from those informing American attitudes.

To anticipate the argument of this essay, Samoan experiences of middle age show few of the negative associations that Americans equate with midlife. Middle age for Samoans is not culturally represented as a crisis related to diminished competence and youth. Nor is it represented as a sudden realization of one's personal mortality and physical vulnerability.

To understand how Samoan experiences of midlife contrast with our own, we need to look at the ways in which Samoan village life structures the activities and roles of different categories of people, and how the social organization of age is reflected in cultural models of life stages. Specifically, Samoan middle age will be viewed in relation to Samoan conceptions of work, activity level, social status, and power.

Rather than understand middle age as a diminution of youthful energy, Samoans appear to understand mature adulthood in terms of a transition between two kinds of status: that associated with physical work and movement and that associated with passive authority. Though a Western stereotype of "traditional" societies suggests reverence for elders, Samoans, particularly young Samoans, evince distinctly ambivalent views of old age. Yet unlike the modern American case, ambivalence about old age appears from our sample to have little to do with the perception or the experience of middle age as the onset of old age.

SAMOAN CATEGORIES OF LIFE STAGES

Samoans do not appear to use chronological age as the main basis of classifying someone. While birthdays (particularly those commemorating "Sweet 16" and or becoming an "adult" at twenty-one) are now celebrated among more urbanized Samoans, villagers do not often commemorate birthdays, and many older Samoan informants professed no knowledge of their own ages.[4] Since birth certificates are routinely provided for hospital births, and proof of age is now required for school attendance, some of these older Samoans may have been embarrassed that ignorance of their age identified them as poorly educated and rural rather than urban dwellers.

The dissociation between life stage and chronological age tends to increase with age. While infancy and childhood are invariably assumed to be age related, the senior statuses are more likely to be evaluated on the basis of a person's social standing, social role, or even activity level rather than on their chronological age. Thus, for example, people may be classified as "old" when they become dependent upon their children, irrespective of their actual age or appearance. One informant I interviewed, a thirty-year-old village pastor, could not pinpoint an age at which he considered his parents old, but focused rather on who cared for whom:

Q. When do you call a person "old" here in Samoa?
A. It's hard for me to identify a certain stage. When a person becomes a chief, gives orders, arranges family matters, he can call his parents "old people." I now take care of my parents and I call them "old." Just like they were taking care of me when I was in school. In age my parents are only fifty-five and forty-five, but I call them "old" because I am in a stage of being responsible for taking care of them. Since I'm working now, I have

to give back the care they took of me. We are not like you. We go away and have our own families, but we return the care for [our parents].

Infancy and Childhood

Samoan infants are called *pepe,* while newborns are called *pepe meamea.* Infants are classified in terms of their relative helplessness and dependency upon others. Thus, a common distinction made between an infant and a child is that the child can walk and is relatively free and mobile, while the baby is carried about by others. Infants are also not held to be responsible for their actions, while children are. Samoans frame this distinction as one of having or not having "judgment" (*mafaufau;* Mead 1928a). Judgment involves being responsible for knowing the difference between right and wrong or between appropriate and inappropriate behaviors.

Examples of good and bad judgment often involve behaviors around food and feeding. Thus, one informant said that people have judgment when they carry out properly common chores such as preparing food. "If they see a horse needs to eat and a person moves a horse to where there is a lot of grass, that's judgment."

Having no judgment (*lē mafaufau*) was also illustrated in terms of food: "If we bring food inside a house, eat while walking inside of a house, this is what we mean by *lē mafaufau.* The person doesn't look after social relations properly" (*e lē tausia le vā feiloa'i*). Only people who are held responsible for their actions can be criticized as having "no judgment." Negligent children are often berated for lack of judgment. An infant on the other hand would be called *valea*—"stupid"— a term also used for mental defectives.[5]

The transition from "infancy" to "childhood" is understood in a number of different ways. Children are assumed to be competent speakers and listeners. As Elinor Ochs has shown, unlike their American counterparts, Samoan caretakers do not normally act as if infants can understand what is said to them. Caretakers thus do not take the part of an infant in speaking for them, translating babble into coherent utterances. Nor do they speak to them as if they understood what was being said (Ochs 1986). "Children" (*tamaiti*) on the other hand are assumed to be linguistically competent. Children are also assumed to be competent walkers. As we shall see, mobility is one of the key defining features of Samoan conceptions of childhood.

Whereas infants are not normally distinguished by sex, children are.

Though the general term for children (*tamaiti*) is also the term for "little boys," Samoans often distinguish between a boy child (*tama'i-titi*) and a girl child (*teine'ititi*). This is because by age 6 or 7 children have begun to play more and more in single-sex groups (Mead 1928b), and girls are encouraged to wear some kind of garment to avoid nudity. Girls are also expected to stay closer to home than boys, to look after their younger siblings (*tei*), and to perform routine household chores. Consistent with the Samoan sexual double standard, girls are usually watched more carefully than their brothers.

As is true throughout Polynesia, Samoan "childhood" often begins abruptly upon the birth of a new sibling, at which time a child experiences an abrupt loss of direct parental contact and affection. While infants are often indulged by adults, children are not. This transition is often associated with the loss of immediate access to food at meals. While very young children may eat with the adults, and are sometimes seen on the laps of their fathers and mothers, children past age 3 or 4 must learn to wait for their food until everyone else has finished. Indeed, as part of their growing domestic responsibilities, children are commonly found preparing food for the elders and then fanning the flies off their elders' meals. This sudden loss of access to both parental affection and food has been noted by researchers throughout Polynesia (Levy 1973; Ritchie and Ritchie 1989). It would appear to have a major impact on Samoan personality development and may help to explain the well-known Polynesian obsession with eating, particularly with the idea of unrestricted access to abundant food sources.

Youth

The third life stage that Samoans distinguish is *tagata talavou,* "youth." As in all of the older life stages, there are significant ambiguities in this designation, reflecting a growing importance of social rather than biological attributes. *Talavou* means literally "unmarried," but it is usually assumed to imply that an individual is "not yet married" and thus it implies a relatively young age. An unmarried older person, or one who has been widowed, would never be called *talavou.*

An alternative designation for youths is *taule'ale'a* (plural, *taulele'a*), which specifically refers to the fact that the youths had not received a chiefly title. The term usually refers to males, but may also designate a young, untitled woman. The category *taule'ale'a* is what Lakoff (1987) terms a radial category, with one central and several peripheral members. The central or prototypical taule'ale'a is a young, untitled male who, as a member of a village *'aumaga* (untitled men's organization) serves the village chiefs as well as his own family. Other less central members of this category include untitled young men not living in a traditional village and therefore not directly serving chiefs, untitled women, and older males who have no chiefly title. I have never heard an untitled older woman referred to as a *taule'ale'a*. Technically, a man holding a chiefly title from another village, but without a title in his residential village, could be considered a *taule'ale'a* in the latter village, but I doubt that such a classification would actually be made.

As we shall see, Samoan youths are associated with physical strength, service to elders, and a developing capacity for judgment. The young men of traditional villages belong to the *'aumaga* and are sometimes known as the "strength of the village" (*'o le mālosi 'o le nu'u*). Young men are also known as *tama*, or boys, a term that implies unmarried status and youthful age but may infrequently refer to older unmarried males (including priests). While the term *tama* implies un-married status, it does not normally connote virginity (unlike the equivalent term for girls).[6] Samoan youths often pride themselves on their physical strength, toughness, sexual adventurism, and physical courage. In this way they epitomize the macho ideal that Freeman (1983) stressed in his refutation of Mead's characterization of Samoan ethos.

Young girls, on the other hand, have a more complex status in a traditional village. The common term for girls is *teine*, and a teenage girl may be distinguished from female children by the designation *teine matua*, or *teine talavou* (unmarried girl). The term *teine* is complex because it refers at once to age, marital status, and virginity. Like the term *taule'ale'a*, the category of *teine* has a radial structure, where the central member is young, unmarried and virginal. Noncentral exam-ples of *teine* would include older, unmarried women (including nuns) and married women when they return to their natal villages and take part in activities of the village *aualuma* (girls' association). In formal discourse, a Samoan girl may be referred to as a *tama'ita'i* (often trans-lated as "lady"), implying a young or unmarried girl of rank.[7] The term *fafine* (cf., Hawaiian *wahine* or Tahitian *vahine*) is used to denote a married woman or one who has had a child and is thus known to have lost her virginity.

While young men are unambiguously associated with physical strength, sexuality, courage, and a high degree of activity placed in the service of the community, their sisters have a more complex cultural status. Like young males, Samoan girls are held to be energetic, smart, and liable to be easily distracted from good judgment. Yet the parallel between young males and females is not culturally emphasized as one might expect. This is due to the emphasis in Samoan thought on the sanctity of girls as understood in their role as sisters. As generations of anthropologists have pointed out, Samoan culture stresses the sanctity of sisters in relation to their brothers (Mead 1928b, [1936] 1966; Good 1980; Schoeffel 1978, 1979; Shore 1977, 1981, 1982, 1989; Holmes 1974; Freeman 1983). The epitome of the unmarried female in a village is the *taupou*, a titled girl who presides over the *aualuma* of a village and over the making of kava during a *fai kava,* a kava ceremony. As I have emphasized elsewhere, the traditional symbolism associated with this sacred status of sisters, and particularly the *taupou*, suggested passivity, stillness, and a ritual binding up of sexual and reproductive powers in the service of the community (Shore 1981, 1982, 1989; see also Schoeffel 1978, 1979.) While a more elaborate exploration of this symbolic association of sisters with a kind of stillness and passive power is beyond the scope of this essay, we shall examine below its more general implications for the ambiguous status of Samoan middle age.

Adults (Middle Age)

The fourth general life stage identified by Samoans is that of *tagata matua,* or adult. The term refers literally to "mature person" and thus exhibits even more ambiguity than the terms for child and youth. In fact, so ambiguous is the designation *tagata matua,* that one might reasonably claim that Samoans have no clear term specifying adult or middle-aged status. *Matua* is inherently a relative term and may designate in different contexts a maturing infant, an older child, or an elderly person as well as an adult. For example, one informant described the term *matua* in relation to a developing sense of good judgment in youth.

> We call *matua* the person who uses judgment. His mind is *matua.* A fifteen-year-old can be called *tagata matua* if they have reached the point where their judgment is right. *Matua* is a general word we can use for fourteen- to fifteen-year-olds. They know how to use the mind right, can judge, choose, do work.

One of the reasons that Samoans lack an unambiguous term for middle age is that adults are commonly known in relation to their particular social or political statuses rather than in terms of a general age classification. One is a chief (*matai* or *ali'i*), an orator (*tulafale* or *failauga*), a teacher (*faia'oga*), a wife of a chief (*faletua* or *āvā matai*), a titled lady (*taupou*), a carpenter (*tufuga*), or a pastor (*faife'au* or *feagaiga*). The notion that one is chronologically middle aged or even an adult is embedded in these achieved social statuses, but the idea of chronological age almost never becomes the salient basis of classification.

As suggested by the proliferation of specific adult social roles, middle age is ideally the time of life when one is most deeply embedded in family and civic affairs. Political machinations and status competition within and between descent groups have always been highly developed features of Samoan life, and interest in local and family politics reaches its apogee during the middle years of life. Whereas youths are often more interested in nonpolitical events such as romantic adventures, entertainment, and sports, middle-aged Samoans often become passionately and even obsessively engrossed in matters of political power and social status. The focus of this interest for villagers is often the local political structure, while urbanites tend to focus on national government politics. Political maneuvering, intrigue, scandal, and gossip are the currency of Samoan middle age. It is also at this time that men and women have maximum family responsibilities, both to their own children and to other close relatives.

Old Age

Unlike middle age, old age is lexically clearly marked in Samoan. Old men are *toea'ina,* and old women are *lo'omatua* (or *olomatua*). Once again, however, these categories are not exclusively age designations. The prototypical *toea'ina* is an old man, passing his days sitting in a house braiding coconut fiber into sennit. Yet the terms for "old man" and "old lady" also imply something about relatively diminished activity levels and increasing passivity. So there are clearly cases when someone who is not chronologically old may be called "old person" by virtue of their relative social status. This ambiguity is nicely illustrated by a thirty-year-old informant, in discussing his changing relations with his own parents:

Q. At what age might a person be said to be old, *toea'ina* or *lo'omatua?*

A. About forty-five and up. All depends on the situation. If I have many kids, that means that I will relax and let the kids help me. But if a person has only a few kids, they are not yet grown up with jobs, then he can continue on taking care of himself and his family.

Q. If my son can support me when I am forty, then am I considered *toea'ina?*

A. Yes, "old" in the stage of working. It seems your son is now taking the part you did for him.

While elderly Samoans often retain other professional or political statuses, it is notable that as they get older the referential terms *toe'aina* and *lo'omatua* become used with increasing frequency.[8] Additionally there are some specific terms for older chiefs and other officials. A particularly important elder orator may be designated as a *tu'ua.* An elderly *ali'i* may be called *ali'i matua.* A retired or elderly pastor is called *faife'au toea'ina.*

Old age in Samoa is ideally associated with a settled and deep judgment, with a dramatic decrease in physical activity, and with the assumption of a dignified passive status both politically and in terms of everyday work. Here is how a middle-aged man described this status:

> An old person can't go out of the house. They sit in the house. What we call a *matua tausi* is a person who is cared for by other people and doesn't go out of the house. In my family the old man does light chores. In other families elders weave mats. In some families elders sweep the house. They do things at their own pleasure.

Elders with political experience and status often take on a status of advisor (*fautua*) to the active heads of the family or village. As we shall see, this kind of backseat councillor role, a passive type of authority, is an important aspect of a Samoan theory of power and has several significant institutional manifestations in Samoa. Thus, rather than automatically slipping into obsolescence, elders who are in good health and of sound mind have a ready-made status they can assume that is compatible with their increasing physical frailty.

Ideally, elders are accorded respect (*fa'aaloalo*) by juniors by virtue of their age, their experience, and their wisdom. There is another term, *ava*, which refers specifically to the respect that the young owe to their elders. So far, I have outlined what amounts to a highly idealized portrait of the status of Samoan elders, one stressing a respected status associated with a kind of passive authority. We shall soon see, however, that our data on attitudes toward different stages of life suggest a picture that is somewhat more complex. To understand some of these complexities, I turn from these generalized portraits of Samoan life stages to a discussion of the results of our survey.

SURVEY 1: YOUTH EVALUATES AGE

We collected 187 pairs of essays from high school students at three different grade levels. Form 3 students were fourteen to fifteen years old; form 4 students were fifteen to sixteen years old; form 5 students ranged from sixteen to seventeen years old. These groups are obviously not to be taken as a cross-section of the population at large, but a school setting was the only place where we were able to get a number of people to take the time to write so extensively. Sampling youth opinion on the most and least desirable stages of life had two important purposes. First it enabled us to determine the categories that young Samoans use in classifying people by life stage, since these were elicited rather than assumed by the essay assignment. These categories then became the basis of the checklist questionnaire that was handed out to a much broader range of villagers.

The second use of these essays was to construct a portrait of aging from the perspective of a single age group, in this case from youths. This portrait could then be compared with the more general results of our checklist survey to clarify the extent to which we can generalize about Samoan attitudes toward aging, irrespective of the age group of the respondent, as well as the kinds of changes that attitudes toward aging undergo between different age cohorts.

Positive and Negative Ratings

Of the 186 essay pairs we collected, 45% were from males and 55% were from females. Third form students composed 22% of the sample, while 50% were in the fourth form, and the remaining 28% came from the fifth form. About 30% of the essays were written in English, the remainder in Samoan. The life-stage categories that we abstracted from these essays that became the basis of the broader survey were translated as (1) baby, (2) child, (3) youth, (4) adult and (5) elder. The essays were subjected to a content analysis. Since the students were asked to evaluate the best and worst life stages, we were able to quantify positive and negative ratings for each of the five life-stage categories. The graph

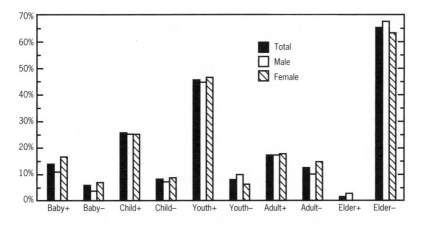

FIGURE 1 Positive (+) and negative (−) responses for all associations, by gender

in figure 1, above, compares positive and negative ratings (percentage of responses) for each of the five life-stage categories. Comparisons are given for total responses and for male and female responses.

As shown in figure 1, the three younger life stages, baby, child, and youth, are each rated more frequently as positive than negative. There is a significant increase in the percentage of positive responses as we move from baby to child to youth (15%, 25%, 45%, respectively). This trend reverses for the two older stages, adult and elder. Positive associations were made for adulthood with slightly greater frequency than were negative associations, but far less frequently than in relation to either child or youth stages. And most dramatic of all was the overwhelming frequency of negative associations with the last category, elder; in fact, there are almost no positive associations with elders. There are no significant gender differences in these responses patterns.

These figures suggest a youth-oriented culture rather than one oriented toward the value and status of old age. These patterns will be illustrated even more dramatically when we do a content analysis of specific associations with life stages below. Remember that these data, with their strong preference for youth over age, come exclusively from students ages 15–18 and cannot be taken as a general measure of Samoan values.

To see if form level (and thus specific age group) has any significant bearing on these patterns, I compared positive and negative responses for each of the five life stages broken down by year in school. Figure

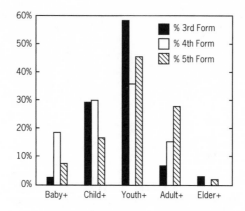

FIGURE 2 Percentage of positive responses by year in school (form 3, form 4, and form 5)

2, which shows the form-level patterns for positive responses, shows some significant but puzzling differences in response patterns by year in school. For instance, a significantly smaller percentage (2%) of the form 3 students, listed "baby" as the most desired of life stages than did the form 4 students (18%). Figure 2 also illustrates that this somewhat younger student cohort indicated a preference for the youth life stage beyond that of either of the other form levels. These borderline youths would seem to be distancing themselves from childhood and identifying with the youth category with particular frequency.

The other significant pattern shown in figure 2 is the stepwise increase in positive identification with adults as the students get older. While the adult category was preferred by a minority of all these youths, its adherents were much more likely to be found among the older rather than the younger cohorts of students. This suggests that these students tended to identify positively with older life-stage categories as they approached them.

The patterns for negative responses (fig. 3, below) showed no similar form-level patterns. The overwhelming negative associations with the elder category are in clear evidence here.

Specific Associations with Life-Stage Categories

From my readings of the student essays, I also constructed a set of specific "associations" students made with each of the life-stage categories discussed. From these I was able to compare the relative frequency of these associations for each stage of life.

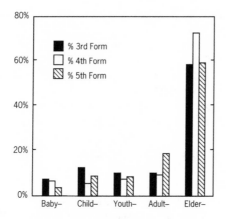

FIGURE 3 Percentage of negative responses by year in school (form 3, form 4, and form 5)

Specific comments were grouped into categories that were then compared across the entire sample in various ways. The frequently mentioned associations that became the basis of the analysis are as coded in table 1. Figures 4–8 below chart the frequency of these associations with each of the five life-stage categories. Each chart orders the associations in order of the frequency with which they were mentioned in the essays.

These figures suggest a distinct portrait of each life stage. Many of the associations tend to be judgmental rather than simply descriptive, which is to be expected from the nature of the question put to the students. The important domains on which these evaluations appear to be based stress (*a*) passivity versus productivity, (*b*) physical attractiveness, (*c*) energy level, and (*d*) key mental characteristics and feelings. Table 2 compares the most frequent associations with each life stage.

SURVEY 2: CHECKLIST OF ASSOCIATIONS

The second survey we conducted employed an extensive checklist of twenty-eight possible associations with different life stages. Informants were asked simply to check off all relevant associations they made with each of the five named life stages (baby, child, youth, adult, elder).[9] Informants could make as many or as few associations with each life stage as they wished. Information was collected on family membership, gender, and age of each respondent.

TABLE 1. Attributions from School Essays

Code	Attributes Mentioned in Essays
PASSIVE	Cared for by others; receiving rather than giving; consuming food without having to work; getting attention from others
NO WORK	No chores or serious labor to perform
EASY FOOD	Easy access to food, to being fed rather than to making food
ATTENTION	Parental affection, being the object of other people's nurturance or regard
SITS	Stays home; does not move about the village
FREE	Not under the authority of others; does what one wants to do; self-indulgent
BURDEN	Others care for an individual at the cost of their own energy or well-being
EASY LIFE	No work, no worries, carefree
PROTECTED	Someone's welfare is guarded by a caretaker
HAPPY	
SAD	
UGLY	
CAN'T SERVE	Unable to perform services for others
IGNORANT	Lacks knowledge, wisdom, experience
USELESS	Has no useful function or purpose
BAD MANNERS	Disrespectful, rude, aggressive
DESTRUCTIVE	Violent behavior causes social or physical damage
HEALTHY	Relatively free from illness, weakness
STRONG	Physically developed and energetic (youth); healthy and willful (baby)
NO FAMILY	Free of serious familial obligations or authority
SCHOOL	Attends school
TROUBLES	Life tends to entanglements, difficulties, worries, cares
MOCKED	Children tease, make fun of
INDEPENDENT	Can make own decisions, no need to rely on others' judgments

The following data are based on 210 completed questionnaires collected from a cross section of villagers. Of the 210 respondents, 53% were male and 47% were female. In tabulating the results respondents were grouped into five age groups. Figure 9 shows the distribution of respondents by age group, and figure 10 shows the gender composition of each age group.

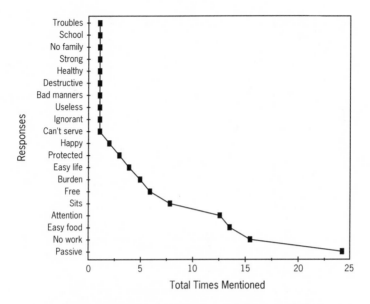

FIGURE 4 Frequency of associations with life stage "baby"

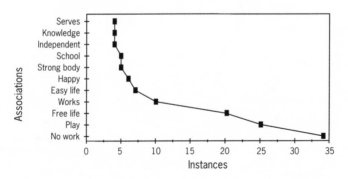

FIGURE 5 Frequency of associations with life stage "child"

Associations Used in the Checklist

Respondents were ask to consider the appropriateness of twenty-eight different possible associations with each life stage. These associations represent an elaboration on the list of associations derived from the analysis of the student essays. Each of the twenty-eight associations is listed in table 3 and, where necessary, a brief explication of the Samoan concept is provided.

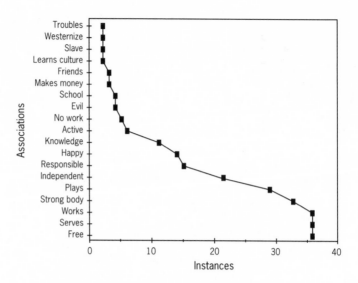

FIGURE 6 Frequency of associations with life stage "youth"

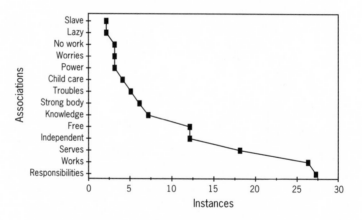

FIGURE 7 Frequency of associations with life stage "adult"

Results of the Survey

I calculated the total percentage of respondents and of checked associations for each of the five life stages. The scores were then ranked in order of frequency of response for each of the five life stages. The results for each life stage are graphically presented in figures 11–15.

As for survey 1 results, the most frequently checked associations for each life stage are listed in table 4. Comparing these frequent associations from survey 2 with those made by the students in survey 1 (table

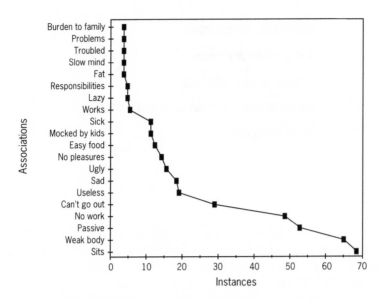

FIGURE 8 Frequency of associations with life stage "elder"

TABLE 2. Frequent Life-Stage Associations, Survey 1

Baby	Child	Youth	Adult	Elder
FREE	NO WORK	FREE	RESPONSIBILITIES	SITS
HAPPY	PLAY	SERVES	WORKS	WEAK BODY
PASSIVE	FREE	WORKS	SERVES	PASSIVE
NO WORK	WORKS	STRONG	INDEPENDENT	NO WORK
EASY LIFE	EASY LIFE	PLAYS	FREE	CAN'T GO OUT
ATTENTION		INDEPENDENT		USELESS
PROTECTED		RESPONSIBLE		SAD
SITS		HAPPY		
BURDEN		KNOWLEDGE		

NOTE.—Associations are listed in descending order of frequency.

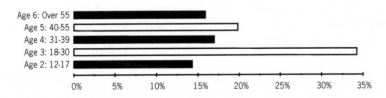

FIGURE 9 Total sample by age categories

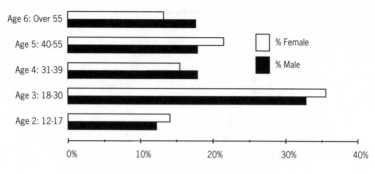

FIGURE 10 Age categories by gender

2) shows much similarity, but also reveals several interesting differences. Associations for baby and child are very similar for both samples. Table 5 compares the sets of frequent associations with several categories in both surveys.

Associations with youth.—It is apparent that respondents to survey 2 (the cross section of all villagers) view youth as a somewhat less positive and more problematical stage of life than those answering survey 1 (the school children). These young people rate youth somewhat more positively and as having more freedom than does the Samoan population at large.

Associations with adult.—While the specific associations are different in each survey, there is no significant contrast between the general pictures of adult life held by those participating in surveys 1 and 2. Both view middle-aged Samoans as hard-working, respected, self-controlled, responsible, and active. A similar comparison for the life-stage category elder, however, shows a significant shift in associations stressed by the two samples.

Associations with elder.—While both surveys stress associations of passivity and immobility with old age, survey 2 participants interpret this positively in relation to dignity, political authority, and being feared and respected. No such positive associations are evident in the student essays, which clearly devalued the status and authority of the elderly, associating their passivity with weakness and a lack of social usefulness. Many of the student respondents associated old age with being mocked by children. Thus it seems that youths overvalue the desirability of their own stage of life compared with the more general population, and they devalue the status and social usefulness of the old.

TABLE 3. Expanded Attributions, Survey 2

	Attribution	
English Code	Samoan Phrase	Concept
CHORES	e fai fe'au	Normally does chores for the family/village
CLEVER	aamai	Knows how to do things; skilled
CONTROLLED	āmio pulea	Exercises self-discipline; self-control; moderation
CONTROLS FAMILY	e pulea 'e 'aiga	Authority; power; responsibility; leadership; chiefly title
DIGNIFIED	mamalu	Respected, reserved bearing; noble status or manner
EDUCATED	a'oa'oina	Schooled, trained
EVIL BEHAVIOR	amio leaga	Bad acts; willful; illicit sex; antisocial behavior
FREE LIFE	olaga sa'oloto	No obligations or responsibilities; one does what one pleases
HAPPY LIFE	olaga fiafia	Pleasure, satisfaction, joy
HARD LIFE	olaga faigata	Life full of difficulties; obstacles; challenges; problems
NO JUDGMENT	lē māfaufau	Does not use good judgment; does not attend well to other's guidance
OBEDIENT	usita'i lelei	Obeys those in authority; pays attention
ONEROUS LIFE	olaga mafatia	Physically exhausting life; worn out; tired out
PEACEFUL LIFE	olaga filemu	
PEOPLE FEAR	'ua fefefe ai tagata	
PROTECTED LIFE	olanga puipuia	Watched over by others; not responsible for own welfare
PROUD	mimita	Full of oneself; showy; high self-opinion; seeks attention
RESPECTED	'ua fa'aloalogia	Deferred to; acknowledged as important; viewed with awe
ROAMS	tafao solo	Wanders, plays, irresponsible; not serious
SERVES	tautua	Provides for family, chiefs, elders, village, etc. Subservient to others' needs

TABLE 3 (*Continued*)

	Attribution	
English Code	Samoan Phrase	Concept
SITS	*nofonofo*	Housebound; stays put; socially inactive; physically immobile; still
SMART	*poto*	Intelligent, knowledgeable
STAYS HOME	*nofonofo i le fale*	
STRONG	*mālosi*	Physically strong, energetic, healthy, fit
STUPID	*valea*	Mentally incompetent, no/poor judgment
WEAK	*vaivai*	Lacking physical, moral or mental strength; puny; passive
WELL-BEHAVED	*aga lelei*	
WORKS	*fai galuega*	Labors, works, holds down a job

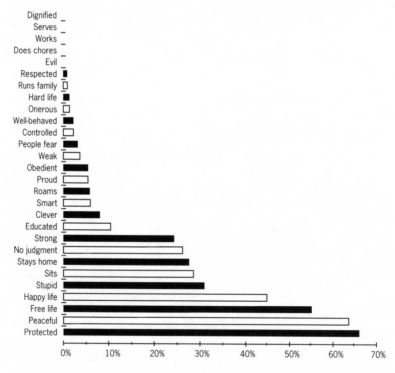

FIGURE 11 Percentage distribution of associations with life stage "baby"

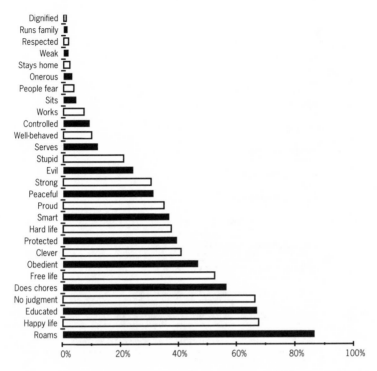

FIGURE 12 Percentage distribution of associations with life stage "child"

The tendency for the valuation of the authority and status of the elderly to increase with age is depicted in figure 16. In this graph, key associations for the elder life-stage category are illustrated by age group. The responses for the positive traits of RESPECTED, RUNS FAMILY, and DIGNIFIED all show a general increase with age of respondent. The exception is the middle-aged group (group 5) whose frequency of positive ratings for old age did not increase from the next youngest cohort. This group might well experience some conflict with their elders since it is a group with whom they share authority. This ambiguity and potential conflict may account for their ratings.

A comparison of the ratings of associations for adult and elder life stages is very revealing in relation to the problem of the status of middle age in Samoa. In figure 17, the response patterns for all associations in relation to adults and elders are charted. These patterns become clearer when we isolate two dimensions of comparison: activity level and political authority. The association patterns for *activity levels,* comparing the ratings for youth, adult, and elder life stages, are found in

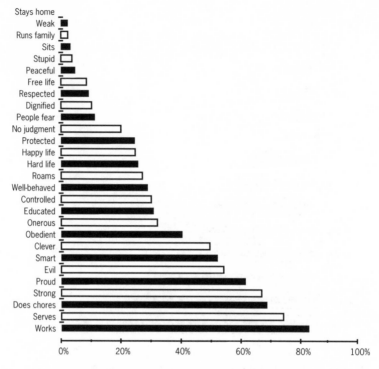

FIGURE 13 Percentage distribution of associations with life stage "youth"

figure 18. Adult ratings shadow those of youth, but with consistently lower frequencies. Both the adult and youth categories rate relatively high in indices of activity, movement, and work. The ratings for elder, on the other hand, contrast dramatically with these patterns, rating consistently the lowest on indices of activity, work and movement. Also revealing are the patterns for associations dealing with political authority, social status, and respect (fig. 19). On these dimensions, adults and elders are much closer in their relatively high ratings. On these power/authority/respect indices, youth patterns contrast markedly with those of adult and elder.

Taken together, these patterns suggest that Samoan adulthood is conceived of as a kind of "middle age" in a very specific sense. Aging appears to be classified by Samoans along two complementary gradients. The one, associated with activity levels, movement, energy expenditure and labor, I shall term *activity indices*. The other, associated with political authority, power, social status, deference and respectability, I term *power indices*. For infants, both activity indices and power indices

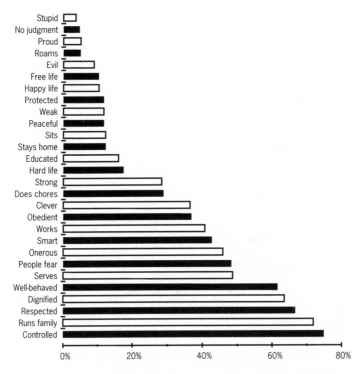

FIGURE 14 Percentage distribution of associations with life stage "adult"

rate low. Childhood and youth are marked by relatively high ratings for activity and low ratings for power. Middle age is relatively high for both indices, whereas elders rate high on power and low on activity. The maximal contrast is between the elder life stage (high power, low activity) and the youth life stage (high activity, low power). Middle-aged Samoans are conceived of as elders in relation to power indices and as youth in relation to activity indices. The relations between the Samoan conception of life stages and the gradients of power and activity are represented graphically below (fig. 20).

DISCUSSION

To understand the cultural implications of these ratings, we need to discuss the more general Samoan concepts of activity and power. Properly interpreted, these data have a lot to say about the privileged place of "middle age" in traditional Samoan life. I have isolated dimensions that appear to shape Samoan perceptions of aging that reflect a complex Samoan theory of power. Elsewhere, I have explicated this

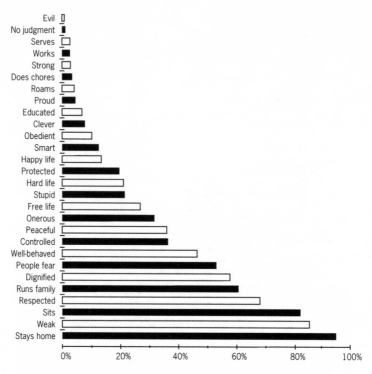

FIGURE 15 Percentage distribution of associations with life stage "elder"

TABLE 4. Frequent Life-State Associations, Survey 2

Baby	Child	Youth	Adult	Elder
PROTECTED	ROAMS	WORKS	CONTROLLED	STAYS HOME
PEACEFUL	HAPPY	SERVES	RUNS FAMILY	WEAK
FREE	EDUCATED	CHORES	RESPECTED	SITS
HAPPY	NO JUDGMENT	STRONG	DIGNIFIED	RESPECTED
STUPID	CHORES	PROUD	WELL-BEHAVED	RUNS FAMILY
SITS	FREE	EVIL	SERVES	DIGNIFIED
STAYS HOME	OBEDIENT	SMART	FEARED	PEOPLE FEAR
	CLEVER	CLEVER	ONEROUS LIFE	WELL-BEHAVED
	PROTECTED	OBEDIENT	SMART	CONTROLLED
	HARD LIFE		WORKS	PEACEFUL

TABLE 5. Associations with Various Life Stages, Both Surveys

Youth		Adult		Elder	
Survey 1	Survey 2	Survey 1	Survey 2	Survey 1	Survey 2
FREE	WORKS	RESPONSIBILITIES	CONTROLLED	SITS	STAYS HOME
SERVES	SERVES	WORKS	RUNS FAMILY	WEAK	WEAK
WORKS	CHORES	SERVES	RESPECTED	BODY	SITS
STRONG	STRONG	INDEPENDENT	DIGNIFIED	PASSIVE	RESPECTED
PLAYS	PROUD	FREE	WELL-BEHAVED	NO WORK	RUNS FAMILY
INDEPENDENT	EVIL		SERVES	CAN'T GO OUT	DIGNIFIED
RESPONSIBLE	SMART		FEARED	USELESS	PEOPLE FEAR
HAPPY	CLEVER		ONEROUS LIFE	SAD	WELL-BEHAVED
KNOWLEDGE	OBEDIENT		SMART		CONTROLLED
			WORKS		PEACEFUL

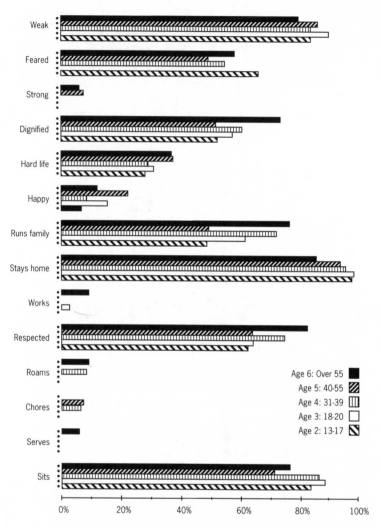

FIGURE 16 Associations for life stage "elder" by age category

theory of power in considerable detail (Shore 1976b, 1977, 1981, 1982, 1989; see also Mageo 1989), and in this limited space I offer a summary of those discussions.

Samoans, like other Western Polynesians, have a dualistic conception of power that informs the organization of many of their institutions. Power is thought of as having two dimensions, "passive" power and "active" power. These complementary forms of power underlie

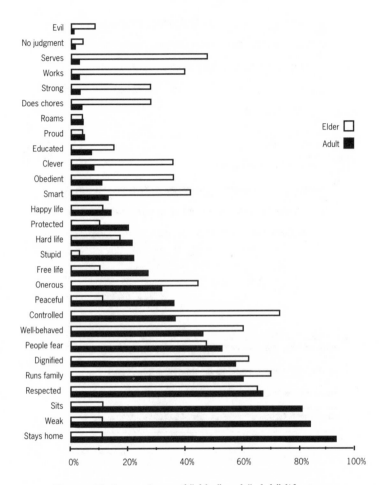

FIGURE 17 Comparisons of "elder" and "adult" life stages

the tendency throughout Western Polynesia toward dyarchy (Marcus 1989; Shore 1989; Howard, n.d.).[10]

In terms of political organization, this dualistic theory of power is manifested in distinctions between sacred chiefs and either warrior chiefs or orators. In Samoa specifically, the relevant distinction is between sacred *ali'i* and their orators (*tulafale*). In conception, *ali'i* "sit" (*nofonofo*) while *tulafale* "move" (*gāioioi*) on their behalf. Passive power, a kind of potential energy, is called *mana* by Samoans as well as elsewhere in Polynesia. Active authority, however, is termed *pule*, a word with a wide distribution in Western Polynesia (Shore 1989).

The associations between the *pule* of motion and the *mana* of

129

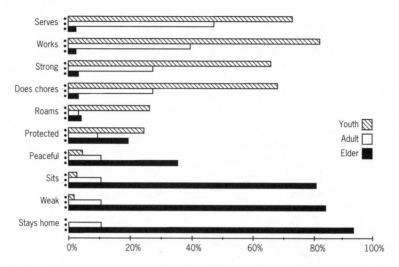

FIGURE 18 Activity indices for "elder," "adult," and "youth"

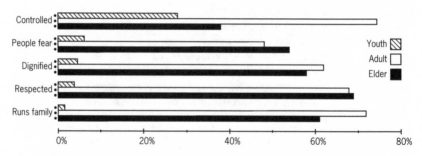

FIGURE 19 Power/authority/respect indices for "elder," "adult," and "youth"

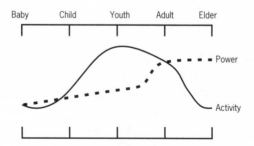

FIGURE 20 Aging/activity indices across life stage categories

stillness are ubiquitous in Samoan discourse. Young men are "the strength of the chiefs" (*matai*), and move in service to them. Similarly orators move in service to the *ali'i*, who sit. In formal oratory, an orator "stands" and "speaks" on behalf of an *ali'i*, who "sits" behind him. The sacred *taupou* (sometimes called the "sitting *taupou*") suggests passive power both through her highly stylized ceremonial demeanor and her associations with virginity—sexual fecundity withheld and redirected for cosmic ends. Traditionally, political districts were divided into two sides—sometimes called *ituau* and *alataua* (Shore 1982). In times of war, these "sides" of a district has complementary roles, the *ituau* leading the fighting, the *alataua* remaining still in their houses, blinds lowered, lending support to the activity through prayer (*tapua'i*). The juxtaposition of activity and immobile prayer is still evident in modern Samoa. When someone embarks on a long journey, those remaining behind are said to remain as *tapua'i*.

Reviewing the data reported above, it is apparent that this discourse of power also shapes the way Samoans conceive of the sequence of life stages. Babies, like elders, "sit" or stay at home but, unlike elders, have no power. Children are distinguished from babies by increasing movement. Children roam (*tafao solo*), play, and do chores (*fai fe'au*). They are not mindless (*valea*) like babies, but their *mafaufau* judgment is often unsteady and poor. Youth are strong and energetic and work (*gālue*) rather than do chores. They are less carefree than children, and their judgment is somewhat steadier, but still subject to whim and desire. They have limited power in their special spheres (youth organizations) but are generally without recognized authority and status in the larger political context. They serve the chiefs, their parents, and elders.

Gender Attributes

This ideology of power also has important implications for Samoan gender beliefs. Young boys are allowed to roam about the village relatively freely, while their sisters, as they develop from babies into children, are increasingly restrained in their movements, more confined to the household compound, and increasingly subject to norms of modesty, particularly in their relationships to boys. The prototypical girl in Samoan culture is the *taupou*, a chief's daughter with an important maiden's title. The term also means "virgin," connoting the sexual restraint and the symbolic redirection of her reproductive potency for village status. In formal discourse she is called the sitting maiden (*tau-*

pou fa'anofonofo), a reference to her symbolically passive status. It is interesting that the symbolic status of the high chief (the *ali'i*) suggests a feminine gender status. The *ali'i* has a relatively passive sort of power in relation to the orators. In formal settings, the *ali'i* wears the same headdress (*tuiga*) as the *taupou*, a headdress that is made from auburn hair cut from a red-headed girl.

So the associations of active power to "male status" and passive power to "female status" are less clearly a way of distinguishing men and women than of distinguishing symbolically male and female social statuses. Thus while the statuses of sister, *taupou*, and *ali'i* are all symbolically feminine, those of brother, orator, and orator's wives are symbolically masculine in relation to the first three terms, respectively. While girls as sisters are linked with passive power, and their movements are socially constrained, women past childbearing age are often freed from this constrained status. In fact, old women in Samoa are often far more likely than their male counterparts to express publicly bawdy humor and irreverent attitudes.

This dual gradient defining active and passive forms of power plays a major role in the construction of the status of Samoan middle age. In middle age people are both politically powerful and physically active. It is middle age that the two axes of power come together for Samoans in a way that is true for no other status. From a cultural perspective, Samoan midlife suggests no crisis; rather it offers an intersection of "powers" that no other stage of life unites in the same way. Mead's (1928a) much-discussed conclusion that Samoan youth is characterized by an absence of "storm and stress" turns out, if these data are accurate, to be an inaccurate description of the status of Samoan village youth in the mid-1970s. Whatever the contribution of biologically grounded maturational factors (see Freeman 1983), a cultural analysis of Samoan aging suggests that many Samoan youths are caught between the demands of impending but yet-unattained adulthood and the pleasures and relative freedom of a childhood that is no longer theirs. The consistent tendency of young people to devalue the status dimensions of age and to overvalue (from a more general Samoan point of view) the importance of activity reflects the developmental trajectory represented above (see fig. 20). Here the status of youth maximally (high activity, low power) contrasts with that of their elders (high power, low activity). Similarly, Samoa cannot be accurately described as a simple gerontocracy that places unilateral value on the status of age. The Samoan view of age accords the diminished physical powers of the elderly a kind of cultural respectability in terms of an ideology of power that valorizes passivity and inactivity in terms of a theory of sacred power that links the status of the elderly with the privileged status of maidens, *ali'i,* and other parallel roles.

But it is inaccurate to characterize Samoan status ideals unilaterally in terms of increasing "dignity" and *mana.* A more accurate character- ization is that Samoans have a bipolar notion of status, and that aging involves a status reversal in which passive power (in the expanded sense used here) as a marker of status begins to replace activity potency as a marker of status.

Samoan society has long revealed considerable tensions between a kind of secular and populist ethic that stresses physical prowess, mili- tary might, and manipulative politics and a sacred chiefly ethic that stresses ascribed rank, sacred power, and passive dignity (Freeman 1983; Marcus 1989; Shore 1982, 1996b; Wendt 1983). This tension has been particularly notable in the historical relations between the power of orators and that of *ali'i* in Samoan politics, where one notes an increasing encroachment of orator power on the traditional authority of *ali'i* titles (Shore 1982).

In modern Samoan society, these ambiguities figure in the compro- mised status of elders, whose authority and power can be based only upon the chiefly ethic stressing "passive power" but who share with babies the lowest status in relation to activity indices. Thus they are ambiguous figures, subject to both respect and to ridicule. The elderly are ridiculed not only by some children, and by the judgments of youths in their essays, but also by Samoan comedians, who often target the elderly as the butt of political satire (Shore 1996a, 1996b; Mageo, n.d.; Sinavaiana 1992).

The same cannot be said for the status of middle age. While middle- aged Samoan men and women undoubtedly confront some of the same anxieties that trouble modern Americans about loss of youth and strength and about the growing awareness of their own mortality, none of these "crises" is given strong public representation in the cultural construction of aging in Samoa. They are not culturally modeled as they are for Americans. Samoan aging is not understood as it is for Americans in terms of a one-dimensional trajectory in which physical passivity becomes simply a loss of youthful vitality. Samoans evaluate aging in relation to two complementary dimensions, in relation to which middle age has a privileged place. If the data in this study tell us anything, it is that Samoan middle age appears to be the one time in Samoan life where the dual trajectories of activity and passive power converge. If the "coming of aging" in Samoa is associated with storm and stress, it is those stresses that are intrinsic to Samoan status competition, social obligations, and political intrigue. But these activities, the special province of Samoan middle age, pull middle-aged Samoans into the heart of life, not onto its margins. Whatever they felt in their more private moments, the middle-aged Samoans that I knew best showed little time and inclination for the kind of introspective soulsearching about impending decline that is common in contemporary America.

CONTEMPORARY TRENDS

These data are old and focus on a rural community. Samoan life is gradually being transformed, with increased emphases on Western conceptions of work and status and with a large proportion of young Samoans seeking a life overseas (Shore and Pratt 1984; Franco 1991). We do not have any data to track the expected changes in Samoan conceptions of life stage. Nor do we have data on middle age experiences among urban and overseas Samoans. One would predict, however, an increasing stress on what I have termed "activity indices of power" at the expense of the traditional notions of "passive power." These predicted shifts would suggest some degree of loss of status for the elderly, and a shift of status toward the youth and adult categories. Tracking such potential changes would be an important goal for future aging research in Samoa.

NOTES

1. On Samoan social organization see Duranti (1983), Ember (1962), Freeman (1983), Gilson (1963; 1970), Good (1980), Holmes (1974), Keen (1978), Krämer (1902), Mageo (n.d.), Mead (1928a, 1928b, [1936] 1966), Meleisea (1987), O'Meara (1990), Schoeffel (1978, 1979), Shore (1976a, 1976b, 1977, 1982), and Tiffany (1971). On aspects of early Samoan socialization see Mead (1928a, 1928b), Sutter (1980), Ochs (1986), Freeman (1983), Schoeffel (1979), and Mageo (1988, 1992).

2. It is interesting to consider the attempt of the travel and leisure industry to valorize leisure by seeing it as a kind of productive activity (going places, doing things, accumulating experiences) rather than the absence of activity.

3. Body size in modern America is often linked to assumptions about energy level, productivity, and competence. Physical fitness is held to be a virtue not only because of its intrinsic health benefits, but because it indexes an active and competent individual. Conversely, obesity is devalued not only because of its health risks, but because it is presumed to model "softness," a lack of productive competence (overconsumption of food, lack of self-control, failure to exercise). In this cultural

context, middle age inevitably triggers anxieties about key indices of productive competence: sexual potency, energy, knowledge, and economic productivity.

4. A few informants provided what were surely wildly inaccurate ages. When a young Samoan member of our team politely suggested to an old woman that her claim of being fifty-five might be off by about twenty years and that she appeared to be seventy-five years old, the woman responded, "Well, maybe that's true." She seemed genuinely ignorant of her age and did not realistically associate a chronological age with her own physical and social status.

5. Particularly offensive behavior on the part of children and youths can sometimes result in people referring to them as *vālelea* (plural of *valea*), in the same way that we might describe behavior as "idiotic" with no literal reference to a clinical condition of idiocy. A senile old person, on the other hand, may be referred to nonjudgmentally as *valea*, implying that, like an infant, the person is not responsible for her behavior.

6. I have heard Samoan youths jokingly refer to a boy as a *tama mo'i*, a real boy, implying lack of sexual experience. I do not know whether this is an old Samoan term or a playful derivation from *teine mo'i* (or *teine muli*), which explicitly denotes virginal status for girls.

7. The equivalent respectful term for young men of rank is, interestingly, *ali'i*, which also means chief or nobleman. In other words, in polite discourse, girls and sisters remain distinguished from women and wives, while boys are categorized with older, married, and titled men.

8. In address, elders may be called *tama* (father) or *tina* (mother).

9. The questionnaires were composed in Samoan with English translations. The named life-stage categories were in Samoan: *pepe*, (baby), *tama'ititi* (child), *tagata talavou* (youth), *tagata matua* (adult), and *toea'ina* or *lo'omatua* (elder).

10. See Errington (1989) for a discussion of a similar dual conception of power among the Bugis of Sulawesi. The Polynesian pattern may well have more general Austronesian roots.

References

Duranti, Alessandro. 1981. *The Samoan Fono: A Sociolinguistic Study*. Pacific Linguistics, ser. B, 80. Canberra: Australian National University, Department of Linguistics, Research School of Pacific Studies.

Ember, Melvin. 1962. "Political Authority and the Structure of Kinship in Samoa." *American Anthropologist* 64:964–71.

Errington, Shelly. 1989. *Meaning and Power in a Southeast Asian Realm*. Princeton, N.J.: Princeton University Press.

Franco, Robert . 1991. *Samoan Perceptions of Work: Moving Up and Moving Around*. New York: AMS Press.

Freeman, Derek. 1983. *Margaret Mead and Samoa: The Making and Unmaking of an Anthropological Myth*. Cambridge, Mass.: Harvard University Press.

Good, Carolyn G. 1980. "The Rat Brothers: A Study of the Brother-Sister Relationship in Samoa." M.A. thesis. University of California, Berkeley, Department of Folklore.

Gilson, Richard. 1963. "Samoan Descent Groups: A Structural Outline." *Journal of the Polynesian Society* 72:372–77.

———. 1970. *Samoa, 1830–1900: The Politics of a Multicultural Community*. Melbourne: Oxford University Press.

Holmes, Lowell D. 1974. *Samoan Village*. New York: Holt, Rinehart & Winston.

———. 1983. *Other Cultures, Elder Years: An Introduction to Cultural Gerontology*. Minneapolis: Burgess Publishing Company.

Howard, Alan. N.d. "History and Myth and Polynesian Chieftainship." Manuscript. University of Hawaii, Department of Anthropology.

Keene, Dennis. 1978. "Houses without Walls." Ph.D. dissertation. University of Hawaii, Department of Anthropology.

Krämer, Augustin. 1902. *Die Samoa-Inseln*, 2 vols. Stuttgart: E. Nägele.

Lakoff, George. 1987. *Women, Fire and Dangerous Things: What Categories Tell Us about the Mind*. Chicago: University of Chicago Press.

Levy, Robert. 1973. *Tahitians: Mind and Society in the Society Islands*. Chicago: University of Chicago Press.

Mageo, Jeannette. N.d. "Undersides of Self and Sign: Self Model Theory and Samoan Culture." Manuscript. Washington State University, Department of Anthropology.

———. 1989. "*Amio/Aga* and *Loto:* Perspectives on the Structure of Self in Samoa." *Oceania* 59:181–99.

———. 1992. "Male Transvestism and Culture Change in Samoa." *American Ethnologist* 19 (3): 443–59.

Marcus, George. 1989. "Chieftainship." Chap. 6 in *Developments in Polynesian Ethnology*, edited by A. Howard and R. Borofsky, 175–211. Honolulu: University of Hawaii Press.

Mead, Margaret. 1928a. *The Coming of Age in Samoa*. New York: William Morrow.

———. 1928b. "The Role of the Individual in Samoan Society." *Journal of the Royal Anthropological Society* 58:481–95.

———. (1930) 1966. *The Social Organization of Manu'a*, 2d ed. Honolulu: Bishop Museum Press.

Ochs, Elinor. 1986. *Culture and Language Acquisition: Acquiring Communication Competence in a Western Samoan Village*. Cambridge: Cambridge University Press.

O'Meara, J. Tim. 1990. *Samoan Planters: Tradition and Economic Development in Polynesia*. Fort Worth: Holt, Rinehart & Winston.

Meleisea, Malama. 1987. *The Making of Modern Samoa*. Suva: University of the South Pacific, Institute of Pacific Studies.

Ritchie, James, and Jean Ritchie. 1989. "Socialization and Character Development." Chap. 4 in *Developments in Polynesian Ethnology*, edited by A. Howard and R. Borofsky, 95–136. Honolulu: University of Hawaii Press.

Schoeffel, Penelope. 1978. "Gender, Status and Power in Samoa." *Canberra Anthropology* 1 (2): 69–81.

———. 1979. "Daughters of Sina." Ph.D. dissertation. Australian National University, Department of Anthropology.

Shore, Bradd. 1976a. "Adoption, Alliance and Political Mobility in Samoa." In *Transactions in Kinship: Adoption and Fosterage in Oceania,* edited by Ivan Brady. Honolulu: University of Hawaii Press.

———. 1976b. "Incest Prohibitions, and the Logic of Power in Samoa." *Journal of the Polynesian Society* 85 (2): 275–96.

———. 1977. *A Samoan Theory of Action: Social Control and Social Order in a Polynesian Paradox.* Ph.D. dissertation. University of Chicago, Department of Anthropology.

———. 1978. "Ghosts and Government: A Structural Analysis of Alternative Institutions for Conflict Management in Samoa." *Man,* new ser., 13:175–99.

———. 1981. "Sexuality and Gender in Samoa: Conceptions and Missed Conceptions." In *Sexual Meanings,* edited by S. Ortner and H. Whitehead, 192–215. Cambridge: Cambridge University Press.

———. 1982. *Sala'ilua: A Samoan Mystery.* New York: Columbia University Press.

———. 1989. "Mana and Tapu: A New Synthesis." In *Developments in Polynesian Ethnology,* edited by A. Howard and R. Borofsky, 137–73. Honolulu: University of Hawaii Press.

———. 1996a. "The Absurd Side of Power in Samoa." In *Changing Leadership in the Pacific: Essays in Honour of Sir Raymond Firth,* edited by R. Feinberg and K. Watson-Gegeo. London: Atlone Press.

———. 1996b. *Culture in Mind: Cognition, Culture and the Problem of Meaning.* Oxford: Oxford University Press.

Shore, Bradd, and Martha Pratt. 1984. "Communicative Barriers to Samoans' Training and Employment in the United States." U.S. Department of Labor, Employment and Training Administration, Office of Research and Evaluation, Washington, D.C.

Sinavaiana, Caroline. 1992. "Where the Spirits Laugh Last: Comic Theater in Samoa." In *Clowning as Critical Practice,* edited by William E. Mitchell, 192–219. Pittsburgh: University of Pittsburgh Press.

Sutter, Frederick. 1980. "Communal vs. Individual Socialization at Home and in School in Rural and Urban Samoa." Ph.D. dissertation. University of Hawaii, Department of Education.

Tiffany, Walter. 1971. "Political Structure and Change: A Corporate Analysis of American Samoa." Ph.D. dissertation. University of California, Los Angeles, Department of Anthropology.

Wendt, Albert. 1983. "Three Faces of Samoa: Mead's, Freeman's and Wendt's." *Pacific Islands Monthly* (April), 10–14.

The Return of the "White Man's Burden": The Moral Discourse of Anthropology and the Domestic Life of Hindu Women

Usha Menon and Richard A. Shweder

The central aim of this essay is to characterize the life course images and domestic life of Oriya Hindu women living in extended households in the temple town of Bhubaneswar in Orissa, India. The essay is divided into three parts.

In the first part of this essay we examine Oriya women's conceptions of the ideal phases in a woman's life. Oriya women do not conceive of a middle phase of life defined by chronological age (e.g., 40–65) or by markers of biological aging (e.g., poorer eye sight, menopause, loss of muscle strength) that would correspond to the English phrase "middle age." Yet, Oriya women do have a well-differentiated conception of the normal and desirable phases in a woman's life. Their ideal life course scheme includes a phase called *prauda* or "mature adulthood," which begins when a married woman takes over the management of the extended household and ends when she relinquishes control and social responsibilities to others. Although *prauda* is a condition that a married Oriya woman is likely to achieve by her early thirties and likely to hand over to others by her late fifties, age and biology per se are not the defining characteristics of Oriya life-phase transitions. The underlying logic of the five-phase scheme elaborated below is a logic of social responsibility, family management, and moral duty. In the first part of the essay we describe this scheme.

In the second part of the essay, we review some recent anthropological representations and moral evaluations of the lives of rural Hindu women more generally. Since the 1970s, a growing number of anthropological studies have examined the lives of Hindu women (to name but a few, Fruzetti 1982; Dhruvarajan 1988; Papanek and Minault 1982; Sharma 1980; Roy 1975; Jacobson 1982; Jain and Bannerjee 1985; Liddle and Joshi 1986; Wadley 1980; Wadley and Jacobson 1986; Bennett 1983; Kondos 1989; Minturn 1990; Jeffrey et al. 1988; Raheja and Gold

We gratefully acknowledge the support of the MacArthur Foundation Research Network on Successful Midlife Development (MIDMAC).

139

1994). Many of these studies are implicitly, if not self-consciously, "feminist" in orientation and rely on moral concepts such as social inequality, patriarchal oppression, subjugation, exploitation, and resistance to depict Hindu women, their lives, and their situations. In explicating and critiquing the feminist view, we identify two kinds of ethnographic portraits—the passive victim and the clandestine rebel—that have emerged from such studies.

In the third part of the essay, we raise some doubts about these recent representations and moral evaluations of the situation of rural Hindu women. We aim to recover a set of local moral meanings that have tended to be lost in the writing or invention (the "making up") of a feminist ethnography of Hindu family life. We do this by relying on Oriya women's own descriptions of their workaday lives and their own ratings of psychological well-being and physical health. Apart from women's descriptions of their daily routines, we also make use of observations of daily life in the family, of cooking and worship, of events like births and marriages, and the everyday conversations that one of the authors (Usha Menon) had with these women outside the interview situation. We relate women's daily routines to the different phases in an Oriya woman's life, and we contextualize the lives of Oriya "housewives" and trace some connections that exist between family statuses over the life course and the achievement of a sense of personal well-being (*hito*).

Our strategy in this final part of the essay is to rely on indigenous and locally salient Oriya moral concepts to reveal a hidden and unexamined presupposition implicit in many portrayals of Hindu women. That unexamined presupposition is the tenet of "the moral superiority of the West," the presumption of a white man's (or white woman's) burden to liberate others from the darkness of their own cultural traditions. We describe the ways in which Oriya Hindu women derive meaning, purpose, and a sense of power from their family life practices, and we point out some of the important differences between the moral sensibilities of "Westernized" feminist writers and the moral sensibilities of the "non-Westernized" Hindu women whose lives they have sought to depict.

As we shall see, the overriding moral significances of the domestic life of Hindu women perceived by many Westernized ethnographers (and projected into their writings about exploitation, victimization, and resistance) are not the moral significances constructed by local Oriya women, whose voices and subaltern notions

140

of the moral good (including their ideas about service, duty, civility, and self-improvement) articulate a vision of life in society that Westernized feminists appear ideologically unprepared to represent sympathetically.

THE ORIYA SAMPLE

Our investigation was done in the neighborhood surrounding the Lingaraj temple in Bhubaneswar, Orissa, the "Old Town" as it is known locally. This medieval temple (it dates to the tenth or eleventh century) is one of the contemporary residences of the Hindu god Siva and his divine family. The temple is an active pilgrimage site and a necessary stop in the itinerary of pilgrims on their way to the famous Jagannatha ("juggernaut") temple forty miles away in the coastal town of Puri.[1]

Data for this paper come from two spells of fieldwork conducted by Usha Menon: the first done in 1991 and the second in 1992–93. In 1991, ninety-two Oriya Hindu men and women were interviewed about their conceptions of the life course and about the kinds of events and experiences that they considered typical and/or significant in a person's life. They were also asked to assess their past and present life satisfaction and their expectations for the future.[2]

The results of this initial spell of research highlighted three important issues. First, Oriya Hindus tend to describe life in terms of changes in roles, duties, and responsibilities. They rarely speak of life in terms of the growth and development of a child's capacity to speak or walk and they never mention first menstruation or menopause, although the former is marked by explicit rituals and marks the beginning of restrictions on girls' movements, apparel, and companions. Second, Oriya Hindus have well-articulated conceptions of the two- and five-phase models of the life course, which are described below.

Third, Oriya Hindu women of all ages tend to see mature adulthood as, relatively speaking, the most satisfying period in a woman's life. This finding appears to be distinctive of the Oriya Hindu cultural world; for instance, it differs quite remarkably from research done with American women.[3] According to Paul Cleary's unpublished results (see fig. 1), American women exhibit a steady, linear decline in anticipated future life satisfaction as they move from young adulthood to advanced middle age. According to our results (see fig. 1), however, Oriya Hindu women have different expectations. In fact, unlike American women, who view young adulthood—the period of life when individual capacities for autonomous, independent action are at their peak—as the

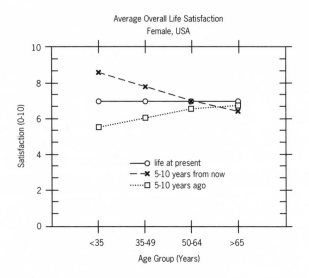

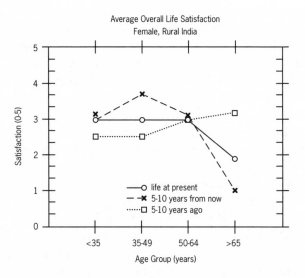

Figure 1 The American data were collected and analyzed by Paul Cleary and his associates at Harvard University. We are grateful for the opportunity to use this unpublished material as a point of comparison with the data from India.

more satisfying period in life, mature adulthood is the period that elicits from Oriya Hindu women the greatest anticipation of positive life satisfaction. As we shall see, there are indigenous meanings and understandings that can help us understand their evaluations.

Those findings from the fieldwork in 1991 provided the background for a second spell of fieldwork conducted by Menon a year later. Since Oriyas tend to describe their lives in terms of changing roles and responsibilities, the later research focused on women at different phases in the life course who were occupying different family roles, performing different duties, and bearing different responsibilities. And since mature adulthood is perceived by many women to be the most satisfying period in a woman's life, the second set of interviews and observations tried to explicate the values and meanings that these women attach to this particular time of life and the ways they define "satisfying life experiences." Because we believe that shifts in these women's roles, responsibilities, and personal well-being can be most clearly witnessed within the context of joint living arrangements, informants for the second spell of fieldwork were selected from extended households.

Joint living arrangements (a three-generation family consisting of adult brothers, their parents, wives, children, and unmarried sisters) are a phase of the developmental cycle of all families in the temple town of Bhubaneswar. One significant difference between joint and nuclear living arrangements in India lies in the fact that joint families are most certainly the cultural ideal. Indians prefer such living arrangements whenever they are possible. In Old Town, joint families usually break up when either the old father or grandfather (the head of the household) dies or when the old widowed mother or grandmother dies. At this time, the adult sons set up their own nuclear families with their wives and their children. Yet with the marriage of their sons and the birth of their grandchildren, their families extend and become complex, and the cycle of joint living arrangements begins again.

Our sample of Oriya informants for this phase of the research consisted of thirty-seven Hindu women belonging to ten extended households, ranging from nineteen to seventy-eight years old. These women follow traditional age-related family roles, those of "new" daughter-in-law, wife, mother, "old" (or senior) daughter-in-law, mother-in-law, grandmother, widow. A couple of unmarried adult daughters also form part of the sample; they were interviewed to provide a same-age control group and counterpoint to the experiences of new daughters-in-law.

Of the ten families selected, seven are Brahman; one is a Chassa (a cultivating caste), another a Teli (a merchant caste) and the last a Maharana (a caste of carpenters). Except for one Brahman family, the families are fairly well off: they own agricultural land and other property—houses and shops—that earn rent. Signs of this relative wealth can be seen in the fact that all families have at least one motor scooter, perhaps two, as well as televisions, refrigerators, and other household appliances.

The number of members in these families vary from six to twenty, with the average being thirteen. Of the thirty-seven women, there are twenty-two daughters-in-law, thirteen mothers-in-law, and two daughters; two of these daughters-in-law belong to four-generation households and so are mothers-in-law to the newest generation of daughters-in-law. In terms of education, a generational effect is clearly noticeable: mothers-in-law rarely have more than three or four years of education while almost all the daughters-in-law have completed ten years of formal schooling. There are, moreover, five mothers-in-law who state that they are unable to read or write; of these, three are non-Brahmans while two belong to a caste (Badus) whose status as Brahmans is contested by other Brahmans in the community.

Using open-ended, loosely structured interview schedules, women were asked to describe their daily routines, the degree of control they exercised over their own actions and bodies as well as the actions and bodies of others, their sense of belonging to their families and being part of a meaningful communal life, and the extent to which they felt they had achieved well-being. In order to measure the extent to which these women experience well-being, responses are keyed to the following mode of estimation. Ordinary folk in Old Town often speak of having "not even one *anna* of control over what happens in life"[4] or of having "fully sixteen *anna*s of happiness in childhood," and so when it came to asking women how healthy they were or how much well-being they thought they had, we framed the question in these commonplace terms. Therefore, the answers we typically heard were, "Six annas of good health [*svasthya*]" or "Four annas of well-being [*hito*]."

Almost without exception, the women were candid, articulate, and eager to participate; consequently, the interviews are long and detailed. None lasted for less than an hour. Some went on for more than two hours. The reasons for this candor and eagerness are not hard to understand. We believe most women saw the interview situation as an opportunity to engage in a kind of therapy or a criticism of family members.

144

They permitted themselves to speak their minds with relative freedom to an interested stranger who spoke their language but who did not share the constraints of their lives. While most interviews were one-on-one conversations in secluded rooms, the feeling that the rest of the family was close at hand, within earshot, was not easy to shake off. Often, when the women felt that they were saying something particularly critical of other family members, their voices would drop, but at other times they would deliberately raise their voices so that their complaints could be heard by other members of the family. Thus, most new daughters-in-law spoke in low undertones while mothers-in-law and sometimes old daughters-in-law spoke loudly and self-confidently, often even aggressively. All interviews were in Oriya, audiotaped, and later transcribed and translated.

Between Birth and Death in Orissa, India: Some Local Women's Views

Diagram 1 is a schematic representation of the phases of life (*avastha*) as described by sixty-six Oriya Hindu women (predominantly Brahman) living in extended households in the temple town of Bhubaneswar. All the women were interviewed by Usha Menon in the summer of 1991. During the interview, they were presented with a sheet of paper on which there were two dots, designated "birth" and "death." The women were asked to fill in the space between the two dots by narrating the most significant events and experiences in a typical person's life and in their own lives as well.

Some women initially resisted the request, indicating that it is really boring to talk in broad generalities about things that are obvious about life. As one elderly woman put it (a woman who was in the fifth and last phase of life, the *briddha avastha,* or stage of completion), "What can I tell you about those kinds of things? You know about them. Everyone does. You are born, you grow up, you grow old, you die. Do you want to hear that?" Other women were initially skeptical about the task on the grounds that "each person's life is different from everyone else's" and that "it depends on what kind of family you are born into, what your caste is, whether you're a boy or girl, whether you are the oldest child or the second or whatever, what your capabilities are, what karma you have brought with you." Nevertheless, Oriya women are quite adept at storytelling, and with just a bit of coaxing, they in fact had much to say about how a woman's life proceeds between life and death in rural India.

DIAGRAM 1. Oriya Women's Conception of the Life Course

Lifeline

	Birth	Knows right from wrong (7–9)	Marriage (18–20)	Takes over family management (30–39)	Relinquishes family management (55–60)	Death
Two-stage model		*bapa gharo* (Life in father's house)			*sasu gharo* (life in mother-in-law's house)	
Five-stage model		*pila* (undisciplined child)	*kishoro* (morally formative youth)	*jouvana* (sexually active)	*prauda* (mature)	*briddha* (completed)
Quality of role		Pet	Guest	Servant	Manager	Dependent
Rank in family		High	High	Low	High (peak)	Low
Control over others		High	Low	Low	High (peak)	Low
Assimilation in the family		High	High	Low	High (peak)	Declines
Served by others?		Yes	Yes	No	Yes	Uncertainty

Restrictive life?	No	Yes	Yes (peak)	Yes	No
Burden of responsibilities	Low	Low	High	High	Low
Worry about welfare of others?	No	No	Yes	Yes (peak)	Disappears
Perceived stress	Low	Low	High (peak)	High	High
Karmic consequences of one's actions	Low	High	High	High (peak)	High
Capacity to reason	Absent	Present	Present	Present (peak)	Declines
Time of suffering?	No	No	Yes	No	Yes
Perception of life-satisfaction trajectory		I will be worse off in next phase	I was better off in last phase and will be much better off in next phase	I was worse off in last phase and will be worse off in next phase	I was much better off in last phase and will be much worse off in next phase

The tales told by these sixty-six Oriya women reveal an alternative cultural conceptualization of the phases of the life course, one based on the logic of social responsibility, family management, and moral duty. In their narrations, Oriya women tend to divide the life course into either two, four, or five phases. These three types of conceptualizations (the two-, four-, and five-phase models) form a nested hierarchy of differentiated cultural models of the life course. The two- and five-stage models are schematically represented in diagram 1.

In the context of our general concern with documenting the breadth versus the narrowness of the cross-cultural and historical distribution of the idea of "middle age," it is the four- or five-phase model that interest us the most, because within these models there is a life phase known as *prauda* or "mature adulthood." We shall have more to say about the Oriya conception of mature adulthood below. First, however, we briefly comment on the most basic or rudimentary Oriya model of a woman's life, in which the life course is partitioned into only two phases: life spent in "my father's house" (*bapa gharo*) and that spent in "my husband's mother's house" (*sasu gharo*), the most common bipartite characterization among Oriya women who divide their lives into only two phases.

In extended households in Orissa, India, married sons continue to stay at home with their parents, but daughters, after an arranged marriage, move out. From the point of view of the daughter who is marrying out, the marriage ceremony is the most significant phase boundary in her life. It is at this point that an Oriya woman's socially recognized status shifts from being "a child who is some man's daughter" (*jhio pila*) to being "a sexually active female who is some other woman's daughter-in-law" (*bou*). As a *jhio pila*, an Oriya female is assumed to be sexually dormant (even after she is biologically mature) and lives under her father's protection. As a young *bou*, she is expected to be reproductively and sexually active and live under her mother-in-law's command.

Ideally, this fundamental phase shift from father's house to mother-in-law's house takes place between eighteen and twenty years of age. However, age per se does not mark the boundary between these two basic phases in life. Rather, it is marked by the numerous changes in social responsibilities attendant upon marriage, including, among other things, the responsibility to serve and be sensitive to the in-laws' needs and to become sexually active for the sake of reproducing the family line. Unlike young American females, who want to be referred to as "women" (rather than "girls") as soon as they move out of their parents' homes and into a college dormitory, a sexually inactive Oriya thirty-year-old who is still unmarried and lives under the protection of her father is socially categorized as a "child." She becomes a "woman" by getting married and by willingly and dutifully placing herself under an older woman's authority.

For the women in our study, the story of the life course, then, is the story of domestic life in someone else's house (first father's, then mother-in-law's). The fact that Oriya women are housebound, however, is not viewed by them as a mark of their oppression. Quite the contrary. The domestic realm is highly valued in Oriya culture, and domestic space (*ghare*) is understood as a kind of sacred, uncontaminating space and is contrasted with public, or outside, contaminating space (*bahare*). Men spend time outside the home and, therefore, are always at risk of becoming coarse (*asabhya*) and uncivilized (*abhadra*). It is by virtue of being able to remain indoors that Oriyas, both men and women, believe that women are more refined than men, more capable of experiencing civilizing dispositions such as "humility," "restraint," and "shame" (*lajya*), and less likely to display crude emotions such as "anger" (*raga*) or "mocking laughter" (*hasa*).

The four- and five-phase models elaborate on life in the two houses, presenting us with a more differentiated view of a woman's life course. In the five-phase model, life in one's father's house is divided into two phases: first, the undisciplined early childhood phase (*pilaliya*), when the daughter is indulged as a kind of adorable yet uncivilized family pet, and the second, the morally formative yet tender youthful phase (*kishor avastha*), when the daughter-child becomes a kind of resident guest in training and is given anticipatory instruction in the social responsibilities and duties of married life. The first phase ends at approximately seven to nine years of age. when the daughter-child is now thought capable of praying on her own, of distinguishing right from wrong, and of being sufficiently mature to have a conscience about the social responsibilities associated with domestic life; the second phase ends at marriage. (The four-phase model joins the first two phases and labels them "pila.")

Life in one's mother-in-law's house is divided into three phases: the first is *jouvana*, or young adulthood, when the sexually active young daughter-in-law is expected to have children and to serve the needs of her husband's family members; the second is *prauda*, or mature adulthood, when a woman takes over all the responsibilities for family management, including planning and control; and the third is *briddha*, or the age of completion, when a woman gives up the management of the family, becomes dependent on her kin, and begins to anticipate life in yet another house, the house of *Yama*, the house of the god of death.

In diagram 1 we have listed some of the characteristics of each life phase as revealed in these women's narratives. We have focused on those that are potentially relevant to perceived life satisfaction or well-being, for example, assimilation into the family, dominance within the family, being served by others, having control over the actions of others, and so forth. The sixty-six Oriya women in our sample represent four of the five life phases. As a measure of perceived life satisfaction, they were asked to estimate the ratio of good and bad events in their current lives, in the past five to ten years, and five to ten years into the future. The perceived life satisfaction of the fourteen oldest women (e.g., those over sixty who are in the last phase, that of *briddha*) can be summarized as follows: "My life was much better off in the past and it will be much worse off in the future." The perceived life satisfaction of the nineteen young daughters-in-law, those women under thirty who are in phase 3 (*jouvana*) can be summarized this way: "My life was better off in the past and it will be much better off in the future." Neither *jouvana* (the early married phase) nor *briddha* (the last phase of life) are valued times for women in this community. By way of contrast, it is the *prauda* (mature adulthood) phase that is highly prized. Married women in their twenties look forward to it with anticipation. The elder women look back on it as that phase of life that preceded their decline.

Prauda may seem vaguely reminiscent of "midlife" or "middle age." Yet that impression is surely misleading, for mature adulthood is not defined by biological age and does not normally extend beyond the ages of fifty-five or sixty. *Prauda* begins when a married woman takes over the management of the extended household and ends when she relinquishes control and social responsibilities to others. According to these Oriya women, *prauda* is the phase in life when dominance, control, planfulness, and responsibility for others are at their peak. The perceived life satisfaction of the twenty-eight women who are in the *prauda* phase can be summarized this way: "Compared to where I am now I was worse off in the past and I will be worse off in the future." In absolute terms it is when Oriya women are "mature adults" that they report the greatest life satisfaction.

When pressed, Oriya women can estimate descriptively normative age boundaries for each of these phases of life. *Prauda,* for example, is likely to begin when a woman is in her early thirties and end when she is in her late fifties. Nevertheless, as we have mentioned before, age per se is not the defining characteristic of Oriya life phases, and other biological markers such as menarche or menopause are rarely mentioned when these women talk about the phases of life. The underlying logic of Oriya life phases is a logic of social responsibility, family management, and moral duty and it is in such terms that a woman's "mature adulthood" in rural India is culturally defined.

We now turn to a discussion of the way Hindu family life and the domestic careers of Hindu women have been represented in recent scholarly literature, where, for the most part, the "native point of view" has either been subordinated to, or appropriated by, the moral framework of the currently popular "feminist" point of view. First we discuss the two types of constructions of the lives of Hindu women that are most prevalent in feminist ethnography. Then we offer an alternative construction derived from an alternative point of view.

Writing about Domesticity: The Moral Foundations of Ethnographic Representation

Feminist Discourse about "Hindu Women": A Brief Overview

Feminist scholarship is, of course, neither uniform nor homogeneous in its goals or beliefs. Nevertheless, in the context of South Asian studies, there are certain assumptions that seem to be widely held among anthropologists who approach their subject matter from a feminist point of view: that is, that patriarchy is bad and is responsible for the subordination of women; that women can be grouped into a unitary, coherent, already-constituted category made up of gendered persons who have the same objective interests and similar subjective desires; that male dominance and female subordination are not only morally outrageous but also seem to exist in almost every context; that Hindu cultural meanings systematically and regularly devalue women.

Armed with these tenets, scholars who study India from a feminist point of view seem to divide into two kinds: those who view Hindu women as passive victims of patriarchy, and those who view Hindu women as active rebels against it.

The scholars who portray Hindu women as passive victims (e.g., Kondos 1989; Dhruvarajan 1988; Jeffrey et al. 1988) focus on the differences that they, as Westernized observers, see in the life circumstances of the female Hindu "other," and they are sensitive to (and feel great empathy for) the situations of the most unfortunate of Hindu women.

There is much that these scholars dislike or even disdain in Hindu society. For example, they blame Hindu religion (which they interpret as mere ideology rather than as a sacred and factual explanation of social and physical phenomena) for the "subordination and subjection" of women (Kondos 1989, 162), for clouding the consciousness of its victims, and for withholding from Hindu women a political discourse of protest, insurgency, and victimhood. Such feminist writers tend to project an image of "the Hindu woman" as tame, domesticated, bound by tradition, intellectually unsophisticated, and sexually constrained. In this view, she is a woman who has little control over her actions or her body, a woman whose life is completely contingent on others.

Thus, Dhruvarajan, while describing her book's objective, writes,

> By elaborating on the philosophical underpinnings and the beliefs regarding the nature of men and women it is based on, it shows how women's dependent position on men is legitimized, how the ideology manipulates the motivational structure of women to accept their position as underlings of men, and how it strips them of the willpower necessary for self-reliance and personal growth. (1988, 108)

Kondos, in her study of upper-caste Nepali Hindu women, concludes that "feminine success is predefined and not open to variation, for a woman cannot be successful in any other way or in any other terms except those specified by the structures (the domicile, the laws, the cultural imperatives to produce sons and to die before her husband)" (1989, 190). Jeffrey et al. reveal their intellectual predispositions when they write that "Swaleha (one of our research assistants) responded to Patricia's exasperation over women's self-abnegation with the comment: 'But you see, the men here have subdued their women so completely that the idea has perched in women's minds that they are indeed inferior'" (1988, 157).

The foregoing image of the Hindu woman as passive victim is set in sharp contrast to another representation that is implicit in the writings of these feminist scholars: the image of the Western or Westernized academic woman as educated and cosmopolitan, as having control

152

over her body and her sexuality, as autonomous, and as having the freedom to make informed decisions on her own. The message conveyed by these authors is that the discrepancy between the two images (the tradition-bound housewife vs. the cosmopolitan, liberated scholar) is a measure of the failure of Hindu society to recognize and live up to a set of obvious and universally binding moral ideals (autonomy, equality, privacy, individual rights, and social and economic justice), which have been recognized and are being institutionalized in the West. In ethnographic constructions of this sort the native point of view remains unvoiced or tends to be subordinated to a feminist point of view.

Yet not all scholars who study India portray Hindu women as passive victims. Recently, there has become available in the literature an alternative construction or invention—the Hindu woman as active rebel. Those who represent Hindu women this way, as proto-Jacobins or cryptorevolutionaries, perceive in Hindu women a set of "liberated" attitudes and reactions against patriarchy that are very much like their own. These ethnographers detect "subversion" and "resistance" in Hindu women's songs, poetry, and ordinary conversations. They portray Hindu women as having a bawdy sense of humor, taking pleasure in their sexuality, and relishing their female nature. They represent these symbolic actions as ways for women to express their disenchantment with patriarchy and as indications of an incipient or clandestine movement within Hindu India aimed at undermining received gender roles (see Raheja and Gold 1994). According to this representation of South Asian moral attitudes and beliefs, Hindu women speak in multiple voices and elaborate both dominant male and subversive female perspectives. At some fundamental level, however, Hindu women, it is claimed, share with Western feminists insights that enable them to identify the ultimate cause as well as the proximate instruments of their oppression—patriarchy and men. In ethnographic constructions of this sort, the native point of view is equated with, and thereby appropriated by, the feminist point of view.

Is There a Distinctive (Nonfeminist) "Native Point of View"? Local Oriya Discourse about Hindu Women

There can be little doubt that the cultural practices of rural India in general and the family life practices of rural Hindu women in particular are a challenge to the cognitive, moral, and aesthetic sensibilities of Euro-American observers. For example, most married Oriya Hindu women living in the temple town of Bhubaneswar are sequestered in family compounds, where they assume a major responsibility for the humdrum routines, tasks, and duties of domestic life. Chandrama, a twenty-three-year-old Oriya woman who has been married for the last five years and is the eldest daughter-in-law in an extended household of twelve, tells us about a typical day in her life. What she has to narrate about her daily routine is typical of a day in the life of an Oriya woman in the *jouvana* phase of life:

> As soon as I get up, I sweep out the house and then I go to the bathroom. I clean my teeth, have a bath, and then I start the breakfast. Once the breakfast is done, people come in one by one to eat. I serve each of them breakfast. Once that is done, we have our breakfast together. *Bou* [husband's mother] and I eat together. And then, I start preparing lunch—what we'll be eating at two in the afternoon. Once that is done, again people come in one by one to eat. By three, we would also have eaten and I would have washed up after lunch. Then, I come and sleep in the afternoon. I sleep for an hour. I get up at four. I again sweep out the house and then I go down to start making something to eat with tea. I knead the *atta* [wheat flour] and make *parathas* or *rotis* [different kinds of bread]. Again, people come one by one to eat. I serve them and then it would be sun-down by now and I offer *sandhya* [evening worship] before I start cooking the night meal. I am usually cooking till nine in the night. Then I go and watch the serial on TV. After that, at about 9:30, everyone will come to eat and I serve them. And then we eat. After finishing eating, we go to bed. The dishes are left as they are till morning. I just keep them till the morning when I wash them. In the morning, the first thing I do is take out and wash the *ointha* [polluted by leftovers] dishes, then I leave them out in the sun to dry, while I sweep out the kitchen, wash it out, and then take the vessels back in again.

Q. Would you like to add anything more to what you've just said?

A. No, nothing else.

Q. What about *puja* [worship]? In the morning do you do *puja* after your bath? Give water to the *tulasi* [basil leaf, representing the goddess] or offer water to *surjya* [sun god]?

A. No, I do nothing. *Bou* does all that. All I do is wash the feet of our *burhi ma* [husband's father's mother] and drink the water after my bath and before I go to make breakfast. I used to do it for *bou* and *nona* [husband's mother and father] in the beginning but they stopped me from doing it. They said that it was enough to do it for *burhi ma* and get her blessings. But apart from that I don't do any *puja*. I offer *sandhya* but that is only in the kitchen— *bou* offers it in the *puja* room and over the rest of the house.

As every interpretive anthropologist knows, a storyteller's intent is not always equivalent to a listener's response. One theme of our essay is that, from the point of view of "authorial intent," Chandrama's chronicle of her daily routine is really a narrative saturated with locally salient yet universally recognizable moral meanings about her self-conscious engagement in a project of doing *sewa,* or service, for her husband's family. Her narrative is about the positive moral implications of voluntarily enduring the specific life phase (and hence temporary) responsibilities of a family *sevaka* (a devoted servant of the divine).

One of the things this storyteller, Chandrama, does not know, however, is that some of her listeners will be cosmopolitan, "liberated" Westernized scholars who will reflexively perceive her *sewa* as humiliating subservience, oppressive subjugation, or abusive exploitation. Minimally we can expect that the daily routine of an Oriya "housewife" as described in this narrative will appear at first blush to give new meaning (both literal and figurative) to the idea of the "daily grind." At least that is the first impression it is likely to create in the minds of many cosmopolitan and liberated academic observers.

A second theme of our essay is that first impressions can be misleading. This is especially true when those impressions have been formed or take shape under the influence of a relatively thin theory of moral goods, such as the honorable yet incomplete (and hence "partial" or "biased") "morality of autonomy" privileged by Western liberal thought. In this case the (objectively) partial yet (subjectively) totalizing moral significance projected (and then perceived) by Western and Westernized feminist ethnographers as they gaze upon the lives of "unliberated" Hindu women are almost neocolonial in character, for those significances carry with them the implications of a moral imperialism or a "white (wo)man's burden" to emancipate and uplift Hindu family life and to disenthrall "uneducated" and "superstitious" Hindus of their "unjust" and "oppressive" gender roles.

In this essay we wish to suggest, however tentatively, that the Oriya

Hindu women of the temple town of Bhubaneswar are neither passive victims nor subversive rebels, but rather active upholders of a moral order that Western feminists have largely failed to comprehend. High on the list of virtues and values in the moral order upheld by Oriya women are chastity, modesty, duty, self-discipline, the deferment of gratification, self-improvement, and the ideal of domestic "service" (*sewa*). Low on the list are liberty and social equality.[5]

This essay is about the cultural agency displayed by the Oriya Hindu women of the temple town as they go about their daily lives, agency that supports and affirms rather than denies or undermines the cultural order. These women are not cultural robots who go through life mechanically and unthinkingly. Rather, they are self-reflecting people who acknowledge the constraints they live with, recognize the choices available to them, and are well aware of the costs and rewards of conforming to cultural norms.

Hito, the Oriya term for well-being, is an analytic category familiar to the women who participated in this study. Defined very broadly, it refers to the state of being satisfied with the way one's world has turned out. A more nuanced definition, one that includes the indigenous meanings that this term conveys to Oriya women, will emerge during the course of this essay. It is that nuanced definition that enables us to critique the rather dismal feminist representations of the lives of Hindu women and to relocate Oriya domestic life within an alternative moral order. (On the idea of plural moral goods such as autonomy, community, or divinity and alternative moral orders see Shweder [1990, 1994], Shweder et al. [1990], Shweder et al. [1997], Haidt et al. [1993], and Jensen [1995]. On the idea of plural moral goods such as fairness, sympathy, duty, and self-improvement and alternative moral orders see Wilson [1993].)

Our representation of women's lives in Oriya households highlights the way a woman's access to and achievement of well-being (*hito*) systematically varies across the life cycle. There are periods when an Oriya housewife is so valued within the family, when her activities are so significant for the material and spiritual prosperity of the entire household, that her own sense of well-being peaks; and there are periods when she is less essential to the household's well-being, and her own sense of well-being declines. No Oriya Hindu woman's life is uniformly a success or uniformly a failure, just as there is no woman in this community who always makes her own decisions or one who never does. These are facts well recognized by the women themselves. Oriya women will tell you that success or failure, control or lack of control, well-being or distress characterize different phases in a person's life and ultimately mesh together to form the fabric of a self-disciplined life. This essay is thus an attempt to describe the moral texture of that self-disciplined way of being in the world as understood by Oriya woman.

Understanding the Cultural Construction of Gender in a Hindu Temple Town

For the sake of our analysis we shall define a "culture" as a reality lit up by a morally enforceable conceptual scheme or subset of meanings instantiated in practice (Shweder 1996). In this section of the essay we introduce the reader to the alternative cultural reality of gender relations in the temple town of Bhubaneswar and to some of the concepts, beliefs, and practices to which the reader must gain access if Oriya gender relations are to be understood as a justifiable or defensible moral reality.

To an outside observer unfamiliar with the concepts, meanings, and practices of the temple town, the women who live there may at first glance seem docile, submissive, withdrawn, and relegated to the background—women without voices. But appearances can deceive, revealing more about the observer than the observed. A closer acquaintance suggests a radically different picture, for these Oriya women do not see themselves as powerless, and they confidently believe that it is they who hold families and society together. Oriya men share this view. In this section, we attempt to show the ways in which such self-understandings grow and develop among these women.

Sudhir Kakar's comment that, in Hindu India, "the preferred medium of instruction and transmission of psychological, metaphysical and social thought continues to be the story" (1982, 1) accurately describes much of indigenous cultural discourse in the temple town of Bhubaneswar. Oriya men and women frequently use stories from the various Puranas (texts about the old times, the often times), as well as regional Oriya folk tales to give logic and meaning to everyday or mundane experience. For most of the Oriya women who spoke at length and in intimate detail about their lives in our data, the stories from the Puranas are far more "real" and relevant to everyday life (and thus more worthy of repetition) than events reported in the daily newspapers.

The female protagonists (divine and human) of these stories—

Durga, Kali, Kunti, Draupadi, Sita, Radha, Savitri, Anusuya—exemplify womanly virtues. Their experiences elucidate a woman's *dharma* and define a woman's *prakriti* (*svabhava*, her nature). Their qualities (*guna*) tell them what it means to be a Hindu woman. Women see these figures as paradigmatic, partly because they represent ideals worthy of emulation, and partly because it is believed that, by virtue of being female, these heroines and ordinary Oriya Hindu women share the same configurations of female substance.

In addition to the Puranic orientation in the temple town, the *Sakta* tradition is also strong.[6] Oriya Hindus of the temple town, both men and women, are liable to say that women embody, as the goddess does, *sakti* (vital energy or power or strength), that they have more of the *guna* in terms of absolute quantities than do men, which is why women can turn the *asadhya* (undoable) into the *sadhya* (doable), the *asambhav* (impossible) into the *sambhav* (possible). Women are commonly described as *saktidayini* (givers of vital energy or strength) and as being *sampoorna sakti* (full of vital energy or strength). Women are depicted as *samsarore chalak* (controllers or directors of the family and the flow of life in this world), as those whose duties include satisfying everyone (*samasthonku santhusta koriba*), maintaining the family (*samsaroku sambhaliba*), ensuring peace and order (*shanti shrunkhala rakhiba*).[7]

Most Oriya Hindus in the temple town believe that social reproduction is the primary task of any group. And they believe that the family represents the most appropriate site for social reproduction. For most Oriyas the idea of a voluntarily childless marriage is a contradiction in terms. (Why would anyone marry, Oriyas ask, if they had no intention of having children and contributing to the reproduction of the group?) Both men and women will say, "We are born into this world to play our roles in *samsara*, to participate in the ebb and flow of life, to build families, to raise children." They emphasize the impermanence of all things in this world, the fact that continual change is the only stable feature of life. They believe that only through procreating and raising children to responsible adulthood does a group achieve immortality.

It is thus not surprising that Oriya Hindu women, and their menfolk too, regard the home and the family—the domestic domain—as a more important sphere of human action than action in the public domain. Since women control and manage all household activities, whether what men earn is utilized effectively and productively depends on the sagacity and capability of the women of the household, particularly the senior-most woman. Men readily acknowledge that women shoulder many more responsibilities than they do (*striro daitya purusa opekhya jyateshtha adhika*) and that the work women do is six times as much as men have to do (*stri jatinkoro karma chho guna adhika*). As a sixty-year-old husband, a father and one of the most articulate of informants says,

> Look at a twenty-year-old man, a twenty-year-old child, he knows nothing, he just roams here and there, but a twenty-year-old girl, she has become the mother of two children, she runs her household and family, she cares for the cows and calves under her care, the children and the house, she cooks and serves her husband, she cleans the children, dresses them, and sends them to school, makes sure that they are well. She manages the parents of her husband, she cleans the house. Compared to a man's, a woman's responsibilities are far more. When you compare men and women of the same age, that is what you find.

In contrast to the premises of modern liberal thought, the view of the world espoused by Oriya women and men is built on a logic of difference and solidarity rather than on equality and competition. To understand the Oriya moral universe as it applies to gender, one must understand that the popular Oriya recognition of the worth of women's work and widespread acknowledgement of greater female effectiveness is not a local idiomatic Oriya expression of a feminist viewpoint, for, quite emphatically, neither women nor men in Orissa believe that women and men are equal.

Indeed, most Oriya women and men find the notion that one should be indifferent to gender or treat the genders as though they were the same as either incomprehensible, amusing, or immature. For these Oriyas, the most common metaphor for society is the human body: no organ is exactly substitutable for any other and yet all work together so that the body functions efficiently while life endures. Most Oriya women and men believe that of all the *jatis* (castes) in the world, male and female are the only authentic *jatis* because male and female are the only two *jatis* whose fundamental differences cannot be transcended.

For Oriya Hindus then, "difference" and "interdependency" are givens. Yet, this "difference" and the character of the interdependence are not fixed or global. The prerogatives and privileges enjoyed and the power exercised by women and men are fluid, varying, as A. K. Rama-nujan (1990) has said, with particular contexts. Men, in terms of the constitution of their bodily substances, have disproportionately more of the *sattva guna* (qualities of transparency, lucidity, coherence) and so are regarded as "purer" and because of this relative purity enjoy certain privileges in some situations (e.g., they can approach divinity with fewer restrictions); while women, because they possess more of all the *guna*s in absolute terms, exercise considerable power and control in other situations (e.g., they manage household finances and activities with little interference). We document and elaborate these points below.

Some Oriya Women's Discourse about Well-being

In this section, we rely on the voices of thirty-seven Oriya women from our broader sample to construct a representation of the way personal well-being is understood and defined by women who belong to this orthodox Hindu community, whose practices and institutions are premised on moral goods and ethical virtues other than those privileged in feminist writings and Western liberal thought.

Family role (rank and status) appears to be the significant variable in determining an Oriya woman's well-being. As noted earlier, considering the fabric of adult life across the life course, access to personal well-being is at its maximum when an Oriya woman enters the managerial stage of *prauda* (typically as either an old daughter-in-law or as a married mother-in-law). And while most Oriya women achieve this rank or status some time between thirty and forty years of age, biological age per se is not a crucial variable.

Similarly, the sense of well-being reported by daughters and new daughters-in-law varies according to their particular family roles. In Hindu extended households, unmarried adult daughters and new daughters-in-law live in the same family compound and are often of approximately the same age (both may be in their early twenties). Yet their well-being assessments vary widely, with unmarried daughters reporting strikingly higher levels of *hito*.

Because an Oriya woman's duties, responsibilities, social status, and ways of being enmeshed in interpersonal relationships seem to be the major factors giving her meaning, purpose, and fulfillment in life, it is one of our aims as ethnographers of Hindu family life to characterize their moral meanings, to describe changes in those duties and responsibilities over the life course, and to understand how access to those moral meanings is related to personal well-being.

The "Daily Grind": The Moral Meanings of Service to the Family (*Sewa*)

It has been reported that in most societies as a woman ages there is a relaxation in the restrictions under which she lives (cf. Brown and Kerns 1985). While this may be true on a worldwide scale, it would be a mistake to infer that increased "autonomy" is the central moral "good" that explains the association between personal well-being and *prauda* in our sample. We believe that in the temple town a woman's sense of well-being hinges on the particular kinds of family relationships she has succeeded at developing or has failed to develop as she ages.

An important part of the story about *hito* concerns the values and meanings that Oriya Hindus attach to the roles of old daughter-in-law and married mother-in-law. By incorporating such indigenous values and meanings, we will try to construct an ideal-typical model of the development of well-being among Oriya women. We believe this model is culturally salient, although because this model is an idealization, summarizing and typifying thirty-seven Oriya voices, it will not necessarily coincide with the lived experiences of each and every woman.

The most striking feature of the daily routines of these Oriya women lies, we think, in the ways such routines highlight social relational patterns within families. These daily routines bring to the fore the ways in which duties, responsibilities, and opportunities get distributed among women according to the needs of the family. In this section, we discuss and contrast five particular family roles: daughter, new daughter-in-law, old daughter-in-law, mother-in-law, and widow. We discuss the social relational patterns that are revealed by their daily routines.

We begin with the daughter of the family. As an unmarried adult an Oriya Hindu girl enjoys a carefree and relatively irresponsible life. She is far more carefree, in fact, than even her brothers, for whom, given the unemployment statistics in India, the pressure to obtain an adequate source of livelihood makes these years of early adulthood very difficult. An unmarried adult girl is indulged. She has no prescribed duties. Whatever she does, she does voluntarily. The daily routines of the two daughters in the sample makes this abundantly clear. (Although there were only two unmarried adult women in our sample, over the years, the authors have observed this pattern of behavior in scores of families). As Sudhangani, one of the unmarried adult daughters, says, "After eating rice, I may stitch something or I may knit or if I wanted to, I may watch some TV or I may go to sleep. I do things like that."

And as the other daughter, Ameeta, says explicitly, daughters have no responsibility towards anyone in their fathers' households. "My responsibility? What responsibility? I have no responsibility. As long as my father and mother are alive, I have no responsibility toward anyone."

At the same time, however, they are aware of their positions as temporary residents in the *kishoro* stage of life; their permanent homes are elsewhere. Although these unmarried girls have few illusions that life in the homes of their mothers-in-law is initially going to be anything less than strenuous, the interviews communicate quite plainly the sense of positive anticipation they feel as they look ahead to becoming daughters-in-law.

Now let us consider the situation of a new daughter-in-law. The differences in well-being between daughters and daughters-in-law are quite striking. Daughters report almost double the level of personal well-being reported by daughters-in-law. This reflects, perhaps, the comfort, the sense of belonging, that daughters feel in their fathers' homes, a feeling of comfort that new daughters-in-law lack during their initial years in their husbands' homes. Since these two groups are of roughly the same age, the relationship is clearly not between age and well-being but between the family role occupied and well-being.

Unlike an unmarried daughter of the house, who is in the *kishoro* phase of life, a new daughter-in-law is in the *jouvana* phase and has explicitly understood duties. She is put through something like the domestic Oriya version of military boot camp. The most important of these duties lies in doing *sewa*—service to members of her husband's family. Such *sewa* has, in the Oriya Hindu context, very concrete dimensions. She has to do all the cooking and some of the serving of the food and much of the cleaning and washing, and she must perform explicit rituals of deference to her husband's mother and father. These rituals include massaging their feet daily, drinking the water used to ceremonially wash their feet before eating, and eating out of the *thali* (metal plate) previously used by either her mother-in-law or her father-in-law.

It is crucial to recognize that the meaning of these rituals are easily misunderstood if they are comprehended only within the moral framework of Western individualist liberationist ideals. From the native point of view, these rituals of family life are culturally defined ways available to a daughter-in-law for reconstructing (see Lamb 1993) her physical substance and for expressing her solidarity with the patrilineage into which she has merged through marriage. This is not to say that every Oriya newlywed is temperamentally inclined to life in a boot camp or tolerates harsh treatment without suffering and physical distress. It is to say, however, that within the framework of indigenous South Asian understandings such rituals of deference continue the process of reconstruction of the bride's bodily substance begun explicitly during the marriage ceremonies and symbolized by the new name given the bride at marriage (see Inden and Nicholas 1977). In keeping with Hindu notions of the body, which emphasize the relative openness to external influences (Marriott 1976), the new given name, the marriage ceremonies, and the rituals of deference mark the continual reconstructions that a woman's body undergoes as her bodily substance slowly becomes that of the patrilineage into which she has married.

Such rituals contribute directly to an increase or decrease in a daughter-in-law's sense of well-being. Thus when an angry mother-in-law withholds permission to perform such rituals, all daughters-in-law interpret such refusal as a rejection by the family to her assimilation and experience that rejection with considerable sorrow and distress. The cognitive and emotional reactions of Westernized feminist scholars to such practices do not further, indeed they obscure, our understanding of the local moral world supporting extended family life in India.

Most new daughters-in-law echo Chandrama (see her narrative about her daily routine, above) with only minor variations. In the early years of marriage, daughters-in-law do not worship any gods. For them, it is enough to worship their mothers-in-law and fathers-in-law, earthly gods having the power to withhold or bestow blessings. As Sabitiri, a new daughter-in-law, married for just four months, reports, "At my time in life, it is appropriate that I worship *bou*. What need is there for me to worship any other god? She is my god."

These new daughters-in-law are working up a spiritual ladder to the gods. At this point in their moral careers, they regard the opportunity to worship their husbands' mothers and fathers rather than the gods as opportunities for promotion, not a deprivation. At this stage in the life course, given their position in the family hierarchy, new daughters-in-law appear to have few other responsibilities. As Chandrama says further along in her interview, "For the moment, I have no responsibility. There are so many people older than I am—they take all the responsibility of this household."

Nevertheless, as she herself is aware, *daitva,* or responsibility, is never completely absent. A competent daughter-in-law has to learn to be adept in maintaining harmony among the younger members of the family. She must take on the role of friend and advisor to them. She may even intervene as an intermediary between them and her mother-in-law, when the latter's consent and approval is required but unlikely. And it is this capacity to, as she says, "understand what lies in the minds of the *nanad* and *diyoro*" (husband's younger sisters and brothers) that is the distinctive mark of a successful daughter-in-law, trusted by her affinal family.

Further in the interview, Chandrama describes the restrictions under which she lives. They are fairly severe. She rarely goes out; she hardly meets anyone but family members. Her trips to her father's house are infrequent and depend on the wishes of her husband's mother and father. Even within the house, she is unable to move freely because, given the pattern of avoidance relationships within the family, she has to hide from (avoid) those male affines senior to her husband. As Sandhyarani, another new daughter-in-law says, "All that one does in the house of one's *sasu* [husband's mother] is hide."

Given the stressful circumstances in which new daughters-in-law in the *jouvana* phase live their lives, it is hardly surprising that only a couple of them claim to have achieved substantial well-being, fifteen to sixteen annas of it. The ones who do experience high levels of *hito* live in relatively small families having only seven or eight members and their mothers-in-law are both noninterfering and undemanding. At the other extreme, there are two daughters-in-law who appear to suffer considerable distress, one claiming to have no well-being at all and the other to have only two annas of well-being. For the most part, daughters-in-law have rather low feelings of well-being: if sixteen annas indicates that one has achieved complete well-being, a new daughter-in-law, on the average, has less than eight annas of well-being.

A notable and distinctive feature of these interviews with junior, new daughters-in-law in the *jouvana* phase is fairly clear evidence for the somatization of emotional distress. New daughters-in-law who give themselves low scores on well-being complain of night fevers, chest pains, and swooning. Such somatization is explicitly recognized in local discourse. There are new daughters-in-law who say that they are so sad that they cannot digest their food and this leads to chest pains that cannot be explained by the doctors they consult. Their husbands' mothers and sisters say that these women make no effort to integrate with the rest of the family, that they are angry and resentful of everyone else, and that this anger and resentment hinders digestion of food leading to chest pains.

There are also daughters-in-law who feel so unappreciated in their husbands' homes, so diminished in respect, so anxious to receive regard, that they experience (by their own accounts) a fall in their blood pressure that leads to fainting. Of course, all this has to be seen against the background of a strong cultural aversion to excessive self-concern and reflection about oneself. Generally speaking, people in Old Town believe that too much thinking (i.e., worrying about oneself) is deleterious. They believe that attention to oneself leads in and of itself to illness and physical distress—one makes oneself vulnerable to disease by thinking about oneself too much.

Thus there are multiple explanations for the somatic symptoms of emotional distress, and they vary depending on who is speaking— whether it is the new daughter-in-law or the mother-in-law or the husband's sister. Nevertheless these multiple explanations have one thing in common. They all ascribe the lack of well-being not to the severity of the restrictions under which new daughters-in-law live nor to their having to perform deference, but to their incomplete assimilation into their husbands' families. Oriya women say quite categorically that the greater the assimilation, the greater the well-being that is experienced.

Before a new daughter-in-law gives birth to children, she receives more from the family than she gives to it, and she does not control any of this exchanging. Oriya women state quite explicitly that a new daughter-in-law has to learn to open herself, during this phase, to influences from the family, learn to become as permeable as she can so that her reconstructing and assimilation can occur rapidly and effectively. Those women who are unable to open themselves—and Oriya women recognize such a possibility, saying that often *lajya* (modesty, a heightened awareness of oneself) makes such opening painful and difficult—cannot make use of the opportunities available, even during *jouvana*, for achieving well-being and so feel less well-off.

Let us now consider the situation of an old daughter-in-law. With age, the birth of children, and the entry of younger daughters-in-law, a woman progressively attains a status that is referred to locally as old daughter-in-law—*purna bou*. *Purna* is an interesting word because it also connotes completeness, and, in a sense, it is when a woman matures, becomes a mother, and becomes senior to others like herself that she finally becomes the complete daughter-in-law. While maturing and seniority happen on their own, women actively complete themselves as daughters-in-law by giving birth to children. By providing new members to the families they have married into, they are entrenching themselves within the household, embedding themselves in the families, and laying claim to being heard in family debates and discussions.

In reading the daily routines of these women, it is possible to detect a gradual relaxation in some of the restrictions women experience as new daughters-in-law. The insistence by their seniors that they do a substantial part of the cooking declines. The restrictions on movement, on meeting people who do not belong to the family, grow fewer. Even the emphasis on the performance of explicit rituals of deference grows steadily weaker.

Thus, Dukhi, a forty-year-old *purna bou*, makes very clear her promotion out of the kitchen. When asked if she helps her husband's younger brother's wife (*sana ja*) in the cooking, she says, referring to herself as a *sasu* (husband's mother),

> No, no. I don't have anything to do with the cooking. The *sana ja*, she does all that. We *sasus* don't even enter the kitchen. She will do all the work, won't she? She does the cooking, doesn't she? Why should I do all that? I don't cut the vegetables, I don't grind the *masala*. I don't touch the cooking utensils.

And Pranati, a thirty-three-year-old *purna bou*, says, "If people drop in, then it is my responsibility to serve tea to them, snacks, talk pleasantly to them, till whoever they have come to see is ready to meet them."

Most old daughters-in-law do not strictly observe the rituals of deference toward the mother-in-law. Most *purna bous* explain it as merely a result of increased familiarity with one's mother-in-law, a consequence of the passage of time, and a function of the number of years they have lived within their husbands' families. An alternative, perhaps more plausible, interpretation would appear to be that such rituals are no longer needed: *purna bous* have completed their reconstructions into fully acknowledged members of their husbands' patrilineages. Indeed, nonperformance of such rituals figures as a factor playing into their sense of well-being by underscoring their sense of finally belonging to their husbands' families. As *purna bous*, it is not a question of being prevented from performing such rituals (as new daughters-in-law sometimes are) but rather that such rituals are no longer needed, having served their purpose of completing the reconstruction of the newlywed into a real daughter-in-law.

With the passage of time and the birth of children, old daughters-in-law have merged with their husbands' lineages. Although they are still some time away from being the senior-most woman of the household, they see themselves as well on the way to it. They have begun to take advantage of the privileges that that position is likely to bring with it, privileges that include commanding those subordinate and junior to themselves. A concomitant of this improved position within the family is greater well-being: on the average, a *purna bou* states that she has thirteen annas of well being.

Let us now consider the situation of a mother-in-law. For the average Oriya Hindu woman, her position reaches its apogee when her sons marry and a new generation of daughters-in-law enter the family.[8] A reading of the following daily routine brings home in sharp detail the shifts that occur in duties and privileges when a woman becomes a mother-in-law. Priyambada, a sixty-two-year-old mother-in-law who lives with her own mother-in-law, her husband, four sons, two daughters, daughter-in-law, and two grandsons, describes her day in the following manner:

Getting up in the morning. We get up at 3:30 or 4:00 in the morning. As soon as we get up we wash our faces and then we bow our heads to god. We then clean our teeth, go and defecate. After defecating, we may do some polluting work. And then we go for our baths. While we are returning from our baths, we pluck a few flowers for god. After we return, we pray to god, we light a lamp, *agarbatti* [incense sticks], offer flowers, repeat a few *slokas* [verses] and after that we have some tea to drink. After tea, I arrange the *thali* [tray] that I will be taking to the temple later on. Once I have finished arranging, I turn my attention to cutting vegetables or grinding *masala*—I have to do all that. It varies from day to day. Once that is done, I have to go to the temple. Once I have gone around the temple and returned, I have to see who has come, who has eaten, who has

gone out, who is in the house, and then again, I have the job of
arranging the flowers and other things for god. And then, I may
sit down, go from this room to that, look out of the front of the
house, whatever needs to be done in the house—that has to be
settled, this has to be cleaned and washed. And then comes the
business of serving food and seeing people eat. All the business
of running a house.

And then the children return home from tuition and it's time
to see to their eating, their studies—this would be about three
in the afternoon. Sometimes it may be a little later but my work
of arranging things for the temple goes on. I make the wicks for
the temple lamps, I make garlands with flowers for the deity. I
gather together whatever will be necessary for tomorrow, and
then. I move around the house, from here to there and then we
have tea. I join in the cutting of vegetables for the evening meal.
After tea, I offer *sandhya* [evening worship]. Once I've given
sandhya, I go and lie down. I cover myself and lie down right
here. I only get up at about 9:30 or 10 at night. I eat food then
and go to bed soon after. Nowadays, because it's cold, I cover
myself and lie down, but even in summer, I lie down and close
my eyes. After all, the food won't be ready till 10 o'clock—so
what is there to do but lie down and close one's eyes?

Q. As you were saying, before you go to the temple in the morning,
you bow your head to god?

A. As soon as we get up, early in the morning, as soon as we have
washed our faces with water, we turn to the one or two photos
we have of god and we bow our heads three times. Then we
clean our teeth, after that we defecate. After defecating, before going for our baths we may clean out the house, throw out the gar-
bage, do all that kind of polluting work and then we go for our
baths. On the way back from Bindusagar,[9] we pick a few flowers
and, after returning home, there are again prayers in the *puja*
room upstairs. After doing *puja*, I water the plants that we grow
and then I come down for tea.

Clearly, this daily routine's emphasis is quite different from that of
the earlier ones. Priyambada is freed from the strenuous work of cooking and feeding a large family; in fact, she does more than most mothers-in-law. When she says, "I turn my attention to cutting vegetables
or grinding masala. I have to do that," she is subtly directing our atten-

tion to what she sees as her daughter-in-law's incompetence, her inability to manage the kitchen independently. Furthermore, her work now is more of a supervisory nature, of ensuring that her little community runs efficiently. She has considerable geographical mobility: she goes alone for her daily bath to the temple pond, she worships everyday at the Lingaraj temple, she admits that, during the day, she looks out of the front of the house, watching the world going by—all activities that are strictly forbidden a new daughter-in-law and often limited even for an old daughter-in-law.

Most important, however, is her regular communication with god and her uninterrupted association with offerings meant for divinity. This privilege of approaching divinity without reservation is a direct consequence of her ability to maintain her physical body's purity, an ability that is relatively recent for her and the direct result of two factors.

First, among Oriya Hindus of Old Town, when a son marries and brings his wife into the family, his parents usually cease being sexually active. The job of reproduction has been passed on to the son and his wife. Many Oriya adults are disgusted or feel desanctified by the idea of two generations copulating under the same roof. Priyambada is no exception to this custom and she believes that this cessation of sexual activity makes it easier for her to maintain bodily purity.

Second, she is past menopause, and so there is no time of the month when she is *mara*, polluted or impure. Both of these reasons make it appropriate that as the mother-in-law she is the intermediary between the family and god, a position that she enjoys considerably and is the source of a substantial sense of well-being; the average score for mothers-in-law among our survey is twelve annas of well-being. In fact, there are three married mothers-in-law who say quite categorically that they have fully sixteen annas of well-being.

Let us now consider the situation of a widow. It is as a married mother-in-law that an Oriya Hindu woman's position is least assailable. Yet time is an accuser and a degrader, and with old age and widowhood there is usually a sharp reversal in a woman's situation. As an old widow, a woman is often relegated to the background, expected to contribute nothing to the family and expecting to get little in return.

Sociologically speaking, a widow in Old Town is a nonperson. During the funeral rites for her husband, there are several rituals that emphasize this erasure of her social existence and that mark her entrance into the status of a perpetual mourner whose preoccupations ought to be both transcendent and otherworldly. This erasure of social standing is symbolized by her lack of a family name: as a widow, a woman can no longer use her husband's family name and is known only by her given name (the one given at marriage, not birth) and the title *bewa*, a local contraction of *vidhwa* or widow.

Harsamani, age 78, has been a widow for thirty-six years, and her poignant story of an ordinary day's activities typifies this particular experience of widowhood among Oriya Hindu women of Old Town.

> I get up at three in the morning. I put some water for heating and then I go and defecate. After that I bathe. People would be still sleeping—it would be dark, some people may be awake but others would be sleeping. After bathing, I get back into bed. I cover myself up and go to sleep. I get up only when the tea comes. With tea, there would be something to eat—whatever they had made, maybe some *upma* [dish of farina] or whatever—they will call me and I get up. But I eat lying in bed—do you understand? Sometimes I sit and eat but sometimes I lie and eat. These days the weather is cold and so I wrap myself and go and sit in the doorway. By about ten or eleven, they would have finished cooking and they come and call me. My daughter would have come, she goes to the kitchen and serves for me and herself and the two of us eat together. We eat here in this room. After eating, we go and wash our hands and then we come back to this room. If daughter is not there, they serve me and bring the food here. On days when I'm not feeling well, I get back into bed after eating, I eat *paan* [betel leaf] and I lie down once more. But on days when my mind is active, I sit in the doorway and chew *paan*. I see you going by sometimes, sometimes I see an aunt going by, sometimes a mother, sometimes a grand-mother, and they will say, "You're sitting here?" After sitting for some time, when I again feel cold, I get back into bed, I cover myself and lie down.
>
> Then again tea and snacks will come and I will eat, again my middle daughter will be here and we have tea and snacks to-gether. And then dusk falls, once dusk falls, there is no work whatsoever. You understand? Daughter will put the mosquito net over my bed and once again I lie down all covered up. In the middle of all this the evening meal arrives. At night, what-ever comes, if I feel like it, I eat it. I eat a little of it and then I

170

lie down. *Parathas* [fried breads], milk, curry, fried vegetables, whatever they have made, that is what is served. After eating, then again I make myself some *paan,* I eat one and keep one under the pillow. I lie down. I have no work to do, neither night nor day. At no time during the day do I have any work. I have nothing to do. When I get up in the morning, again I put water for heating, I shit, clean my teeth, I bathe. This is the month of *Magha* (January/February), all the women get up early, bathe, go to the temple, they do what they want to after bathing, I go back to bed. The *nathani-bou* [grandson's wife], she comes and calls me, "Ma, you've fallen asleep, get up, get up, here's your tea and breakfast." Again the tea and something to eat—some days it's *suji* [cream of wheat], some days it's *parathas.*

Q. When do you pray?

A. There's no more praying for me. Why? Do you want to know why? Our gods are kept upstairs. By the time I walk up those stairs, my strength disappears. God is taken care of nowadays by the *bous* (sons' wives). Now that they do all that, what is left for me to do? On days when I have the strength I pour a little water on the *tulasi* [basil leaf] at the back but otherwise all I do is put a few drops of *nirmaliya* in my mouth.[10] Everyday, everyday, I put a few drops of *nirmaliya* in my mouth and then I lie down. Then the same things happen every day—over and over again, the same things.

Q. How often do you go to the temple?

A. I can't go to the temple. It is now two years since I went to the temple. My strength is declining, my body trembles, I may fall down somewhere, and then people will say, *Hou, hou,* people will criticize me for that.

Harsamani appears to have been effectively marginalized by age and widowhood. She is forbidden to provide sustenance to the family, for she is not allowed to cook for and feed others. She is forbidden to provide spiritual sustenance, for she is not allowed to intercede with divinity to ensure the health and prosperity of family members.

The "Auspicious Heart of the Family"

In one of the interviews about roles and responsibilities across the life cycle, an articulate Oriya woman described a mature, married woman as the "auspicious heart of the family" (*parivararo mangaliko antahkarano*). That particular description seems apt as one reads and rereads these accounts by Oriya women of their daily round of activities and their feelings of well-being. As the interviews demonstrate, a new daughter-in-law gradually becomes an old daughter-in-law, and her access to and enjoyment of greater well-being occurs almost imperceptibly as she attains the domestic managerial responsibilities associated with *prauda* [mature adulthood]. A period in which she has many juniors and still commands all sustenance in a household, *prauda* is a peak period in the lives of each of these women.

For a daughter-in-law to grow old (and well), she has to move out of the kitchen. This move out of the kitchen need not be complete or even substantial, but the possibility that she could move out if she wanted to has to exist. However, her ties to the kitchen continue to be strong enough to make her the primary server of food—a responsibility steeped in prestige that emphasizes the central nature of her role within the family. Through ensuring that each member of the family gets his or her fair share of food, she sustains, very concretely, the life and health of the family. If someone should come to the house for social or business reasons and if the men of the family are otherwise busy, she entertains them. She represents the family, underscoring once more her importance. She performs less and less frequently the rituals of deference, indicating her full assimilation into the family. Finally, she begins to represent the family in its relations with divinity: one of the first tasks of any ritual significance that an old daughter-in-law does is to offer *sandhya*, a ceremony performed at sunset that seeks to keep malevolent spirits at bay while inviting Lakshmi, the goddess of wealth and auspiciousness, into the home.

Of course, other factors, physiological and cultural, limit this involvement in household worship: usually, an old daughter-in-law is young enough to menstruate. She is sexually active and she is still involved in the care of her children, feeding and cleaning them. All these factors make it difficult for her to maintain bodily purity and compromise her ability to approach the divine. It is as a married mother-in-law that these factors begin to lose their salience.

With daughters-in-law entering the household, the business of reproduction is passed on to the younger generation. The older couple withdraw from sexual activity, enabling the mother-in-law to maintain bodily purity more easily. This is also the time when one is no longer involved in taking care of the very old or the very young. One's own children are past needing such care. One's own mother-in-law and father-in-law are either dead or their care has been handed over to the newest daughter-in-law. At this time of life, most Oriya women go through menopause, which eliminates impurity caused by menstruation. Finally, for a postmenopausal Oriya Hindu woman, it is both culturally and physiologically appropriate to go to the temple whenever she wishes, to pray whenever she wishes, to perform the daily *puja* for her family without hindrance, and to function as the intermediary who seeks divine blessings for every member of the family.

Apart from this, an older married woman is also relieved of the physical labor of cooking and cleaning for a large family. While she still retains the responsibilities and privileges associated with *prauda,* she continues to administer the affairs of the household and remains aware of everything that happens to family members. The possibility of geographical mobility, of traveling, of going on pilgrimages, and of visiting relatives also contributes in some measure to her heightened sense of well-being. As a mother-in-law, explicit deference is paid to her by the junior women of the household. While this explicit display of social power must surely increase her sense of well-being, it also provides her with a forum in which to express her opinions. By refusing to accept a daughter-in-law's deference she conveys unmistakably her feelings of displeasure and disapproval without saying a word. A mother-in-law, therefore, has greater opportunity to express negative feelings about other family members, and this perhaps does make her feel better. Unlike the other women in the family, she does not, for the sake of family harmony, have to control what she says or does.

There are of course anxieties that may work to reduce the married Oriya Hindu mother-in-law's feelings of well-being. First, there is the prospect of widowhood and all the connotations that Oriya Hindus attach to that condition. Second, there is the process of growing old and losing the ability to care for oneself physically. While the junior wife has to shake off the constraints that are attached to being new to gain in well-being, the mother-in-law loses some of her wellness because she is looking to an uncertain future.

A Culturally Salient Model of Well-being

In general, women expect the middle phase of their lives, that of mature adulthood, *prauda,* to afford them the most satisfying experiences. According to their accounts, during this phase, they will be either the senior-most woman in the household or the next-to-most senior. As such, a woman is dominant—she has control over her own body and her actions, but more important, she has considerable control over the activities of others within the family. She is also very productive during this phase—she is likely to feel and to be felt central to the order and material prosperity of the family. Finally, she feels coherent—her connections and communication with divinity are now regular and uninterrupted. Dominance coming from seniority, productivity emerging from centrality within the family, and coherence resulting from the capacity to approach divinity without restriction are thus three salient measures of well-being for an Oriya Hindu woman. All imply controlling and managing the transactions and exchanges she has with those above, around, and below her, within the household, between the household, and beyond.

There is another, subsidiary aspect of women's well-being that needs to be mentioned here—the skill and competence with which a woman manages and controls these processes and transactions. In Bhubaneswar, as Lamb (1993) reports for Bengali women, the processes of reconstruction and deconstruction that women undergo as they marry, give birth, undergo affinal assimilation, mature, age, and become widows, require them to skillfully manage change if they are to achieve well-being. Those women who are less competent at managing these processes experience low well-being even during the middle phase of their lives, while those who know when and how to expand and encompass others and when to curtail their transactions, withdraw into themselves, or minimize their exchanges are more likely to achieve higher levels of well-being during all phases of their lives.

Furthermore, we suggest that these three measures (dominance, productivity, and coherence) of well-being are not competing but complementary. Having control over one's own activities and the activities of others makes one central to and productive of the family's well-being. Both of these conditions enable one to control one's interactions with divinity and to approach the gods in a coherent, ordered way. When a woman achieves all three, usually during the middle phase of mature adulthood, her well-being is complete.

Variations around the Ideal Model

What we have described is, of course, an ideal model extracted from our interviews. However, even thirty-seven interviews are enough to make the point that this ideal rarely has a perfect fit to anyone's lived experience. There are women in other family roles who claim to have achieved substantial well-being as well as some married mothers-in-law and old daughters-in-law in the *prauda* phase of life who claim to be miserable. For instance, Priyambada, the married mother-in-law whose description of an average day was quoted earlier, says that she does not even have two annas of well-being. She ascribes her lack of well-being to the conflicts within the family, which she believes result from the lack of respect that younger members display toward their elders:

> Everyone thinks he is the superior of the other, everyone thinks he is the family elder, everyone thinks he has to speak out, that he has to say what his opinion is. . . . I'm not preventing others from talking, I'm only saying, "Think of everything, the person who is talking and the consequences of your talking back before you answer."

In a community in which asymmetry of privilege and responsibility has such salience, it is hardly surprising that lack of respect should lead to such a diminishment of well-being. It is also possible that Priyambada was using the occasion of the interview to inform others in the family of her displeasure with what she perceived as discord within the family. Her daughter-in-law definitely interpreted her statements to indicate just that. This daughter-in-law believed that her own conduct was the focus of the mother-in-law's criticism. The daughter-in-law's attribution seems plausible. At the time of the interview it appeared possible that Priyambada was using her low assessment of her own well-being as a means to arouse the younger woman's guilt at being an "unsatisfactory" daughter-in-law.

And the reverse, too, occurs. There are widowed mothers-in-law who continue to be valued and respected members of the family. There are "sonless" (Kondos 1989, 185) mothers who become the mainstay of their husbands' families. There are new daughters-in-law who dominate household affairs almost as soon as they step across the threshold. Even in this small sample of thirty-seven women such examples can be found, demonstrating, we think, quite conclusively that one must be suspicious of simplistic feminist representations (see, e.g., Kondos 1988, 108). Kondos claims that Hindu women lead such contingent lives that only those who produce sons and who predecease their husbands are deemed successful. The following excerpt, from an interview with a seventy-two-year-old widow, Labanya, whose husband died almost forty years earlier, holds particular relevance here. She describes her day:

I get up in the morning. I clean my teeth, I have tea. After having had tea, it's necessary to make sure that the children have gone to school and I go and do that. And then, maybe someone comes over, like you have come over, and I sit and talk. I have become the elder (*murabbi*) in the family, when people come over, I have to sit and talk to them, we discuss things. They may have tea, I may have some more tea. And then, I go for my bath. After my bath, the cooking would be almost finished, and so I eat. After eating, I take some rest, I lie down. I rest till afternoon. At about four, I get up and again, if people come over, I sit and talk to them. I talk to them till the sun sets. After the sun sets, once more tea is made, I drink some tea and then . . . [Long pause] I have no work. So right here, I take some rest. While I'm resting, the children will come, the *bou*s will come and they will say, "*Ma*, come, eat your rice," and so, I go and eat. And then, I go to bed—what else is there to my day? . . .

Q. Do you do *puja*s to God?

A. [Long pause, then finally, hesitantly] Ye . . . s, ye . . . s . . . This elder *bou*, she does all that. I have become an old woman. I can't have a bath that early in the morning. They all have their baths early and then they pray to God. Eldest son, he bathes, he is the *kalasi* [medium through whom the goddess speaks] at the *Thakurani mandir*. He goes there. . . .

Q. Do you offer *sandhya* in the evening?

A. No, I don't offer any *sandhya*. I don't have that responsibility any more. That is a responsibility that the *bou*s have and that they fulfill. I no longer touch the cooking vessels, they do and so they offer *sandhya*. This *bou* offers *sandhya* or if this one can't, then the other or the other or one of the granddaughters, they offer *sandhya*. That is a burden that has slipped from my head.

Q. Do you tell them what to cook?

A. No, no. I don't bother my head with all that. When they first came to this house then I had to teach them everything. "*Arre, ma*, do this like this, do that like that," I used to tell them. "This food won't be enough" or "That is too much," but now I have grown old and they have all raised their families. What is there for me to teach them now? Now that I am old, I eat a fistful of rice that they give me and I sit. What else is left for me in life? Why should I continue to keep all that in my head?

Q. When did you give up giving directions?

A. It is now thirty years since I left all that. Once this eldest *bou*
came into the house, a few years after that, I stopped running
the house. A few years after eldest *bou* came, another *bou* came
into the house, and a few years later, another *bou* came. In this
way, three *bou*s came. They gave birth to children, and they managed running the house. Why should I try to keep the nuisance
and trouble of running the household on my head? All that I do
nowadays is soothe my grandchildren when they cry, carry them
on my hip when they're small, clean them when they're dirty,
see that they go to school regularly. Or when someone wants advice or when someone wants to give or take money, I do that—
that's my business now. . . .

He [eldest son] keeps nothing. He comes and gives me everything. I keep all the money, when he needs money, he asks me.
He needs 5,000 rupees or 6,000 rupees to pay the laborers who
are repairing this house, he comes to me, I give him the money.
Vegetables have to be bought, I give the grandsons the money to
buy the vegetables. I keep all the money. When I go away to
Unit VI to be with my middle son, then I leave some money
with eldest *bou* for household expenses but the rest of the money
is still with me and he [eldest son] will come to Unit VI when
he needs money.

One can see that Labanya is hardly involved in the day-to-day activities of the household and has little contact with divinity. But even a
casual reading of her daily activities makes clear how she continues to
be the center of her family. She holds the family purse strings. Her
sons choose to give her all their earnings. No expense is incurred without her knowledge. More important, according to her account, her
sons and her daughters-in-law make it explicit that they care for her:
they are concerned that she relish what she eats, that her clothes are
decent. They desire her comfort.

And then there is Pranati, an old daughter-in-law, mother of three
daughters, who recognizes that she has disappointed her mother-in-
law and father-in-law by not providing sons for the *kutumba* (lineage).
This affects her sense of well-being, her score of eight annas being the
lowest among all the old daughters-in-law. While this score may reflect
her sorrow at not having had sons, that inadequacy clearly does not
cramp her style when it comes to running the household. She is not
relegated to some corner of the house, ignored and despised because

she is sonless; instead, as one reads her interview as well as those of her mother-in-law and her younger sister-in-law it becomes quite clear that the entire household depends on her for its efficient functioning. She decides what will be cooked. She shops for the entire family, selecting the clothes that others will wear. She entertains guests and relatives when they visit. She plays the lead role when it comes to arranging her husband's younger brother's marriage. Sonlessness, though a matter for personal sorrow, does not determine her position within the family; in fact, it does not even define her as inauspicious. For these women, success and failure are not predefined. Being a widow or sonless are constraining circumstances but they do not absolutely define success or failure.

Labanya and Pranati are examples of ways in which "psyche and culture make each other up" (Shweder 1991, 73). Cultural meanings and possibilities are picked up by these women, each according to her particular talents; they then create their own life situations. Thus Labanya is not just a widow, she is also the loving mother who singlehandedly raised her three sons to adulthood. As such she is entitled to their respect and devotion, an entitlement that she appropriates in full measure. Again, Pranati is not merely a sonless mother. She is also the dutiful daughter-in-law who has never stinted in her performance of *sewa*. As such, she has extended her influence through the family, making her its single most important member. According to Kondos's formulation, these women would be "failures," and yet, by all accounts, they participate fully in running their households and raising their children. More important, they feel good about themselves.

The Question of Subversion/Resistance

On the basis of our experience in Old Town, we have come to harbor the suspicion that the representation of the Hindu housewife as a rebel or subversive is largely a projection of critical ethnography grasping at straws. Quite baldly stated, almost nothing we have encountered in our interviews and observations implies a deep political critique of family or social life or the desirability of subverting the social system. There is an absence of subversive voices in Old Town. While complaint could, perhaps, be regarded as a language of "subversion" and the dragging of feet while performing household chores as acts of "resistance," it is curious that only old daughters-in-law and mothers-in-law do so. New daughters-in-law who have the most to gain from subverting the system do not complain and rarely drag their feet. Some of the reasons, of course, could be that they are trained to suppress their words, to anticipate negative consequences from expressing themselves. It is true that their positions within the family are fragile, and that they have yet to accumulate power or exercise substantial influence. Only an old daughter-in-law or a mother-in-law, secure of her position within the family, could engage in such verbal and nonverbal displays of discontent with impunity.

We believe, however, that a more accurate representation of the situation is that neither complaint nor dragging one's feet can be credibly viewed as subversion or resistance. In Old Town they are just the ways in which confident women express their dissatisfaction or displeasure with what is happening within the family—we do not believe they indicate any desire for radical change.

Ultimately extended families do break up. Each brother lives separately with just his own wife and children. This is the nuclear beginning for a fresh cycle of joint family living. A catalyst is usually needed to set this breakup into motion. Often this is the death of the father or of both father and mother. Yet joint family living remains the ideal. Daughters-in-law, both new and old, continue to live jointly because they are realistic and pragmatic about the options open to them. They make the best of whatever resources they have, realizing that they often gain thereby. Apart from the advantages that these women themselves mention when explaining why they continue to live within the joint family—those of greater economic, social, and personal security and the sharing of household chores and child rearing—an important reason lies in the fact that there *is* room for manoeuvering, for achievement, and for working toward personal goals such as increased power within the family, a greater say in the process of family decision making, a sense of getting newly recruited women and their children to do what one wants them to do, and the possibility of ensuring the future success of one's children.

What is remarkable and worth noting is not the insurgency of these women but rather their attitude of active acceptance. Sudhangini, a daughter who was to be married just six weeks after the interview, in talking of her future life in her mother-in-law's home, says,

> In truth, however affectionate the new family, I will feel
> sad for some time remembering this home but then as one

179

> day passes and then another and then another, the sense
> that this is mine will begin even with respect to the other
> home and the people there. . . . One has to accept every-
> thing as one's own. *Nona-bou* [father-mother] haven't
> given us our *karma*, they have given us only *janma* [birth].
> They have given me birth, and they have also given me
> *sikhya* [learning], they have given me *jogyata* [compe-
> tence], that is my good fortune. Now with that, if I decide
> to do good work in their house, then it will arouse their
> appreciation, but if I don't do good work, they will criticize
> me and that I will have to endure. But it is all in my own
> hands—my *karma* is in my hands. If I want to do good
> and gain appreciation, it is in my hands.

Most people in the Old Town hold to this future-oriented notion
as a major aspect of the karmic process. This sense of having control
over what happens in one's life, of being responsible for one's own
destiny, this belief that "human intentions really do matter" (Babb
1983, 180) runs through several of the other interviews, though perhaps no other woman articulated the idea so fluently. All these
women—daughters, daughters-in-law, and mothers-in-law—recognize the givens in each of their situations. They recognize the factors
that they cannot change. But they also realize that it is possible to work
within an emerging situation for success. In fact, these women see such
compromise and accommodation as admirable signs of maturity.

Furthermore, these women share with other Oriya Hindus a particular way of looking at life. They look on family life as a process, one
that is continuously shifting and changing, never complete or static.
And so, when they marry and enter a household, they do not see themselves as new daughters-in-law for the rest of their lives. They can see
in front of them women at different stages in the life course. They see
themselves as occupying those positions in the not too distant future.
If one has to understand their motivations and actions, one has to
assume their future-oriented, developmental perspective. They do not
see themselves as victims. They are looking ahead into the future, perhaps ten or fifteen years, seeing themselves contributing to and controlling family decisions. Even the very old do not lack this future orientation. Indeed, most people in Old Town see death as merely a
punctuation mark in the process of living numerous lives, and they

are clearly busy at work preparing the way for the life they expect to come next.

Oppressors and Victims? More on Gender Relations in the Old Town

Among Oriya Hindus in the temple town of Bhubaneswar, men and women recognize one other as social actors, equal in importance and effectiveness, whose activities complement their own. To cast men as oppressors and women as victims is to try to establish a false dichotomy, one that does not exist within the Oriya point of view. If one wants to organize Oriya social life in terms of those in control and those controlled, then it makes much more sense to discuss the matter generationally, with the older generation controlling the activities of the younger generation. But even here one needs to temper this statement because age is not valued in and of itself. Only those older people who care for and are responsible for the welfare of others are respected and their opinions valued.

Furthermore, as anyone familiar with life and society in Hindu India knows, men (especially younger men) as well as women live with major constraints. Neither a young man nor a young woman has the right to choose, although they do have some rights to veto. Most Oriya men and women, just like most Hindu men and women in other parts of the subcontinent, do not decide for themselves what Westerners would regard as the two most crucial decisions of a person's life: their professions and their marriages. This is not to say that there is no difference between men's and women's lives, for, most significantly, men can move and interact with others quite freely.

Whether women regard this freedom as an unmitigated advantage is doubtful. Many women pitied the interviewer's predicament, one that necessitated "wandering from door to door looking for people to talk to." One widow, in responding to whether she planned to send her seventeen-year-old daughter to college, said good-humoredly, "Why? So that she will become like you, going from door to door talking to people?"

Sakti: What it Means to be a Woman in the Old Town

Even today, most Oriya Hindus believe that female power (*sakti*) energizes the natural and social world. In ordinary, everyday conversations, women in Old Town describe a woman as the embodiment of adya sakti (primordial power), *matru sakti* (mother power), and *stri sakti* (woman power). According to these women such *sakti* is harnessed for the good of society and the family. It is power reined in, power that is controlled from within, power that is exercised responsibly. A woman is said to hold the destiny of her husband's family in the palm of her hands. If she is irresponsible in her management of the family's resources, the household does not prosper. If she commits adultery, the family disintegrates.[11] These women say that a woman maintains her chastity not because she lives in a joint family and others exercise a watchful eye over what she does, but because she disciplines herself. This is a remarkable assertion, quite unlike what Derne (1993) found among Hindu men in Varanasi, who relied on family structure and external forces to control their behavior. For Oriya Hindu women, to be truly effective, control has to come from within; only this ensures the spiritual and material prosperity of the family.

It is relevant to mention here some of the understandings that Old Town residents have about a popular icon of the goddess Kali in which she is shown with her foot placed squarely on the chest of a supine Siva (for a detailed description of this study, see Menon and Shweder [1994]). When men and women interpret this icon, they describe the protruding tongue of the goddess as the mark of her shame (*lajya*) at having stepped on her husband, her personal god. Acknowledging her husband's social and ritual superiority enables her to become calm, to rein in her power to destroy. Many of those knowledgeable about this icon say that Siva does not do anything to stop her, because, in fact, he *can* do nothing to stop her (Kali is far too powerful). Rather, she *chooses* to recognize what she owes her husband in terms of respect and deference and so stops her destruction. According to the Oriya Hindus of Old Town, her choice is an entirely "autonomous" act.

From the perspective of many Oriya Hindus, Ortner's formulation (1974) nature:culture::woman:man (nature is to culture as woman is to man) seems unnatural. For Oriya Hindus, a woman derives her strength and power from her closeness to nature. She, like nature, creates and reproduces, but such power gathers its full significance only because it is subject to cultural, ultimately moral, control that originates from within her. As Ramanujan points out, the Lévi-Straussian opposition between nature and culture is itself culture bound. In the Hindu alternative, "culture is enclosed in nature, nature is reworked in culture, so that we cannot tell the difference" (Ramanujan 1990,

50). This is yet another of the "container-contained relations" (ibid. 50) that extend to other Hindu concepts and ideas.

So, Oriya Hindu women think of themselves as intrinsically powerful. Simply by being female, by sharing the gendered physiology of the great goddess of Hinduism, they believe they share her power to create and destroy. But, they also recognize that unrestrained exercise of such power inevitably leads to destruction. Such power has to be curbed not by an external force but from within, through a voluntary, autonomous act of self-discipline. We believe that it is this self-discipline that those who perceive the world through Westernized lenses misinterpret as subordination.

Culturally Available Means to Power

Personal growth, then, for these women is not conceived by them to be some kind of process of self-realization that involves detaching themselves from others. Instead, it is a power that involves an increasing denseness in one's relations with others. It depends on one becoming a strong weaver of the fabric of the family.

An Oriya Hindu woman achieves this kind of personal growth in a variety of ways. Behavior that from a Western perspective may be misconstrued as an index of subordination and passivity often lends itself to being seen as something quite different when seen from a Hindu perspective or understood in terms of local meanings. The Hindu notion of the body emphasizes (Kakar 1982; Zimmerman 1979) its relative openness to both improvement and contamination. Thus when a new daughter-in-law takes orders from her mother-in-law or eats her leftovers or massages her feet or drinks the water that has been used to wash the older woman's feet, these practices are not a measure of her subordination or passivity. Rather they are ways she takes into her body potent substances from a superior. Ultimately these internalized substances empower her. Progressively, with time, such behavior increases her influence and control within the family.

Again, *sewa,* or service to others, is a culturally significant way of achieving power. When a woman cooks, serves, and takes care of members of the joint family, she is building relationships in very concrete ways. Many women compared cooking and serving to acts of *bhakti* or devotion, requiring the same degree of concentration and attention to detail as that involved in worshiping God and leading to similar feelings of serenity and contentment.

Self-abnegation or self-denial is yet another culturally salient way of gaining moral authority. While from a Western perspective self-abnegation could be interpreted as a kind of deprivation, that is not what it means to an Oriya Hindu woman. Fasting, eating last, and eating leftovers are seen as ways to garner moral authority. And when, after years of self-denial, a woman requests or decides or commands that something should be so, her husband and her adult sons cannot but accede to her, for no man in the family equals her in moral stature.

Conclusion: The Moral Discourse of Anthropology

Think of the Oriya Hindu woman's life as a movement in three dimensions: outward and upward with time being the third dimension. Her life moves outward because with time she is no longer restricted to the kitchen, and she can ultimately move freely within the house and sometimes go outside the house accompanied by only a child. Her life moves upward because with time it becomes socially and physiologically possible for her to approach divinity.

A new daughter-in-law is essentially locked into the kitchen, which is often referred to as the heart of the household, because it is the place where the ancestral spirits (*pitru loku*) reside and are fed. But with time and age, when she begins to play a greater and greater role in making decisions within the family, she moves to other spaces within the house. She has access to the *puja* room and "higher" gods, the household deities (*ishta devata*). With old age and widowhood, this outward movement is completed, and old widows, who are now peripheral to household affairs, often live in an outer room that overlooks the street. On the other hand, the upward movement is temporarily halted, for although old widows continue to pray, they are relatively inauspicious members of the family who are no longer involved in family rituals. They are free to absolve themselves of their own accumulated spiritual debts for the sake of their own personal salvation but little more.

To represent women's lives is a difficult and complex task. If anthropology as a discipline views itself as a means to understanding one's self and one's own culture by journeying through other selves in other cultures, then it is important that feminist anthropologists understand the dialectic they are engaged in. At the moment, the intellectual insights of feminist anthropology cannot be easily disentangled from their political agenda, for there is a transparent attempt in feminist literature to universalize women's oppression and to indulge in myth-making for political ends. If anthropology is a discipline that studies differences, then it is necessary that feminists devise the means to analyze and interpret differences that they find personally disturbing without disrespecting the objects of their study (see Boon 1994). To ignore the alternative moral goods emphasized and made manifest in family life practice in India, to presume that inner control, service, and deferred gratification amount to subordination and acceptance of oppression, to represent Hindu women in South Asia as either victims or subversives is not only to dishonor these women—it is to engage in little more than a late-twentieth-century version of cognitive and moral imperialism.

NOTES

1. For more on this temple and the community that serves it, see Mahapatra (1981), Seymour (1983), Shweder et al. (1990), Shweder (1991), Shweder et al. (1997).

2. For a complete description of this sample see Menon and Shweder (1994).

3. Paul Cleary and his associates at the Harvard Medical School have collected comparable data on American women. In a large telephone survey women were asked to assess their satisfaction on a ten-point scale.

4. An *anna* is a coin that is no longer in circulation. In pre-Independence India, there were six *paisa* (or *pice*) to an *anna* and sixteen *annas* to a *rupee*.

5. We should, perhaps, clarify that our particular understanding is neither unusual nor peculiar to us. Today in India there is a burgeoning women's movement (see *India Today*, 30 September 1995) that disdains the label "feminism," distances itself from Western-inspired feminist movements, and does not identify gender equality at home or in the workplace as a significant goal. Instead, it seeks to identify potential sources of female power defined in Hindu terms and works to achieve female empowerment within that framework.

6. This is the tradition that worships the Sakti or Devi, the great goddess of Hinduism. Followers believe that the world is energized by her and that in her lies the ultimate meaning of life in this world.

7. For the Oriya Hindus of Old Town, *samsaro* stands for the family, for household life, the entire world of living beings as well as for the never-ending cycle of rebirths and redeaths that characterizes all existence this side of release and liberation.

8. Not all Oriya Hindu women have sons, but traditionally, people in Old Town overcome this by adopting a relative's son, preferably one's own daughter's second or third son. The child is adopted formally into his maternal grandfather's lineage and all ritual ties to his biological father are severed. Dukhi, the old daughter-in-law quoted earlier, and her husband have done just that.

9. The Lingaraj temple bathing tank—literally, "ocean of droplets."

10. *Nirmaliya* is a solution made of water and desiccated *prasad*, which are leftovers of divine offerings from the Lingaraj temple.

11. According to Oriya Hindus of Old Town, the effects on the family of a man

committing adultery are far less profound than if a woman does so, because men are considered to be marginal to the well-being of the family.

References

Babb, L. A. 1983. "Destiny and Responsibility: Karma in Popular Hinduism." In *Karma: An Anthropological Inquiry,* edited by C. F. Keyes and E. V. Daniel. Berkeley and Los Angeles: University of California Press.

Bennett, L. 1983. *Dangerous Wives and Sacred Sisters: Social and Symbolic Roles of High-Caste Women in Nepal.* New York: Columbia University Press.

Boon, J. A. 1994. "Circumscribing Circumcision/Uncircumsion." In *Implicit Understandings,* edited by S. B. Schwartz. Cambridge: Cambridge University Press.

Brown, J. K., and V. Kerns, eds. 1985. *In Her Prime: A New View of Middle-Aged Women.* South Hadley, Mass.: Bergin & Harvey.

Derne, S. 1993. "Equality and Hierarchy between Adult Brothers: Culture and Sibling Relations in N. Indian Urban Joint Families." In *Siblings in South Asia: Brothers and Sisters in Cultural Context,* edited by C. W. Nuckolls. New York: Guilford Press.

Dhruvarajan, V. 1988. *Hindu Women and the Power of Ideology.* South Hadley, Mass.: Bergin & Garvey.

Fruzetti, L. M. 1982. *The Gift of a Virgin: Women, Marriage, and Ritual in a Bengali Society.* New Brunswick, N.J.: Rutgers University Press.

Haidt, J., S. Koller, and M. Dias. 1993. "Affect, Culture, and Morality; Or, Is It Wrong to Eat Your Dog?" *Journal of Personality and Social Psychology* 65:613–28.

Inden, R. B., and R. W. Nicholas. 1977. *Kinship in Bengali Culture.* Chicago: University of Chicago Press.

Jacobson, D. 1982. "Studying the Changing Roles of Women in Rural India." *Signs* 8 (1): 132–37.

Jain, D., and N. Bannerjee, eds. 1985. *Tyranny of the Household: Investigative Essays on Women's Work.* New Delhi: Shakti Books.

Jeffrey P., R. Jeffrey, and A. Lyons. 1988. *Labour Pains and Labour Power.* London: Zed Books.

Jensen, L. B. 1995. "Habits of the Heart Revisited: Autonomy, Community, and Divinity in Adults' Moral Language." *Qualitative Sociology* 18:71–86.

Kakar, S. 1982. *Shamans, Mystics and Doctors.* New York: Knopf.

Kondos, V. 1989. "Subjection and Domicile: Some Problematic Issues Relating to High Caste Nepalese Women." In *Society from the Inside Out,* edited by J. N. Gray and D. J. Mearns. New Delhi: Sage Publications.

Lamb, S. 1993. "Growing in the Net of Maya." Ph.D. dissertation. University of Chicago, Department of Anthropology.

Liddle, J., and R. Joshi. 1986. *Daughters of Independence: Gender, Caste and Class in India.* London: Zed Books Ltd.

Mahapatra, M. 1981. *Traditional Structure and Change in an Orissa Temple*. Calcutta: Punthi Pustak.

Marriott, M. 1976. "Hindu Transactions: Diversity without Dualism." In *Transaction and Meaning: Directions in the Anthropology of Exchange and Symbolic Behavior*, edited by Bruce Kapferer. Philadelphia: Institute for the Study of Human Issues.

Menon, U., and R. A. Shweder. 1994. "Kali's Tongue: Cultural Psychology and the Power of 'Shame' in Orissa, India." In *Culture and the Emotions*, edited by H. Markus and S. Kitayama. Washington, D. C.: American Psychological Association.

Minturn, L. 1993. *Sita's Daughters: Coming Out of Purdah*. New York: Oxford University Press.

Ortner, S. 1974. Is Female to Male as Nature Is to Culture? In *Women, Culture and Society*, edited by M. Rosaldo and L. Lamphere. Stanford, Calif.: Stanford University Press.

Papanek, H., and G. Minault 1982. *Separate Worlds: Studies of Purdah in South Asia*. New Delhi: Chanakya Publications.

Raheja, G. G., and A. G. Gold 1994. *Listen to the Heron's Words*. Berkeley and Los Angeles: University of California Press.

Ramanujan, A. K. 1983. "The Indian Oedipus." In *Oedipus: A Folklore Casebook*, edited by L. Edmonds and A. Dundes, 234–61. New York: Garland Publishing.

———. 1990. "Is There an Indian Way of Thinking? An Informal Essay." In *India through Hindu Categories*, edited by McKim Marriott. New Delhi: Sage Publications.

Roy, M. 1975. *Bengali Women*. Chicago: University of Chicago Press.

Seymour, S. 1983. "Household Structure and Status and Expressions of Affect in India." *Ethos* 11:263–77.

Sharma, U. 1980. *Women, Work and Property in North-West India*. Honolulu: University of Hawaii Press.

Shweder, R. A. 1990. "In Defense of Moral Realism." *Child Development* 61:2060–68.

———. 1991. *Thinking through Cultures*. Cambridge, Mass.: Harvard University Press.

———. 1994. "Are Moral Intuitions Self-Evident Truths?" Special issue, "Symposium on James Q. Wilson's *The Moral Sense*." *Criminal Justice Ethics* 13:24–31.

———. 1996. "True Ethnography: The Lore, the Law, and the Lure." In *Ethnography and Human Development: Context and Meaning in Social Inquiry*, edited by R. Jessor, A. Colby, and R. A. Shweder. Chicago: University of Chicago Press.

Shweder, R. A., M. Mahapatra, and J. G. Miller. 1990. "Culture and Moral Development." In *Cultural Psychology: Essays on Comparative Human Development*, edited by J. Stigler, R. A. Shweder, and G. H. Herdt. Cambridge: Cambridge University Press.

Shweder, R. A., N. C. Much, M. Mahapatra, and L. Park. 1997. "The 'Big Three' of Morality (Autonomy, Community and Divinity), and the 'Big Three' Explanations of Suffering." In *Morality and Health,* edited by A. Brandt and P. Rozin. New York: Routledge.

Wadley, S. S. 1980. *The Powers of Tamil Women.* South Asia Series no. 6. Syracuse, N.Y.: Syracuse University Press.

———. 1986. "Women and the Hindu Tradition." In *Women in India,* edited by S. S. Wadley and D. Jacobson. New Delhi: Manohar Publishers.

Wadley, S. S., and D. Jacobson. 1986. *Women in India.* New Delhi: Manohar Publishers.

Zimmerman, F. 1979. "Remarks on the Body in Ayurvedic Medicine." *South Asian Digest of Regional Writing* 18:10–26.

SIX

Fertility and Maturity in Africa: Gusii Parents in Middle Adulthood

Robert A. LeVine and Sarah LeVine

At the present time, with birthrates in Europe, North America, and Japan at the lowest level for human populations in history and with fertility declining rapidly in much of Asia and Latin America, it may be difficult to understand the perspective of an African people whose dominant ideals of adulthood are organized around the bearing of many children. When world fertility was dropping between 1965 and 1985, many birthrates in sub-Saharan Africa were *increasing* to new peaks for national populations. Kenya led the way, with a crude birthrate of 54 per thousand population in 1979, more than five times that of European countries at that time, and the Gusii people of Kisii District had the highest birthrate in Kenya (table 1). For Gusii parents, the desirability of high fertility, averaging about ten children per women, was unchallenged, and men and women at forty years of age were deeply concerned with continued childbearing. Their experience of middle adulthood, the years from 40 to 60, can only be understood in terms of the meanings of reproductive performance in the culturally organized Gusii life course during the latter part of this century.

The twentieth century has profoundly altered the lives of men and women throughout sub-Saharan Africa. At the century's end, precolonial (i.e., nineteenth century) ideals for the life course are still cherished in many communities, but the social conditions for their realization have changed, creating dilemmas for contemporary adults. Some changes have been caused by dislocation and new scarcities of resources, but others with equal impact have been produced by newfound abundance, opportunities, and the satisfaction of personal goals. The fulfillment of their reproductive goals, for example, has created an ironic predicament for East African parents: having long sought to maximize the number of their offspring for potent economic, social, and spiritual reasons but in an environment full of lethal risks to children, they were able to see child mortality rates finally drop after 1950. But child survival has been accompanied by rapid population growth and resultant scarcities of land, food, and other resources and a more

TABLE 1. Mean Number of Children Ever Born to Women
45–49 Years Old

Location	Number of Children
Kenya (nationwide)	7.17
Kisii District (rural)	9.04

SOURCE: *1979 Population Census of Kenya.* Vol. 2, *Analytical Report,* p. 70. Central Bureau of Statistics, Ministry of Planning and Development, Nairobi.

competitive environment in which to raise children. It could be said that, for most African agricultural peoples before 1950, there was a true scarcity of children and that for many of the same peoples in the following decades, children became abundant and then superabundant. But this is what outside observers say; for East African parents themselves, another pregnancy or delivery usually remains a welcome event, a consummation devoutly desired rather than a terrifying harbinger of poverty, even in middle adulthood when the parents' earlier children are becoming parents.

The conditions of life in sub-Saharan Africa differ considerably from those elsewhere in ways that favor high fertility: outside South Africa (where fertility *has* declined), Africa is the most rural of continents, and rural people everywhere tend to prefer larger families than do urban dwellers. Furthermore, although they are poor by global standards, many rural Africans have experienced rising cash incomes and expanding economic opportunities in recent decades, which makes them feel optimistic about future family resources even when their landholdings are reduced. (There are also parts of the continent, particularly in West Africa, that are still afflicted with high rates of sterility or child mortality.) These environmental factors are important but inadequate by themselves to explain why, particularly in East Africa where the Gusii live, fertility remains high; for a deeper understanding, it is necessary to explore the ways in which environmental realities are translated into the subjective experience of parents through the medium of a local culture. We begin with some informative incidents from our fieldwork among the Gusii of Kenya during 1974–76.

GUSII FERTILITY EXPERIENCE

The Gusii are a people of 1.2 million who speak a unique Bantu language and inhabit a cool, well-watered highland area in the southwestern corner of Kenya, just east of Lake Victoria. They live in dispersed settlements organized by patrilineal descent, with each family devoting itself to agriculture and animal husbandry on land owned by its patriarch. Their geographical location, far from cities and major transportation routes, isolated the Gusii from many of the social changes affecting the rest of Kenya until the second half of the twentieth century, but by the mid-1970s their situation and their responses to change resembled that of many other agricultural peoples in Kenya and other parts of eastern Africa. The demographic situation facing Gusii parents at that time can be illustrated by the predicament of a sixty-year-old man whom we shall call Ombese.

Ombese lived at "Morongo," where we did our fieldwork. His father, one of the original settlers of the Morongo area in the early 1930s, had owned a large hillside of 75 acres, and Ombese as one of three sons had inherited about 20 acres. As he prospered in small business as well as agriculture, Ombese married six wives who, by 1975 had borne more than fifty children, twenty-five of them sons, each entitled to inherit a share of his land. Some of his sons were engaged in modern occupational careers–one was a local school principal, others worked in Nairobi—and Ombese himself was a wholesaler and shopkeeper. But they all still looked to the land for a sustenance and security it could not adequately provide its 61 residents (in 1975) or its potential inheritors. Not content to sink into poverty, most of Ombese's wives and sons supplemented cultivation with a wide range of other remunerative activities. But their frustrations about Ombese's failure to provide them with enough land for a livelihood based on agriculture, as Gusii patriarchs were expected to do, had led to tension and conflict within the domestic group and erosion of family trust. Ombese tended to isolate himself from the family he had spawned, living with his sixth and youngest wife, with whom he continued to have children. Reproductive success on a limited land base had turned prosperity into tension in one generation.

Everyone at Morongo was aware of Ombese's problems and many criticized him for poor or even immoral management of family relationships, but no one, in his family or outside it, thought birth limitation was (or would have been) the proper solution. Indeed, it was not unusual in Morongo for families who had had adequate landholdings in the 1950s to leave each son of 1975 an acre or less on which to raise a family. By the 1979 census, Kisii District (i.e., Gusiiland) had become the most densely populated district in Kenya. But this did not incline Gusii parents toward family planning: the Kenya National Fertility Survey of 1977 found only 1% of Gusii women to be using contraception, the lowest among Kenya's ethnic groups. (This had risen to 15% by 1985, but many were using contraceptive technology for birth spacing rather than for terminating their childbearing.) The Gusii we knew were not only capable of "rational choice" but were constantly and conspicuously strategizing and seeking economic opportunities; all of their strategies for advancement, however, assumed they would have many children.

An incident occurring early in our fieldwork of 1974–76 sheds some light on the role of fertility as an ultimate goal in the Gusii life course. We attended the funeral of a sixty-eight-year-old woman, the mother of a man we knew. A large number of people, perhaps two hundred, were gathered for the ceremony, and a piece of paper was handed around that listed her dates of birth, marriage, and conversion to Christianity, and then the numbers of her children, grandchildren, and great-grandchildren (males and females separately), with the total number of progeny at the bottom. At other funerals we attended, the summation of accomplished fertility was indexed simply by the presence of those known to be the numerous progeny of the deceased (LeVine 1982). The Gusii do not generally consider it in good taste to refer overtly to the number of children or descendants a person has, particularly in the presence of that person. The literate survivors of the old woman, however, decided that the occasion created by her funeral would make the numerical accounting of her reproductive performance an honor that all could pay her rather than (as it would be in everyday social life) a flaunting of accomplishment that might arouse jealousy.

A second incident indicating an interest in quantifying fertility involved a man in his late sixties whom we shall call "Obaita"; his large homestead was even more rent by conflicts among his wives and sons than that of Ombese, and he was also ailing with a terminal disease. Obaita privately told one of our Gusii assistants that he liked to sit at the top of the hill, look down on his homestead, and count the number of people he "had" in his homestead, that is, his wives, his descendants, and their spouses; this counting gave him comfort. We believe that Obaita was revealing what many Gusii people do privately as they grow older, namely comfort themselves with the thought of their successful fertility and that of their children.

The other side of the coin was demonstrated by the funeral of a twenty-eight-year-old unmarried man who died of natural but unknown causes at a Nairobi hospital. Although his father had the funeral announced over the radio, hardly anyone attended, for two related reasons. First, the size of funeral attendance usually reflects the deceased's stage of reproductive maturity—large numbers come to funerals of the elderly, like the woman mentioned above, but no one outside the family comes when an infant or young child dies (LeVine 1982). When a man is old enough to marry but has not done so before death, he is in a sense doubly immature, in that he not only died without issue but also without even having established a jural reproductive union, and nonattendance signifies this tragedy. Second, in this case the young man was living with a woman who was not a Gusii, and he died on the operating table in the hospital where he worked, all of which suggested to his parents' kin and neighbors that he was the victim of a conspiracy by people of other ethnic groups and that anyone attending the funeral might be harmed by the malevolence that killed him. Thus his reproductive failure was compounded by the mysterious and potentially contagious conditions of his death. The funeral was a sad and humiliating occasion for the young man's parents.

It should be evident from these incidents that there is a great deal at stake in childbearing for Gusii men and women: reproductive accomplishment is not only required for ultimate social judgments of maturity in a Gusii community but also intimately involved in the anticipations of success and failure in the life course that regulate the emotions of adults. This is most clearly observed during the middle years of adulthood.

FERTILITY IN MIDDLE ADULTHOOD

A forty-year-old married woman in 1974 was pregnant and told us she was worried about whether the child would be a boy. She had eight daughters and this might be her last chance to have a son. The trouble with daughters for the Gusii is not that they require dowry, as in India; on the contrary, they are supposed to bring in cattle as bridewealth, and although by 1974 one could not count on getting the bridewealth, there was always hope. The problem with a daughter is that, as in much of India as well as Africa, she moves to her husband's place at marriage (even when the bridewealth is not paid), leaving her mother behind. If a woman has no sons, she will be "alone," that is, she will have no daughter-in-law to replace her own daughters as a helper and companion, and without an adult son, she will be unprotected in the factional politics of the Gusii family as well as lacking the resident grandchildren that provide child labor, sociability, and continuity of her line within the husband's lineage. Furthermore, as Gusii women would say in the 1950s, you must have a son so that his son will bury you: the grandson customarily digs his grandmother's grave. And while a woman's grandchildren through her daughters often have an especially affectionate relationship with her that is emotionally expressed at funerals, they do not count in the same sense that sons' children do. (When we asked an old, university-educated Gusii friend how many grandchildren he had, he counted up the number of his sons's children; it had not occurred to him to include the children of his daughters.)

The Gusii talk about a woman who reaches menopause without a son as if it were a death sentence. She will live out her life lonely and unprotected, lacking both the material rewards and the status that come from having a son and imagining a miserable funeral and extinction of her line.

As it happened, the pregnant woman gave birth to a ninth girl and was extremely downcast afterward; later she tried again and gave birth to a tenth daughter. This meant she would have daughters at home until she was almost sixty but not afterward, and as long as her husband did not take a second wife (which he might be tempted to do in order to have a male heir)—she would not have to fight for her rights within the family. Her life was hardly at an end, but it would lack many of the rewards a Gusii woman is entitled to expect during the middle and later years of adulthood.

This was an unusual case; the most frequent problem a Gusii woman faces in middle adulthood is widowhood, which permits her to stay in her marital home but ties her to a leviratic husband who fathers her children (in her late husband's name) until she reaches menopause, after which he may or may not continue to visit.[1] Widowhood creates a serious crisis when the wife has borne no sons by the time the husband dies or afterward; once it is clear that she has reached menopause, she is permitted to take the bridewealth paid for one of her daughters and "marry" a young woman to be impregnated by one of the late husband's patrilineal kin, in the hope of getting a son who will count as son of the dead man (since he would have owned the cattle paid for his daughter). This practice, termed "woman marriage" by Evans-Pritchard (1953) in his study of the Nuer of the Sudan, happened a number of times in Morongo, most recently on our 1988 visit. The advantage to the widow is a second set of chances at getting a son who will not only bring the usual benefits to a mother but also prevent the husband's patrimony, that is, his land and cattle, from being inherited by his collateral kin (brothers and cousins).

"Woman marriage" for widows without sons is one of several special arrangements the Gusii have for permitting persons with unusual reproductive careers to get benefits from childbearing that might otherwise be lost. Another is the provision for a married couple who have had no son until just before the wife reached menopause, for example, when she was forty-five and her husband fifty-five. If their son married in the normal age range of twenty-five to thirty, they might never live to "see" their grandchildren. Thus a Gusii custom called *okoboererwa* permits them to arrange the son's marriage at the age of fifteen to an older woman, providing his parents the consummation of grandparenthood in their own lifetime.

From the Gusii viewpoint, furthermore, the bearing of a son is simply an extension of his parents' reproductive careers; their goal is to be the parents of a man in a fertile and legitimate reproductive union. This was dramatically illustrated at the initiation ceremony of a boy who was his mother's eldest son. Initiation is regarded as a major step toward marriage and fatherhood, and while the boy was in seclusion recovering from being circumcised, the happy celebration of the many adults who gathered to eat and drink was focused on his mother as the mother of a boy who would soon marry and have a wife to bear children that would make her a grandmother and an elder female in the home. Parents are promoted to a higher age status by the reproductive maturation of their sons.

Continuity of a woman's childbearing until an age plausibly associated with normal menopause is regarded as essential by most Gusii women. One exception we encountered in 1975 was a high school–educated woman living outside the rural area who told us she had a tubal ligation after giving birth to her fifth child, and while this was a decision shared with her husband, she told her female friends that she was simply unable to give birth any more, because "they would not understand" why she would voluntarily shorten her reproductive career. Among the rural people of Morongo, anxiety would be aroused by a woman with only five children who could not have more, even if several were sons (as was the case with the woman who had been sterilized). In such a case, it would not be the numbers or the lack of male descendants causing concern but the meaning of reproductive discontinuity as an omen of disaster to the whole family.

Married women are expected to give birth about every two years from the time they first get pregnant (between sixteen and eighteen years old) until some point after forty; some women go on bearing children until fifty or beyond. Under these circumstances, a woman would have her fifth child when she was around twenty-six years old and her tenth child ten years later. (Average fertility is somewhat lower than this implies because of reproductive problems, such as miscarriage and difficulty getting pregnant, which become more frequent as women get older, lengthening their actual birth intervals.) When a woman in her late twenties or early thirties goes three years without getting pregnant, everyone in the family and neighborhood thinks something is wrong: this could be indicative of *emechando*, afflictions. An interruption in the birth sequence, like an abnormal birth (twins, breech delivery, albino) or reproductive dysfunction (miscarriage, child death, male sterility or impotence), means either that the ancestors have been neglected and will escalate the afflictions (to the point of exterminating the family) unless placated or that a witch has targeted the woman or her family for misfortune and eventual extinction. The only way to find out is to consult a diviner and to follow her instructions for ancestral sacrifice or other measures to be taken. These measures, which can include elaborate rituals and the sacrifice of goats or even a bull, are expensive. That they were nevertheless often taken in Morongo, even by people who were not prosperous, indicates not only that those affected believed their lives were in danger but also the political nature of Gusii family life: in a polygynous situation, if the first wife goes on bearing children when the second wife cannot get pregnant again, then their husband has to do whatever seems necessary to rectify the imbalance and avert conflict between the wives and their children. If the man is a monogamist, neglecting the sacrifices and other rituals necessary to get his wife's reproductive career back on track means his own reproductive career will be stalled; he will be criticized by kin and neighbors, and his wife will suspect him of planning to take a second wife. Thus men felt compelled to invest their resources in restoring reproductive continuity in the family.

Another way of explaining the maintenance of reproductive continuity among Gusii men and women is in terms of the quest for personal security. When women gave birth on schedule to "normal" babies, they felt safe from the threat of spiritual affliction or the malevolence of witches. When pregnancy was delayed, or a miscarriage occurred, or the child was delivered feet first, a sense of impending disaster could only be allayed by finding out from diviners what had to be done and then doing it. Furthermore, the diviner herself would say that the only way of knowing if the ritual had worked would be to see what happened during the *next* pregnancy: if that happened on schedule and the baby was normal, it proved that safety had been restored; otherwise, more rituals might be necessary.

A Morongo woman we knew who had a twelve-year-old albino daughter among her five children gave birth to twins and had to be hospitalized because of their low birth weight. On her return home from the hospital, she went into seclusion briefly with the twins and then underwent the elaborate and expensive ritual for twin births (LeVine et al. 1994, pp. 134–38). As she said at the time, however, she would not know if the ritual worked to protect her and the family until she gave birth to her next child. Thus feeling safe from spiritual and interpersonal danger requires the security of knowing that one is capable of continuing to bear normal children. By the time she reaches menopause, however, the focus of concern should be the reproductive competence of her daughter-in-law, who is now responsible (along with the other daughters-in-law) for extending the patrilineal genealogy into the next generation.

If we define the early years of middle adulthood as beginning at forty, it is a period in which a woman may be still bearing her own children, as her older daughters move away to get married, and looking forward to the marriage of her oldest circumcised son; a few years later the son should be married and his wife bearing children, while his mother has become an elder and is approaching the age at which her own childbearing is naturally terminated. Before reaching menopause, she may experience long birth intervals and other reproductive difficulties—more frequent among older women who have had many children—that will give her anxiety and may lead her to seek advice from diviners. But it is obstacles to the son's reproductive career that would be most distressing. The leading diviner of Morongo, a woman in her sixties, said she had not taken up her role as healer until her married son had become insane when she was in her forties; as this made it impossible for him to father children, she took him for medical treatment and performed many sacrifices, none of which effected a permanent cure. She then sought treatment by a healer in a distant place, which restored his mental and reproductive competence. Subsequently, she underwent training as a diviner herself. This total commitment to the son's cure makes sense in a Gusii context, because insanity, like reproductive dysfunction, is held to be a clear sign of ancestral

197

affliction, demanding reparative action to save not only the afflicted person but also the entire family. Thus reproductive success in a Gusii homestead is a sign that relations between the living and the dead are peaceful, that the ancestor spirits are not visiting afflictions on its residents, that they can prosper and multiply. But as experienced by Gusii adults, it is a fragile peace, easily disrupted by what might be considered minor reproductive difficulties elsewhere. Gusii men and women do not speak publicly about their good fortune in childbearing and health; to do so would be flaunting it in front of neighbors or unseen others whose resentment might result in witchcraft and sorcery threatening the lives of the family. But their desire for security in what they experience as an uncertain world made Gusii adults in the 1970s reluctant to give up childbearing as a sign of well-being even as they reached middle adulthood. The woman who had her tubes tied after five children was exceptional as a devout Protestant living in a religious community; to the people of Morongo, her action, perhaps based on a sense of security derived from religion, seemed full of risks they would not take.

The Place of Middle Adulthood in Gusii Cultural Models

So far we have described the experience of fertility for Gusii adults with a minimum of contextual background, depending on anecdotes to show how strong were the feelings and motives that kept fertility high in the 1970s. It should be clear, however, that Gusii men and women act in situations heavily structured by cultural concepts, norms, templates, conventions, and strategies. There is a logic to their actions, but it depends on assumptions only partly revealed. In this section we try to describe as concisely as possible the contexts that make sense of Gusii thought and action in middle adulthood and the place fertility holds in that part of the life course.

Three cultural models constitute the primary contexts of Gusii adult experience: (1) the rules of kinship and marriage; (2) the gender-differentiated stages of life; and (3) the economic, reproductive, and spiritual careers of men and women.

1. *The rules of kinship and marriage.*—Until very recently, kinship provided the primary identity for all Gusii: who you were was determined by the patrilineal descent groups to which you belonged and married into, the legitimate marital arrangements in which you were involved, and your genealogical connections with people within the

descent group (agnates) and those outside it (cognatic kin). It resembled in many respects the classical agnatic pattern described by Evans-Pritchard (1940) for the Nuer, only tidier, as the Gusii had fully localized patrilineages. When two Gusii met who were previously unacquainted, they would hold a brief conversation to locate their relationship to each other in a common genealogical space, and they were then able to retrieve from memory the script for their interaction: a "grandfather" talking to a "grandson"; two "brothers" conversing, and so on. The number of prescriptions and proscriptions for interaction and social relationships was vast, yet it was acquired by all as the omnibus guide to conventional social life. This heavily prescribed world of rules and regulations fit well with Radcliffe-Brown's social anthropology, given his legal-constitutional analysis of society (see Radcliffe-Brown [1952] 1968; Forde and Radcliffe-Brown 1951), so we have a good record of Gusii kinship rules from the first anthropologist who worked among the Gusii, the late Philip Mayer (1949, 1950), a student of Radcliffe-Brown.

Gusii adults talk about their own lives and those of others in terms heavily derived from the kinship system, and they judge each other in terms of the recognized norms governing kin relationships. Their personal strategies tend to operate within these norms, or did as late as the 1950s when kinship provided most adults' identities. In the colonial period, male roles were drastically changed, as warriors were forbidden to operate as such and local elders lost their power to a bureaucratic administration, but it was not until after Kenya's independence in 1963 that social identities other than those of kinship were created by mass schooling, the movement of men into urban occupations, and conversion to Christianity. Even in the 1970s, kinship norms, though eroded, prevailed in rural areas like Morongo.

The cultural model of adulthood embedded in the Gusii kinship system is first of all a patrilineal genealogy that enables a boy to see himself as becoming an ancestor through marriage and procreation. Descent groups are named after their founders; they are actually called names like MwaMoriango, which means "children of Moriango." To be a named ancestor like Moriango, you have to marry a number of wives who have to bear many children, grandchildren, and so on. Anyone's genealogy is actually the success story of its founder, for Moriango's brothers are forgotten and do not have lineages named after them. From a Gusii genealogy (which is entirely oral, except as recorded by anthropologists) you can also learn that fathers own all the

TABLE 2. Gusii Life Stages

	Life Stage	
	Gusii	English
Female:		
	Ekengwerere	Infant
	Egasagaane	Uncircumcised girl
	Enyaroka, Omoiseke	Circumcised girl
	Omosubaati	Young married woman
	Omongina	Female elder
Male:		
	Ekengwerere	Infant
	Omoisia	Uncircumcised boy
	Omomura	Circumcised boy, warrior
	Omogaaka	Male elder

property, control their wives and sons, negotiate bridewealth transactions: men have more power than women, older men more power than younger men, men with more sons more power than other men. In other words, the Gusii genealogy is not only a success story of the founder but a model of what makes for success, and it is "read" that way. It also indicates the role that women play as founders of the several houses (*chinyomba*), that is, factional segments, within the polygynous family of a lineage founder. Women with several loyal sons who become successful in a given area have a lineage segment named after them, within the larger patrilineal descent group (Hakansson 1989).

There are many lessons that young Gusii learn from their own genealogies, but the one we want to emphasize here is the importance of fertility: the ancestors who are remembered, men and women, are those who proliferated according to the rules of the Gusii marriage system; the lines of those with fewer children died out or were merged collaterally. Fertility is an essential ingredient of the genealogical success story, and success means wealth and power through control over people, cattle, and land—but primarily people. In this conception of success, those with adult sons enjoy its fruits, and they are the men and women who have reached middle adulthood, the years from forty to sixty.

2. *The stages of life.*—The Gusii do not partition the life span by chronological age but by stages of life for men and women, with a lexicon of general terms used for these age-sex categories (table 2).

This life plan is a status hierarchy based on relative age in which "higher" (i.e., lower on table 2) means not only better in general social esteem but also the gaining of respect and obedience from those at a lower stage. It is good to get older; there is no equivalent in these terms to "middle aged" in English as connoting decline or obsolescence. In the absence of chiefs or dominant social classes, the "elders" (i.e., those designated as *omogaaka* (plural *abagaaka*) constituted the governors of the community, and while female elders (*abangina*) did not constitute a collective unit, they also exerted authoritative influence among women in the area. In contrast with a fixed hierarchy, however, an age hierarchy necessarily entails mobility, providing incentives for the young to act maturely so as to move up. Each Gusii individual was particularly concerned with the movements of one's peers or age mates (*abagesangio*). For men, this group comprises those born in the same year; for women, those married into the lineage at the same time. For a young married woman whose age mates had all given birth when she had not, or a man whose age mates were married when he was not, the fear of being left behind would become a preoccupation. Thus the local age hierarchy of one's gender was subjectively motivating, with its carrot of higher status and the stick of being left behind.

The gloss "elder" for *omogaaka* and *omongina* is not quite accurate insofar as the English term refers to a person older in years. "Senior" may come closer in suggesting relative status that can be but need not be associated with chronological age. Within the homestead, the same words as terms of address to the most senior man or woman might be better translated "patriarch" and "matriarch," though there are in fact no English equivalents.

The Gusii stages of life are primarily based on reproductive maturity, anticipated in childhood, achieved in adulthood, and extended into the maturation of one's children. The initiation ceremonies, including genital operations, that promote a boy to *omomura* and a girl to *enyaroka* or *omoiseke* mark the end of their status as children protected from sexuality and the beginning or anticipation of their future roles in mating. At marriage, the nubile woman changes to *omosubati,* a young wife, but a man remains *omomura,* a warrior. There follow a number of reproductively significant changes unmarked in stage terminology: when the first child is born (demonstrating the bride's fertility and helping to cement the marriage arrangements), when the first son is born (giving the mother a respected place among the women in her husband's home), and when the first *son* is initiated (and circumcised)—this last being a particularly joyous event for the mother, marking her success in raising a permanent member of the home close to the point of marriage and the bearing of another generation for the lineage (including the grandson who will bury her). But it is the marriage of a child that brings the marked change to elder (or senior) status for both sexes, signified by the fact that someone from outside the clan, unrelated by blood, must now call a man or woman "father" or "mother." This event also points to the imminent emergence of the next generation. As reproduction, growth, and marriage add to the bottom of the hierarchy, those of the parental generation are accordingly promoted.

The subjective salience of this reproductive ideal is indicated by the tragic quality of the events that can undermine its realization. In the case of a woman, it can be her failure to conceive at all, her loss of children during infancy and early childhood, her failure to bear any sons (meaning that all her children will leave at marriage), or even falling behind other women in the family in terms of reproductive performance (LeVine 1979). In the case of a man, it can be the inability to obtain bridewealth for a first marriage or the onset of sterility or impotence so severe that he is unable to impregnate his wives. All of these events are seen by Gusii as threats not only to an adult's well-being but also to his or her movement through the canonical stages of life that confer personhood and maturity in the most fundamental sense. Without living children from a bridewealth marriage, an adult is "nothing"; without married children, one is barred from the expectable status of a senior man or woman. (Thus a thirty-year-old married man with young children who had behaved irresponsibly was excused by Gusii as being morally immature, in the way Americans might excuse a teenager for a misdemeanor; full moral maturity and responsibility are expected only of male elders, who have attained their status through the marriage of their children.) Reproductive failures threatening normal progression up the age hierarchy arouse severe anxiety and, as noted above, impel men and women to restorative ritual action.

3. *Economic, reproductive and spiritual careers.*—The Gusii kinship system and life stages are domains of public discourse in which the normative dimensions of Gusii adulthood are explicitly defined. At a more private and covert level, Gusii men and women have a set of coherent and strongly felt ideas about the desired directions of their lives, ideas not publicly discussed or even verbally formulated but which became clear to us through the actions that people took, as illus-

trated in the anecdotes about blocked fertility, and through observing funerals.

To make this explicit, we formulated career pathways for the Gusii that are recognizable to them but more explicit than they would ever make them (LeVine 1980, pp. 93–100). In our formulation, each Gusii man and woman thinks of himself or herself as having economic, reproductive, and spiritual careers, with goals that are differentiated by gender but similar in their motivational force. For each career, but particularly the economic and reproductive ones, there are clear standards of progress that give one a sense of well-being. When setbacks occur—crop failure, the death of children, the reproductive anomalies—restorative action is taken in the spiritual realm, with the aim of getting the economic or reproductive career back on track.

When the more usual kind of ritual action does not work—that is, animal sacrifices ordered by the diviner or the use of various kinds of magic—then the individual parent, usually a woman in middle adulthood whose son is afflicted (like the diviner described above) or who has had numerous birth anomalies (like the mother who gave birth to an albino child and twins), goes to a far-off place for treatment or through an elaborate ceremony, which, if effective, leads to her becoming a diviner (*omoragoori*) or a ritual practitioner (*omokorerani*) specializing in ceremonies appropriate to the kind of birth anomaly she herself had experienced. This is not separate from her own spiritual career but is a form of sharing with others (for a price) the power she had to acquire in order to eliminate the obstacles to her own reproductive progress. Having achieved a higher level of spiritual mastery that can remedy blocked reproductive careers—and in the case of diviners, economic careers as well—the empowered woman practitioner provides this service to others. Every Gusii has a spiritual career, which can begin before birth in sacrifices neglected by one's father, but it is in middle adulthood that some Gusii, most frequently women, obtain the spiritual power to help others.

CRISES AND RESOLUTIONS IN MIDDLE ADULTHOOD

What did mature Gusii men and women do with their reproductive success during the 1970s? If children are a benefit, how are these benefits realized and experienced in the life of a person who has passed through all the stages of maturation to the desired status of an *omogaaka* or *omongina*? The answers are very different for men and women. Postmenopausal women who had many children and at least one son could concentrate their interests and energies on the sons, their wives, and the grandchildren. Their sons' reproductive careers extended their own and became the focus of their concerns, positive and negative. Having founded a house (*enyomba*) within the homestead of the patriarch, a mature woman could enjoy the relationships with her progeny who belonged to her house.

For a man the situation was more perilous. As he approached the age of fifty and his wife approached menopause, he was tempted, particularly by the incoming bridewealth for his daughters or by his monetary earnings, to take a second wife for several reasons: First, polygyny still carried prestige. It had been the sine qua non for community status, power, and prestige in the past, when a middle-aged man with one wife was disqualified for any leadership role and was even actively despised. Even in the 1970s at Morongo, middle-aged monogamists were sometimes publicly insulted or chided jokingly, particularly by intoxicated men, as being dependent on and controlled by their wives. The male elders had lost most of their political authority in local affairs to government-appointed chiefs and civil servants, but polygyny could at least give them a higher social standing among their peers. Second, some Gusii women turned away from their husbands at menopause, making themselves unavailable for sexual intercourse or cooking (closely associated in Gusii custom) once their childbearing days were over. Thus the husband wanted a younger wife "to take care of him" in his later years. Third, each woman with her children formed a production unit, and it had been the case that, the more wives a man had, the more land he could cultivate; this was the precolonial route to prosperity. Land had become scarce, but the model lived on for many men.

The actual frequency of polygyny had declined since the 1950s. In one neighborhood studied at the earlier time, 44.4% of married men were polygynists in 1956 and only 8.9% were in 1975. But that area included families who were cultivating the chief's land and owned little land of their own even in the 1950s. More prosperous neighborhoods had a somewhat higher rate of polygyny, but the big division was by age. For all of Morongo in 1975, 32.1% of men over fifty but only 5.4% of men twenty-five to fifty, had more than one wife.

Polygyny still brought status and prestige among local men but it also brought serious problems to many of these older men. Gusii women are often unfriendly to their cowives and sometimes try to drive them away in the early stages of marriage. With the land shortage of the 1970s, a man's taking another wife to give birth to future heirs who would constitute another house within the homestead represented a great threat to the first wife and her sons. Conflict among the wives and their groups of sons often resulted in the older men, some of whom had three or four wives, being driven into isolation with just a cow for company, a good deal of alcohol consumption to get through the day, and a sense of genealogical accomplishment for solace.

Among men who entered middle adulthood in the 1970s, there were three fairly distinct paths that can be illustrated from men we knew. In one case, a man whose monogamy was associated with his Christianity suddenly decided when he reached fifty that he would emulate his wealthier cousins and take a second wife. However, he made no special provision for the livelihood and future inheritance of his nine sons, who were furious on both economic and moral grounds. The older sons attacked the father physically and drove the new wife away.

Another man had three wives and children with each one, but only one lived on his inherited land at Morongo; another lived on land he bought in the Kuria country some 20 miles to the south; and a third in Kisii town, where she ran the shop he had founded. Through entrepreneurial activity in the modern sector and the purchase of land outside of Kisii (something unheard of as recently as thirty years ago), this man was able to put distance between his "houses" and provide for them economically, thereby averting open conflict.

A final path that was still relatively rare in the 1970s but seemed the destiny of future cohorts was that of men who had become educated to at least the secondary school level and had been able to get a permanent job in the government or a private firm and who adopted a bourgeois lifestyle. Such men were wealthy by local standards and could afford to have one wife in the city and another working back on the land, which some of them did. But those who were more educated, younger, and had a stronger Christian identity and a greater personal involvement with a modern occupational role were less inclined to opt for a polygynous reproductive career that would put them at the apex of a rapidly expanding genealogy based on multiple marriages.

Thus Gusii culture in the 1970s seemed to offer women at middle adulthood a measure of fulfillment from successful reproductive careers (after ten or twelve home births and some twenty-five years of toiling in the fields)—domestic status, economic security (through their sons), relative leisure, sociability, and the respect of other women in the community. If their continued proliferation through their sons were threatened by afflictions, a compensatory career of divination and healing was available that also offered status, respect, and economic rewards. For middle-aged men, however, the pursuit of Gusii cultural models no longer brought personal fulfillment, since their elder roles had lost authority, and polygyny—once a guaranteed pathway to prosperity, status, and comfort—could be the route to economic disaster and family conflict. They had to look to new occupational and religious identities through which to fashion a satisfactory life in their later years.

Summary and Conclusions

Gusii conceptions of the life span are not based on chronological age and do not include a concept of middle age as an intermediate period of adulthood or a time of incipient decline. On the contrary, the Gusii expectation for men and women forty to sixty years of age is that they have ascended to the highest stage in a gender-specific hierarchy of relative age statuses—through their fertility and that of their sons—and are enjoying the economic and other benefits of maturity as governors of home and community. In this view, their social status is accompanied by a moral maturity that justifies their authority over the younger persons under their control.

During the precolonial period (prior to 1908) and even much of the colonial period (before 1963), Gusii models of the life span were based on assumptions concerning the centrality of fertility that were pragmatically attuned to the indigenous sociopolitical, economic, and cultural conditions of an East African agropastoral people. Men and women pursued reproductive, economic, and spiritual careers that were mutually dependent and complementary, with a spiritual career in middle adulthood compensating for reproductive and economic failures, particularly for women. Institutional changes initiated by British rule and expanding at an accelerated pace with each decade of the twentieth century eroded the pragmatic basis of the Gusii models, converting polygyny and high fertility from economic assets to liabilities, eliminating the authority of male elders, and subordinating kin identities to those based on occupation role, educational attainment, and religious affiliation. For the rural Gusii, and particularly for rural men over fifty in the 1970s, these changes created unprecedented personal dilemmas and family tensions for which no solutions were in sight. Among later cohorts, however, the salience of new identities and the growing acceptance of birth limitation indicated a major change in future Gusii experience of middle adulthood. The recent decline in fertility among the Gusii, as for Kenya as a whole, comes too late and is too modest in scale to diminish the stress of population pressure for rural Gusii, but it suggests that conceptions of adult maturity less centered on fertility will eventually become dominant in the Gusii culture.

Notes

1. The levirate is a customary practice in which a widow is assigned to a reproductive union with a deceased husband's brother or a cousin on the father's side.

References

Evans-Pritchard, E. E. 1940. *The Nuer.* London: Oxford University Press.

———.1953. *Kinship and Marriage among the Nuer.* London: Oxford University Press.

Forde, D., and A. R. Radcliffe-Brown, eds. 1951. *African Systems of Kinship and Marriage.* London: Oxford University Press.

Hakansson, T. 1989. "Family Structure, Bridewealth and Environment in Eastern Africa: A Comparative Study of House-Property Systems." *Ethnology* 28:117–34.

LeVine, R. A. 1980. "Adulthood among the Gusii of Kenya." In *Themes of Work and Love in Adulthood,* edited by N. Smelser and E. Erikson. Cambridge, Mass.: Harvard University Press.

LeVine, R. A. 1982. "Gusii Funerals: Meanings of Life and Death in an African Community." *Ethos* 10:26–65.

LeVine, R. A., S. Dixon, S. LeVine, A. Richman, P. H. Leiderman, C. Keefer, and T. B. Brazelton. 1994. *Child Care and Culture: Lessons from Africa.* New York: Cambridge University Press.

LeVine, R. A., and S. LeVine. 1991. "House Design and the Self in an African Culture." In *The Psychoanalytic Study of Society,* vol. 16. Essays in Honor of A. Irving Hallowell. Edited by L. B. Boyer and Ruth M. Boyer. Hillsdale, N.J.: Analytic Press.

LeVine, S. 1979. *Mothers and Wives: Gusii Women of East Africa.* Chicago: University of Chicago Press.

Mayer, Philip. 1949. "The Lineage Principle in Gusii Society." Memorandum no. 24. International African Institute. London: Oxford University Press.

———. 1950. *Gusii Bridewealth Law and Custom.* Cape Town: Oxford University Press.

Radcliffe-Brown, A. R. (1952) 1968. *Structure and Function in Primitive Society.* London: Cohen & West.

III Diversity, Resistance, and Conflict within the United States

Children of the 1960s at Midlife: Generational Identity and the Family Adaptive Project

Thomas S. Weisner and Lucinda P. Bernheimer

I have always been and still feel connected to it in my heart. I think [the hippie movement is] the best thing that happened. . . . There wasn't any way in which it was harmful.

The hippie revolution in those days—we really could feel we could make a difference in the world. . . . I still believe most of the ideas from that revolution.

I was not really true to myself when I was part of the counterculture. If I had been truer to myself, I would have been straighter.

I don't feel that I belong to a generation. . . . It is probably my open-mindedness that I don't feel part of . . . you know, anything.

I didn't *calcify* the way some of my friends have.

I don't like it [the countercultural generation] now. . . . It isn't like I am locked in the sixties, or whatever.

We messed it up for them [our children], even though we intended not to. . . . We had ideals which we didn't manage to achieve.

. . . for people my age, I think a lot of lives were derailed by the sixties, because when you're in your twenties is a time you're

The Family Lifestyles Project has been generously supported by a Carnegie Corporation grant and a U.S. Public Health Service grant (B397 and MH24947, respectively) to the late Bernice T. Eiduson, principal investigator, and a Carnegie Corporation grant and W. T. Grant Foundation grant (B4189 and 92-1488, respectively) to Thomas S. Weisner, principal investigator. The Division of Social Psychiatry, Department of Psychiatry and Biobehavioral Sciences at UCLA has also provided important support. The authors thank Helen Garnier for data analysis and Maurine Bernstein, Chemba Raghavan, Rebecca Stein, Jennifer Jacobs, Jennifer Furin, and Anne Staunton for interviews and fieldwork. Most of all, we thank the two hundred families who participate in the Family Lifestyles Project. This chapter was completed while Weisner was at the Center for Advanced Study in the Behavioral Sciences (CASBS). He is grateful for financial support at the CASBS provided by the National Science Foundation (grant SBR-9022192) and the William T. Grant Foundation (grant 95167795).

supposed to be doing certain things and for a lot of us, we weren't preparing for real life, or we refused to prepare for real life [as I hope to prepare my teenager now].

I am hippie about money, but not about drugs.

Because I felt so lost, I used.

COUNTERCULTURAL PARENTS AT MIDLIFE

Most members of the countercultural, 1960s generation are now somewhere in their forties or early fifties—at an age Americans consider to be midlife. Since 1974-75, we have had the privilege of following a group from this generation, 150 countercultural parents living in nonconventional family arrangements (communes, single mothers by choice, and unmarried or "social contract" couples). We also have followed a comparison group of fifty two-parent married couples. All the mothers in our study gave birth in 1974 or 1975. We revisited these parents most recently in 1993–94, as their children reached their late teen years, and talked with them about their identification with the counterculture. Our essay describes parents' reports on their generational identity at midlife and their adolescent children's beliefs and circumstances.

We thought that nonconventional family lifestyles might influence midlife beliefs because of the active questioning and high involvement in change characteristic of many such families. Among its other consequences, the countercultural movement certainly opened a new era of negotiations within families, as well as with the normative standards of the culture of the time. Indeed, Glen Elder comments that the renewed interest in life course studies was in part due to the "social discontinuities" of that decade (1985, 15), which led to new formulations in the field of life course socialization (Nesselroade and Eye 1985; Baltes and Brim 1980).

As the quotes above from parents' interviews suggest, generational identity varied in content, salience, and affective meaning. Family troubles, personal problems or successes, drug use, poor or wise economic choices—all influence how generational identity is experienced at midlife. In addition, all these parents now have teenage children, and they see their children's well-being (or lack thereof) as resulting partly from countercultural parental values and life choices. These beliefs about their children shape the parents' feelings about their generational identity.

Furthermore, most parents have retained some values of the countercultural era, such as antimaterialism or egalitarianism. Sixty-three percent responded with a yes or qualified yes to the question, Do you think that the counterculture, overall, has made a positive contribution to society? (Weisner and Garnier 1995). But this leaves a considerable number of parents with less positive views. When we listened more closely to parents' personal and family stories, we found that the countercultural cohort diverged. Over the years, the group has fragmented, producing individuals with many different life trajectories and experiences and with different views of their generational identity.

A number of classic longitudinal cohort studies have followed the consequences for children of a generational cohort experience, and they have also found that effects for children and families varied. Recall, for instance, that the effects of the Depression were not uniform for children or parents (Elder 1974; Elder et al. 1986). There was not a direct correlation between degree of hardship and child outcomes, for instance. Fathers already unstable became more so during periods of economic hardship. Fathers who were more stable and resourceful to begin with were relatively calm under economic calamity. The *predictability* of the home environment mattered, not just the level of family income. Consequences of the Depression also differed for sons and daughters, with sons having a more difficult time in many circumstances. Just as for the countercultural parents in our study, the Depression experience was refracted through the relational and emotional circumstances of the family.

This interaction between family dynamics and sociocultural change is found across a variety of studies of generational change (Elder 1991). Katherine Newman (1988; in this volume) found that the experience of downward mobility for women who were used to the hardships of the Depression or World War II was different from that of women growing up later. The former group were used to deprivation; the latter often did not know what to do when it came. The former wanted material possessions; the latter sometimes said that the experience of economic deprivation was good for them because it got them away from a false materialism. Werner and Smith (1977) found that different adaptive strengths assisted Kauai families at different points in their children's development, and that hardships and calamities on Kauai varied in their effects as a result of family resilience. These kinds of psychosocial adaptive responses also can be found in life course descriptions of upper-middle-class New England men and their families (Weiss 1990).

An important variation in our countercultural sample concerns how involved parents were in the values and practices of the era over time. We compared parents who sustained a relatively high commitment to countercultural values and identity over eighteen years with parents whose countercultural identity declined or significantly changed. The sustained high generational identity group had more satisfying and less troubled family lives and felt that their teenage children had done at least "okay." This group was made up of those who had been most active in their countercultural life. That is, they tried to incorporate their countercultural values into everyday family practice early in their children's lives. Parents who did not bring countercultural ideals into sustained, shared family practice tended to experience a decline in generational identity. Because most countercultural parents in our study began their family life with high countercultural identity, and because family experience and personal struggles varied thereafter, successes and failures in subsequently achieving family goals related to the counterculture account in part for change in the meaning of generational identity at midlife.

One view of midlife is that it is a cultural construction that labels and deeply constrains us. Most countercultural parents in our study were well aware of this aspect of midlife in particular and cultural norms in general. Most parents we talked with did *not* succumb to midlife generational "labeling," "aging," or "staging." They neither damned nor glorified midlife and the counterculture. They were reflective, critical, quirky, and resistant to "cultural discourses" about their generation and midlife. They saw the stages of midlife as events to be critiqued and questioned, just as they had critiqued politics and social convention in their youth. After all, many countercultural parents are comfortable with a critical stance vis-à-vis cultural categories generally, and the concept of midlife was no exception.

This critical stance toward life stages extends to family life and parenting as well as their views of midlife. They perceive that there is more than one plausible, defensible, possible way to be a family or a parent and that experimenting and trying out possibilities is a valuable and important process, a part of their social and cultural identity. They are also living in a social-historical era in America with more available cultural models for family life and life careers than may have ever existed before in history in one society (Weisner 1986a).

These parents did not critique cultural categories (categories of the countercultural era of their youth or categories like middle age now) because they were afraid they otherwise might get trapped in these categories, but because of something more psychosocially powerful. They saw midlife as a time of important adaptive problems for themselves and for their teenage children, a time when they hoped their cultural goals for their children were being realized. During this period, generational identity is filtered through the family project of assisting, or sometimes resisting, teenage development. And adolescents, of course, contribute their own dynamic to the process. They sometimes reject their parents' generational culture, reassess it, and rebel, since adolescents in the 1990s have their own generational culture.

Our evidence suggests that midlife is an important and recognized time of life for the countercultural parents we interviewed, and that it is more than a purely culturally represented fiction. Midlife involves thinking back on one's own youth, as well as attending to the teenage developmental transitions of one's children. Our theory is that midlife also is a joint, yoked transition of adolescent children and parents. Parents experience, define, and respond to midlife in part because of the teenage transition of their children. This transition involves intrapsychic concerns, revisions, and realizations of parents' cultural goals and parents' attempts to provide for safety and continuity in their teens' lives. Reassessments of parents' own generational identities are nested in these midlife projects. Our view is that midlife is a "cultural fiction" only in the sense that cultures provide developmental pathways for our lives that always involve sets of stories, moral values, and activities. However, these cultural developmental pathways are in response to panhuman, universal experiences during the midlife period. These experiences include our children's transitions into and out of adolescence.

We also present some evidence regarding what everyone, including countercultural parents, wants to know: How did the children of countercultural parents turn out? We found that, overall, in educational achievement their teens were doing as well or better than teens from our comparison families (two-parent married couples) and national samples. We have evidence that countercultural parents' cultural goals and values have indeed been adopted by their teens, although not in a straightforward way. We also suggest that a strong generational identity, including a sustained commitment to countercultural values, can actually offer some protection for children and parents alike as they face the often difficult tasks of family life.

MIDLIFE AS AN ADAPTIVE PROJECT

Our view of midlife and generational identity is ecocultural; that is, we believe that development occurs in an ecocultural niche that provides resources, constraints, goals, values, and cultural practices that make development possible (LeVine 1977; LeVine et al. 1994; Whiting and Whiting 1975; Whiting and Edwards 1988). There is a developmental niche for children (Super and Harkness 1980, 1986) and an ecocultural niche for families and communities (Weisner 1984, 1993, 1996; Gallimore et al. 1989). A set of possible cultural careers is a part of this niche (Goldschmidt 1990), possible life trajectories that are the joint product of biology, ecology, history, and culture.

Cultural categories like "midlife," which are a part of our cultural career, do not arise in language and practice at random. They arise because they encode adaptive challenges and problems that emerge at certain times in life. For example, many of the countercultural parents we talked with were responding to their children as they completed high school, were beginning college or work, were leaving home, emerging sexually, developing close relationships (including marriage and childbirth), and struggling for economic autonomy. These projects fall into the three areas of adolescent developmental change that any culture ignores at its peril: the onset of fertility, reproduction, and marriage; participation in productivity, survival, and competence; and the commitment to a morality, ideology, and spirituality (Schlegel and Barry 1991; LeVine 1977; Schlegel 1995).

Midlife is a relational stage of life experienced through one's children as well as a cultural life stage and a personal transition. At midlife, parents try to assist and resist their teen's generational change—the same kinds of changes that happened to them when they were youths first embracing the counterculture. Midlife and the teenage transitions that go with it are jointly predictable perturbations in the development of the parent-child unit across the life course (Chisholm 1983; 1992). This is the sense in which midlife and adolescence are yoked together.

However, adolescence is far more often explicitly marked in cultures around the world than is midlife. Is adolescence, therefore, more clearly a cross-culturally identifiable stage in human development, whereas midlife, being relatively unmarked, not celebrated in ceremonies or rituals, is not? Midlife is not a sharply marked life stage; it has very wide malleability in timing and salience in cultures around the world. We suggest that midlife actually is marked by its being yoked with the adolescent developmental transition. Many cultures have adolescent initiation ceremonies, or relatively early marriage and associated negotiations and ceremonies soon after puberty, and there are accompanying changes of residence, transfers of property, and realignments of kin and affinal relations as a result. All these kinds of cultural markers are coded ethnographically and thought of as adolescent linked. But who is arranging all those ceremonies? Transferring that property? Rearranging where family members live and sleep? Having grandchildren in their lives? Parents at midlife, of course. Midlife transitions *are* there in the ethnographic record, but are described and *represented* as the adolescent and marital transitions of parents' adolescent children rather than as distinctive life stages of the parents themselves.

Our study, like all the chapters in this volume, is culturally, historically—and in our case, generationally—situated. Our sample are all parents with teenage children. Hence parents' reflections on their lives and their pasts in the counterculture era were mixed with their observations of how that era affected their children and their family life. Generational identity for parents brings into sharp focus the problems their adolescents are experiencing. This makes the yoked intergenerational aspects of midlife no doubt more salient for our particular study and for our parent and teen participants. We also interviewed more mothers than fathers, and perhaps women experience midlife as more family and child centered than do most fathers. And this is a cohort study by design—it frames children's lives and their parents' circumstances in a particular American ecocultural place.

But the nature of our sample and cohort, even though sociohistorically specific, nonetheless makes more vivid certain features of midlife and generational identity that we believe are very widespread: the yoked teen/parent transition; the importance of processes of assistance and resistance for teens and parents; and the importance of family-mediated experience for a positive, continuous generational identity. However, we do not intend by our focus to suggest that other features of midlife (e.g., bodily changes, spiritual renewal, commodification, or gender role changes) are unimportant. Adults without children or living apart from their children, as well as teens estranged from parents, have variant experiences no doubt, as do ethnic minorities and other subgroups and communities.

IDENTITY, SELF, AND GENERATIONAL EXPERIENCE

The countercultural generation experienced a set of presumptively similar formative experiences at a similar age, and this is what defines them as part of a generational cohort (Newman 1988, 287 n. 17). A countercultural, or 1960s, generational identity is, by definition, shaped by collective experience, not least because of its appropriation by the media and political debates. The countercultures of the late sixties and early seventies included two central goals: an exploratory, spiritual, hedonistic, drug-using, experimental lifestyle; and political activism, antiwar and protest movements, and a moral critique of society. The birth cohort of our study (people born 1942–55, approximately, who lived through their late teens and early adult years during the countercultural turmoil of the 1960s and 1970s, and became parents in 1974–75) cannot avoid taking a position regarding this generational identity; ignoring it is a position. An individual's generation is among the set of cultural and physical characteristics—gender, race, region, clan and family, birth order, ethnicity, language, religion, and physical appearance—that often seems to matter to identity.

Generational identity is one of the social sites for the self. It is the set of representations (about present and past cultural experiences) that is held in the mind and used to organize understandings of self. Did you demonstrate against the war? Serve in it? Did you join a women's group? Did you smoke much dope? Were you a hippie? Did you sleep with a lot of people? Did you live in a commune or a collective? Generational identity includes a sense of accountability for both the past and the present. Generational identity is recast throughout life to serve the strategic interests of the person and the self; it is elaborated or suppressed depending upon the audience or the pain of the experiences.

A personal generational identity is formed with all the varied capacities of the mind. It is repressed, denied, feared, and idealized through psychodynamic processes. It is used to tell stories about the past, stories that take on a life of their own, accounting for our present and shaping the future. Generational identity provides a cultural model used to drive action and organize memory. It is used as a template to appraise, evaluate, and make strategic, locally rational choices about current relationships, political events, and children's lives. What this means is that

218

even if a generation shares similar collective historical and demographic experiences, the mind will uniquely refract and transform those experiences. The same is true for developmental transitions—a unique ideoverse is formed out of those transitions by each person. The common experiences remain but are altered both by common mental processes that transform them and by the unique life experiences that refract their meanings.

THE COUNTERCULTURE GENERATIONAL IDENTITY

What *were* those presumptively formative, commonly shared experiences that shaped a countercultural generational identity? First of all, the counterculture generational identity was morally and emotionally charged at the time, and the counterculture, hippies, and 1960s idealism remain as hotly debated now. Newt Gingrich made sure to mention that he was opposed to "it," and that "it" is the cause of many of the political and social ills he sees in the nation. George Will (1995) wrote a column, titled "A Bad Era," damning 1960s generational "irresponsibility" in parenting in a *Newsweek* issue reporting the death of Jerry Garcia. Bill Clinton now and again invokes the "Kennedy legacy" as his formative influence; he is from the age cohort of the 1960s, however gingerly he identifies with it.

The consequences of the counterculture are debated, including whether there really were any consequences. Whatever one's judgment of the time, or one's beliefs about its consequences, it is said to have a central core of beliefs and values (Berger 1981; Flacks 1988; Gitlin 1993; Gottlieb 1987; Keniston 1968, 1971; Miller 1991; Partridge 1973; Reich 1970; Roszak 1969; Tipton 1982; Yinger 1982): free, drug taking, self-enhancing, experimental, morally aware, emotionally labile and externalized, politically radical, antiwar (especially Vietnam), pro–Civil Rights, egalitarian, antimaterialistic, pronatural, antiauthority, spiritual, and communitarian.

Just in reviewing this list, we have some reason to wonder about the homogeneity of the 1960s generational identity. The counterculture had many "generational units" in it (Mannheim 1972); that is, subgroups with very different experiences. Gitlin and Kazin (1988, 49) defined counterculture ideals as in "constant flux—civil rights, student, anti-war, countercultural, feminist, gay, and none of the above." The countercultural generation was influenced by a political movement (Gitlin 1993), a moral search for personal meaning (Bellah et al. 1985), a desire for the "natural," open, and free (Berger 1981; Reich

1970), by the baby boom, by the economic expansion of the time (East-erlin 1980), by the search for new forms of religious and spiritual ex-pression (Rochford 1985; Weisner 1986b), and by the particular sub-sets of American youth who formed it. Yet, whether out of convenience or conviction, the generation often is portrayed as a "tribe"—coherent, continuous, perhaps scattered and wiser now than then, but still a spiri-tual tribe. As one member of the generation put it:

> We are still a generation far more united than divided. . . .
> I felt like nothing so much as an anthropologist visiting
> her own tribe. For the Sixties generation is a tribe with its
> roots in a time, rather than in a place or a race. Like many
> human tribes, we were founded on a vision. We share a
> culture; we share a religion, though many would not call
> it that; and so we approach the 'power age' of forty, and
> a second chance to make an impact on the world, we share
> a fascination with our origin myth, the experiences of
> the Sixties that, to a great extent, made us who we are.
> (Gottlieb 1987, 8–9)

The two core principles of the counterculture most often mentioned are the exploration of all aspects of life and continuing progressive moral critique of self and others. The parents in our study certainly mention both of these a lot. For Todd Gitlin (1993) and two recent television series, one on Berkeley activism and the other on the sixties, the core of the counterculture was political activism, with experimenta-tion (cultural and otherwise) coexisting uneasily. Gitlin expresses his experience of the essence of the era in terms at once grandiose and egocentric—just the way the era was for many. To him, the 1960s "took their point from the divine premise that everything was possible and therefore it was important to think, because ideas have conse-quences. Unraveling, rethinking, refusing to take for granted, thinking without limits—that calling was some of what I loved most in the spirit of the Sixties" (Gitlin 1993, 7).

The counterculture's ideals, ideas, and ideologies were not original; most came from diverse sociohistorical origins, and many were contra-dictory. The sources for countercultural ideals include at the least ear-lier American communitarian thought (see, e.g., Bellah et al. 1985; Zablocki 1980), American populism, European socialism, and folk un-derstandings about the primitive and, thus supposedly, natural way to live (Yinger 1982; Erasmus 1977; Reich 1970). As one well-known member of the 1960s generation, Billy Joel, put it, with regard to politics in particular, "We didn't start the fire/It was always burnin'/Since the world's been turnin'."

The counterculture would be seriously misunderstood, however, if viewed solely as a collection of positive values, freeing ideologies, radical politics, self-expansion, tribelike cohesion, and spiritualism—as do recent videos (Law 1990), film series, and books (see, e.g., Bellah et al. 1985; Tipton 1982). If you look more closely and talk with participants, you will hear other, darker sides to the counterculture: violent, grotesque, health-endangering, exploitative, sometimes sexist, and cruel. The counterculture could and did *hurt*. Many parents in our study experienced some of these injuries and gave painful reports about the damage done to themselves and to others. Many regret such aspects of their past and present and blame the 1960s and its aftermath for their bad experiences. Listening to a broad range of countercultural parents, not only the financially successful and those with sustained values, does not leave us with a romantic or consistently positive view of the 1960s era.

These varied strands of the counterculture reflect what we heard when we talked with parents at midlife about their generational identity. Parents disagreed about every aspect of the period, including whether they still had a countercultural identity at all. Their moral evaluations of the period, their descriptions of what it meant to them and what it *did* to them, were highly diverse. The countercultural generational identity at midlife is complex, refracted by troubled lives, mixed with thoughts of their teenagers' present circumstances and possible futures. Our results are not inconsistent with findings from several other studies that have examined the effects of participation in social movements of the 1960s and 1970s in later life (DeMartini 1983; Fendrich and Lovoy 1988; Jennings 1987; Marwell and Aiken 1987; Nassi 1981; Whalen and Flacks 1989). Participants in such movements, like most of our parents, report a continuity of values, continued political activism (although at lower levels of activity), a less fervent expression of ideology, and much more modest or selective implementation of values in everyday life.

Although the content of what parents mean by a countercultural generational identity varies, and its valence has often changed, generational identity is still salient. Most of our parents are still largely liberal, progressive, feisty, experimental, quirky, going against—countering—society. Many are still making a lasting impact on society at midlife.

Those who sustained this kind of countercultural generational identity were generally less troubled in other areas of their life since the 1970s, and were more successful at putting their values into practice in their family and personal life. Before turning directly to data on generational identity, we first summarize our study population and some of the measures we used; next we turn to our qualitative data on parents' generational identities at midlife and then to the question parents and others alike seem most often to want to know: How did the children of the children of the sixties turn out?

The Family Lifestyles Project has followed a sample of 200 conventional and nonconventional European-American families since 1974–75 (Eiduson and Weisner 1978). We contacted two hundred mothers during their third trimester of pregnancy and have been following them, their mates, and their children ever since. Attrition has been phenomenally low. When we contacted these participants in 1992–94, we reached 100% of the mothers, 98% of the teenagers, and 48% of the fathers or other mates.

At the time of recruitment, 150 families were in nonconventional family arrangements, including fifty single mothers, fifty social contract couples (not legally married), and fifty in communes or group-living situations. The nonconventional families were located by using snowball and network sampling, by advertising in alternative media of all kinds, and by obtaining referrals from clinics and obstetricians preferred by countercultural clients. We also tramped through the hills in northern California where many communards had set up camp. Our comparison sample of fifty two-parent, legally married couples comprises forty parents located through a random sample of obstetricians in major urban areas of California and an additional ten located through staff contacts.

The total sample represents a range of lower-working-class to upper-middle-class European-American families. All parents were between the 20th and 90th percentile on the Hollingshead combined socioeconomic and educational scale when selected. The average age of the mothers at the birth of the child was twenty-five years old, with a range from eighteen to thirty-two. Their birth cohort centered on 1949 (plus or minus seven years), placing them squarely in the middle of the countercultural period. Fathers (i.e., the child's biological father) were slightly older, with an average age of twenty-eight and a range from nineteen to forty-two. Mothers had completed an average of fourteen years of education and fathers sixteen years by the time the child was six. Seventy-five percent of the children were firstborn.

All the parents were selected without any knowledge of the parents' socioeconomic status (SES); nor did we know beforehand the parents' parents' SES. We did not know parents' commitment to various countercultural values until after they were selected (based solely on their nonconventional family lifestyles) for the study and then interviewed. Hence, there were no formal selection criteria that could have resulted in a sample of persons with an advantaged background or with a particular set of value orientations or kind of generational identity.

Of the mothers who started out as single parents, 39% were still single mothers when their teenagers reached eighteen. Of the social contract couples, 36% were still in that family arrangement. Only 14% of the families who had been in communes at the start of the study were still living in communes. Of the two-parent, legally married couples in the comparison sample, 73% were still married in 1992–94.

Figure 1 illustrates the overall change in families in the longitudinal sample over an eighteen-year period. When the study started, the women were in the third trimester of pregnancy and each lifestyle (single, social contract, communal, and two-parent married) comprised roughly 25% of the total sample. Married couples rose to 52% of the total by the end of the eighteen-year period, whereas communards dropped precipitously to 4% and social contract couples to 11%. Single parents first dropped and then increased steadily to a current 28% of the total sample. A new category, "unstable" family situations, appeared once the study began. These were families that changed frequently and for whom we could not establish a predominant lifestyle pattern. After early instability in a large number of the families, the persistently unstable group declined to 5% after eighteen years.

MEASURES

Parents were interviewed shortly before their child was born, and at child ages 1, 3, 6, and 18. These were semistructured interview/ conversations: parents' and teens' comments about generational identity, the counterculture, and values are drawn from these interviews for use in this chapter. Parents and children were interviewed at home at age 18, and at offices at the University of California, Los Angeles,

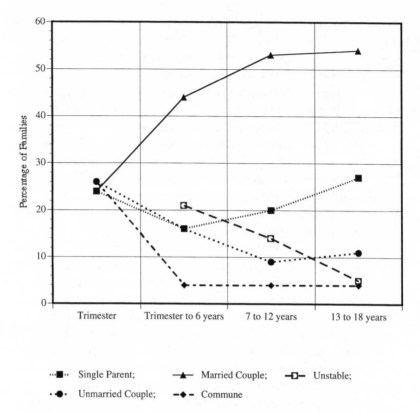

FIGURE 1 Percentages of family lifestyle arrangements from trimester to eighteen years of age

at ages 1, 3, and 6. (Families also were visited at home when the children were six months, eighteen months, and five years old, but these data are not included here.) Parents also completed questionnaires asking about values, countercultural orientation, drug use, and child rearing, among other topics. Adolescent children were interviewed as well about their own values, drug use, school and peers, and social and political attitudes. A representative subset of countercultural families participated in ethnographic visits, and some of these field notes have also been included in the study.

Values.—We initially defined eight values that characterized the countercultural movement: alternative achievement goals, pronaturalism, humanism, a present rather than future orientation, an acceptance of nonconventional authority, gender egalitarianism, low interest in scientific and rational understanding, and antimaterialism (Eiduson et al. 1973). Weisner et al. (1983) and Weisner and Eiduson (1986) studied "pronaturalism" in the Family Lifestyles Project sample. Pronaturalism includes a complex of values and practices, such as environmental concern, emotional openness, and a "laid-back, mellow," relaxed interpersonal and socioemotional orientation. Eiduson et al. (1982), Weisner and Wilson-Mitchell (1990), and Weisner et al. (1994) report on gender egalitarianism as a value and a practice: families changed domestic tasks and roles, provided androgynous clothing, toys, play styles, and media for children, and encouraged mixed-gender play and friendships, for instance. However, there were only mixed results, more pronounced for girls, from familial efforts to socialize their children and change familial roles, in gender-egalitarian ways.

We assessed each parent's value orientations during the third trimester and at the child's ages 3, 6, and 18, using open-ended interviews. We asked parents directly about the eight values listed above. We also had parents complete values-rating scales (Weisner and Garnier 1992). Items for these scales were drawn from published scales, as well as from our project measures. We also asked parents about their commitment to a nonconventional lifestyle and to nonconventional values, and parents' answers are presented in the qualitative summaries in this chapter.

Drug use of teens and parents.—We assessed teenagers' and parents' drug use through the use of standardized interview and questionnaire items at the child's ages 3, 6, and 18.

School achievement.—The children's school grades and enrollment histories were obtained in first, second, sixth grades and the third or final year of high school; SAT scores were also obtained for all teens who took the test.

Social and political attitudes.—We asked the adolescents to complete the Student Information Form (Astin et al. 1993), which asks a wide range of survey questions concerning student attitudes. For the past twenty-eight years, a national sample of students entering U.S. colleges has completed this survey. We also asked teenagers about their beliefs and attitudes in our open-ended interviews and during ethnographic visits.

Interview questions and field notes on generational identity.—In addition to quantitative analysis of values, drug use, school achievement, and social attitudes for all two hundred participants in the study, we drew a subsample of forty-two nonconventional families from the study for intensive qualitative analysis based on parents' self-reported countercultural commitment. We examined our field notes and qualitative interviews for patterns of response to our questions regarding generational identity: In the course of listening to what parents and teenagers said, fieldworkers used probes and thematic topics to expand understanding.

• How do you see the broad social movements that were occurring at the beginning of the project in 1975 [seventeen, eighteen years ago]—radical politics, feminism, alternative families, freer sexuality, drug use, folk music, new religions, and so on—in retrospect?

• How do you now view your own countercultural participation and family lifestyle choice?

• How would you rate your (and your spouse's) commitment to counterculture? (1 = no commitment; 7 = strong commitment) And why?

• Looking back now, how do you see the countercultural movement? In what ways was it beneficial/harmful? What has replaced it today, if anything? What are some examples? Do you think there should be something like it today? Something replacing it? What should it be?

• How have your lifestyle choices influenced your life today?

• Do you feel that you carry a generational identity? Is it important to you? Why? If not, is there a reason why you do not see yourself as part of a generation? Are there generational categories or labels that are not a part of your identity? How do you see your generation as distinct from your child's generation? How do the two differ?

PATTERNS IN COUNTERCULTURAL COMMITMENT OVER EIGHTEEN YEARS, 1975–93

Five patterns of change in generational identity over time.—The questions about countercultural commitment had been asked at the beginning of the study, and repeated seventeen years later at our teen follow-up. We compared the two responses and examined the patterns and directions of change in countercultural identity over this period for every family. These data were used to group the parents in our study into five categories: those who declined in their countercultural, generational identity (HiLower), those who sustained a low sense of that identity through the study (LoLo), those whose countercultural identity remained strong and consistent throughout the years (HiHi), those who currently called themselves "boomers" and were not any longer countercultural in orientation regardless of their prior countercultural experience (HiBoomer), and an "other" category composed of parents who were unable to classify themselves clearly or who had varied views of their generational identity—for example, that their identity stems from the 1950s rather than the 1960s and 1970s (LoOther).

There are differences in SES and other characteristics across the five groups, but they are trends; none were significant by chi-square test. Sixty-nine percent of the HiHi group was in the upper two quintiles on SES when the study began compared to 40% of the HiLower; 50% of the HiLower was in the middle quintile. The Boomer group was also higher in SES. When we revisited the families in 1992–94, the HiLower and other currently lower generational identity parents were slightly lower in SES, but again, not statistically significantly lower. The HiHi and Boomer mothers were also slightly older than the other groups were in 1975: HiHi mothers were twenty-six (plus or minus 3.8 years), for instance, compared to a mean of nearly twenty-five (plus or minus 4.3 years) for the HiLower mothers, but these are nonsignificant trends.

We focus most of our analysis on the two predominant patterns: families with higher, more sustained countercultural commitment over the eighteen years of our study (HiHi); and lower, more varied, declining identity (HiLower). But first, we summarize the fuller, more complex portrait of the entire sample and each of the five patterns of generational identity.

HiBoomer families (19%).—Some parents had a strong commitment to a countercultural identity in 1975 that was replaced by a "baby boom" identity by 1993. These parents reported their generational identities as belonging to the baby boom era, rather than the countercultural era. One single mother talked about her identification with the "role-playing thing." It made her think that she had a certain path to take and then, when the 1960s happened, "it just showed me that I had a whole world to choose from." Another commented, "I think the 60s was my response to what happened in the 50s." Those identifying with the baby boomers mentioned the difficulty they had in finding work as young adults. "I was in the middle of that huge cohort of job hunters," said one of the parents. Several of those parents who identified with the baby boomers continued to describe their lifestyle as "compatible with" but not part of the 1960s generation.

LoLo families (11%).—These parents had a relatively weak commitment to a countercultural identity in 1975 that remained low through 1993. Said one parent, "I feel like there's a lot of depravity in our generation. . . . I think we have a generation of people who are crooks." A father identified himself as part of the 1990s, not some earlier period. "It's just evolution, so to speak. Everybody evolves . . . they thought this way then, they think this way now." Our case materials suggest that these families with low generational identity were more changeable and troubled in their family circumstances. In fact, their low generational identity from the start was related to their more chaotic, unstable lives.

LoOther (18%).—Some parents had a relatively weak commitment to a countercultural identity in 1975 that was replaced by some other identity or by an inconsistent response by 1993. These parents often reported themselves as having a partial 1960s generational identity but only in retrospect: they only now see how the 1960s may have changed them. One mother commented that she no longer saw herself as "an isolated person, but as really a part of a broader group. In my generation . . . I've had some really true friendships with people. I look back at all that stuff basically fondly now." Others reported that they gained some spiritual renewal from that period but were not directly interested or involved in the counterculture.

We now turn to a more extended view of the two predominant groups of parents composing 55% of the sample: those with a relatively high countercultural commitment at midlife (HiHi), and those with a declining countercultural identity by midlife (HiLower).

HiHi parents (31%).—Many of the parents in this group were still living a life that reflected countercultural values. Although they certainly were not homogeneous, these parents shared a certain moral orientation toward what life's goals should be and how one should live in the world. In varying degrees, for instance, most parents in this group still placed little value on material things and a great deal of value on spiritual or personal growth. Many had very little disposable income, but, on the other hand, few lived in poverty. For instance, one single mother supported herself and a 12-year-old daughter on less than $20,000 a year, but their economic status was not a major concern of hers. They felt a certain pride in frequenting secondhand clothing stores; it became something of an adventure. As another mother commented, "I find wonderful stuff that other people spend weekends shopping for in shopping malls. Andrew [her son] probably has more clothes and more toys than most people but they just happen to be used." Another single mother turned down well-paying jobs if they sapped too much of her creative energy; her priority was writing fiction and poetry and she did not want to be emotionally and mentally drained by a tedious nine-to-five job. These same women, however, as they approached midlife, wondered how they would feel about their economic situation as they got older. "I really want a house" said one. "I feel like I'm going to be forty-nine years old. It's not like 'I deserve it,' but then I think, 'this is really only reasonable, to own your own house.' "

Some in this group were doing extremely well financially, living an affluent lifestyle. Although these people were grateful for their economic security, most felt some guilt about their situation. One mother felt apologetic for living in an upper-class suburb in southern California. She insisted that her values were not the same as those in the rest of her community. Another mother struggled with labels: "Because of Eric's job we do have money, we ride in limos because he's in the music business, so we have that yuppiness—but money's not the only thing to me." She later decided she could best be described as a "hippie-yuppie." About half of those in the high-commitment group started off in 1975 with somewhat higher SES than the countercultural sample as a whole and stayed there. The other half started off with a somewhat poor SES and got better off.

Danielle is an example of a mother whose economic status improved. She offered one of the statements that opened this chapter: "I think [the hippie movement is] the best thing that happened." She also commented regarding the counterculture, "I feel that in my heart we are brothers and sisters; that we are one and that we are divine." Her story illustrates a sustained commitment to countercultural values, in spite of changes in her family lifestyle:

> Danielle entered the project in a social contract relationship. When her daughter Sarida was born, she married the father "to make things easier for the child." The family lived in rural northern California in a cabin with water and a woodburning stove but no electricity. By the time Sarida was four-and-a-half, her parents had separated and Danielle was living as a single mother. At the six-year visit,

Danielle was living a more middle-class lifestyle, still in northern California. She was again in a social contract relationship and lived with her partner for four years before he was killed in an automobile accident. Over the next seven years, she dated several men but did not live with any of them. She returned to school for a doctorate in family therapy and moved to Hawaii to set up a private practice. She started living with Roy when Sarida was seventeen and married him the following year.

At the eighteen-year visit, Danielle talked about trying to maintain her 1960s values related to spiritual awareness while living a comfortable middle-class life. Although she enjoyed her professional and financial success, she worried about keeping a balance between achievement and spiritual growth. She marks the beginning of her spiritual growth to using psychedelic drugs in the 1960s. "It was in psychedelics that I first experienced the divine." At that time, she made a decision to reject the values of her very wealthy family. "It was the best thing I did, because our values are so different."

Danielle is a strong believer in "the mind-body connection." She practices meditation and studies metaphysical philosophy. When she was diagnosed with chronic fatigue, she sought treatment at a holistic clinic and now uses acupuncture and lives a "totally pure life" (no drugs, very little alcohol) to control her symptoms. She has made a conscious effort to pass these beliefs and practices on to Sarida and believes she has been successful. Danielle is still strongly gender egalitarian and proud of being involved in the Green Party, a new environmental political group.

Spiritual or personal growth was important to many other parents in the high-commitment group. Their spirituality traveled many paths: following a vision quest according to Native American practices; practicing meditation; returning to the Catholic Church and finding comfort in liturgical ritual; finding spirituality in nature; studying tai chi chuan; joining a secular Jewish community. Several parents had very negative feelings toward organized religion: "I think it [religion] comes from peoples' fear and their inability to cope. To me religion is the most backward way of dealing with the world."

Although only about 8% of counterculture families were still in communes by 1992, three out of four of these families were in the HiHi group seventeen years later (the remaining former communards are all parents who no longer have a countercultural identification and are often disaffected and bitter [HiLower]). Many in this group continued to value various forms of communal living, usually in rural settings. In one case, a divorced mother became quite successful at selling real estate. The first property she bought was a fourplex; she had no interest in living in a single-family situation, so she used two of the units for herself and rented out the other two. Her tenants have become part of her extended family. One of the fathers purchased a plot of land with seven other people, each of whom had a family dwelling on the land. He described his living situation as "semicommunal." Several families still owned parts of the land they had lived on during the 1960s and 1970s and made a point of returning periodically to reunite with former commune members. Those who no longer live in a community residence sometimes still retain their contacts and spiritual commitments to their group.

Children often diminished the intensity and practice of parents' generational identities. One couple was committed to maintaining their family in a stable, married, noncountercultural lifestyle so as not to expose their children to a difficult and changeable lifestyle similar to the one the father had experienced as a child. He felt that this commitment had a positive effect on his children. "Our children think that we were a couple of hippies. . . . We've told them all the stories of our lives after they were born, and before. They like that . . . they think it's funny."

Sarah and Jack were living in a social contract relationship at the start of the project. They married when their child Tanya was a year old due, in part, to their concern that, should Sarah die, Jack might be denied custody of the baby. Jack also felt that a legal marriage was important so that society would not look down on Tanya and treat her badly.

Over the next ten years, Jack and Sarah had two more children and moved from California to Washington state and then to Hawaii. By the eighteen-year visit, the couple had divorced, and Tanya and one of her brothers were living with Jack in the family home that Jack had built. Jack was doing quite well as a contractor. His focus was on "maintaining the stability of what we have left of our family . . . with the house and keeping everything going on day to day, for the children." Although he still professed a strong commitment to the counterculture, some of his values had changed. Before he had had gender-egalitarian views; now he felt that women should stay home with their families and men should be the breadwinners. He decried the current economic situation that forced women to join the workforce in order to maintain a decent standard of living.

As parents, members of this group had emphasized certain values with their children: social responsibility, environmental concern, anti-materialism, and open and honest communication within the family. A minority had smoked pot with their children. Other parents had been very open about their past drug use but made it clear to their children that they would prefer that the children did not follow in their footsteps. Others were comfortable with their child smoking pot if the child was "sensible and responsible."

Not surprisingly, many of the teens in the high-commitment group praised the open lines of communication in their families and felt they could discuss any topic with their parents. Jennie, for example, felt her family was different from most American families. "To me, I think we're more spiritual—we're willing to talk about things. I think we're more communicative than most kids and their parents." Janna explained that she was always honest with her parents. "Because when you start hiding things, then subconsciously it can build up with guilt in your mind. And that's what makes you wig out later in life. . . . I think if you're open, even with drug use, I think you're a lot happier. I think you feel better about what you're doing."

These teens also felt fortunate to have been raised with so few rules. Mutual respect marked the relationships between parents and children; one teen commented on how much he appreciated never being talked down to as a child. Some teens, however, were not sure they would raise their children with so much freedom. And others were determined to provide their families with more financial security than they had had growing up.

One teen said that she had a reputation for having the "coolest mom," especially during junior high school and high school. Her friends would discuss things with her mother—such as drugs and sex—that they could not discuss with their own parents. On the other hand, it was hard having a mother who could not afford to send her even five dollars, as was the case when a teen was in San Francisco, unemployed, and "living off Top Ramen." She also wonders whether it would have been better for her to have had more boundaries growing up.

Other teens described their parents' countercultural values as somewhat of a burden. Jane was annoyed by her parents' constant emphasis on social responsibility. She felt her parents were unfairly critical of her for not doing more to help the disadvantaged, and she felt guilty for not working at a soup kitchen. She also found her mother's anti-materialistic views annoying. She saw nothing wrong with spending money on new clothes, as opposed to always going to secondhand stores. For the most part, though, the teens in the high-commitment group respected their parents' values as well as their lifestyle. "I never saw my parents as that different from other people," Nell commented. "Except that my dad had longer hair than most people's parents. It's not like it's a different lifestyle. I think it's actually a better lifestyle . . . growing your own vegetables and having your own goods and chicken for food."

HiLower (24.5%).—Another group of midlife parents had reported a high commitment to the counterculture from the time their child was born until the child was roughly age 6, but significantly less commitment by the eighteen-year interview. Their stories detailing the causes for this decline often included ideological changes, personal struggles with drugs, and interpersonal problems. Many parents had lost the conviction that countercultural identity mattered to them. Such an identity became irrelevant, feared, or blamed for their current troubles.

Some parents no longer particularly identified with the 1960s because they did not feel, in retrospect, that they had been "true to themselves" at that time. These parents look back on their countercultural identity in 1975 as a false identity. Jessie, one of the mothers in this group, thought that if she had been truer to herself she would have been "straighter." She struggled to raise her daughter as a single parent. Her midlife is improving—but not because of the sixties in her view.

> At the time of the first interview, Jessie was in a social contract relationship "out of love" for the father of her daughter. She and her partner separated when their daughter Lissa was four years old. Jessie remarried when Lissa was twelve and moved with her new husband to Oregon. She returned to school, got a bachelor's in geology, and entered graduate school. At the eighteen-year visit she reflected on her past. She said that she now felt that living in a social contract relationship was "morally wrong"; she was more comfortable in a traditional marriage. Her experience with drugs in the 1960s was largely a charade; while her partner took acid, she would break off a little and "pretend" to take it. When she met her present husband, she felt relieved to be returning to the values of her family of origin.
>
> Jessie was apprehensive about Lissa becoming sexually active at too young an age and had urged Lissa to be careful with drugs. She knew that Lissa smoked pot and went to parties where they took the drug "ecstasy." She told Lissa, "I don't want you taking drugs. . . . I've seen a lot of people destroyed."

A number of parents with declining or denied generational identity had been heavily involved in the drug scene of the 1960s and 1970s. In a few cases, drugs continued to play a central and negative role in their lives. At the extreme, one family was temporarily homeless after both parents had lost their jobs. At nineteen, their teen was working full-time and giving most of her earnings to her parents. She told the interviewer that she was afraid her parents were using the money to buy drugs. Another single mother had struggled with drug addiction most of her child's life. She felt that she started using drugs as a reaction to her chaotic home life. "Because I felt so lost, I used."

Others had been involved with drugs, but stopped using them during their pregnancy. If they started up again, they stopped when their children were young. One single mother stopped when her child was born. "It was just time to take a break," she commented. Another mother stopped before she was pregnant even though her close friends were still smoking heavily. "I did it to experience a different kind of consciousness; I didn't know who I was; I was just darn sure I didn't want to be like my parents." To those parents in our study who had been involved with drugs, much of the overall counterculture era was clearly associated with the drug scene; once they stopped using they no longer felt committed to that period. For them, the positive features of the counterculture were submerged by the negative effects of the drugs or family struggles they associated with drugs.

Some of the parents expressed real bitterness about the era and their experience of it, which they felt led to a troubled life. They strongly but negatively identify with their generation in an angry way. One mother commented, "It wasn't real easy. It would have been okay if I wasn't drinking or using. I think it would have been just fine. But then if I wasn't [using], I don't know if I would have been in that kind of a movement." She felt that the countercultural movement was "okay," but that many people—including herself—were "really lost."

A number of parents followed the values and practices associated with the counterculture, but not because of the social movements of that time. They resisted defining their life choices as due to having belonged to a generation. One said, "It's not what we [in our communal group] were doing at all [i.e, participating in the counterculture]. I guess in that respect I have always been a countercultural person but I never thought of it as the counterculture." Another said, "There have always been countercultural *people* and there always will be." These parents resist being associated with a 1960s generational identity because they feel that the countercultural lifestyle is broader than the 1960s generation or any social movement.

> Nora and Dan, for example, were living as a social contract couple in 1975. Nora made clear then that she did not consider herself as living an alternative lifestyle. She "was just doing what was natural; it's just who I am." At twenty-two, she was an experienced and expert midwife held in high regard by many of the community obstetricians. She described marriage as a "silly institution," saying that she and Dan were "married in the deepest sense of the word." The family subsisted on public assistance, with Nora and Dan sharing childcare tasks and Dan doing most of the housework.
>
> By the eighteen-year contact Nora and Dan were still together as a social contract couple. They had four children

between the ages of thirteen and twenty. Dan was working in the defense industry with computers, Nora had gone back to school to get licensed in midwifery, the children were all in school or employed. She still had a thriving practice in midwifery; many of her clients now were illegal immigrants, who were comfortable with midwives and needed inexpensive care, whereas in the past most were counterculture families who wanted a "natural" childbirth in their homes. She talked at length about the values she had tried to instill in her children: gender egalitarianism, a strong belief in the inherent value of all human beings, concern for the environment, liberal political beliefs with an emphasis on improving conditions for the underclass, and a skepticism about the intentions of governments. She rejected the notion of a generational identity, insisting that what she cultivated was a "human identity." She commented that she herself was raised in a countercultural manner when she grew up in the late 1940s and 1950s, and the 1960s just seemed routine to her.

Some parents thought that carrying a generational identity of any kind meant a lack of personal growth and self-enhancement. To them, living within cultural categories restricted self-development; it implied living in the past or persisting in a stage one should grow out of. These parents recognized their generational identity but denied most of its relevance to their current lives. This is itself, perhaps, a countercultural trait: always questioning the past, always reconstituting aspects of meaning and identity. One parent did not identify with what her same-age countercultural-era friends were going through. "It has something to do with not living in a big house in the suburbs but also that I didn't *calcify* the way some of my friends have." Another mother said "I don't like it [the countercultural generation] now. . . . It isn't like I am *locked* in the sixties, or whatever."

Other parents now felt that they should have been identified with some other group. An identity of resistance *was* central to them but it was not the counterculture movement that was central. One mother had started to feel that she did belong to a generational group—but not the 1960s generation: "I only identify with women who are fifty, who have been molested, who are discovering their power, and learning to . . . come into their own, playing drums, who are growing and look-

ing to each other for support." In a related fashion, other parents identified with one aspect of the counterculture (such as feminism) but
rejected the others (such as spiritual concerns or drug use)—indeed,
denied the value and utility of these aspects of the counterculture. Thus
they had a very qualified generational identity, specific to one or another strand of the counterculture.

Toby considered herself a feminist, not a 1960s countercultural
product. She said that she had never considered herself a hippie. "To
us, the hippies were lazy, they didn't do anything. That was not me.
I studied alternative things and was interested in a new world. I still
am, but now more so on an individual level. Feminism taught me this.
It's making a lasting impact on people as individuals that is important."

For some, the commitment to the counterculture was replaced by
a spiritual awakening. One mother, who had been part of a commune
when her child was born, became involved with a New Age church after
having a vision during which she spoke in tongues. At the eighteen-year
interview she was deeply committed to her religion. Another mother
joined a yoga community after years of reading and searching for truth.
She looked back with disbelief at her countercultural days: "To just
live as a hippie is very selfish. You were doing it for yourself; you
weren't thinking about anyone else."

> For Wendy, commitment to the counterculture and
> spiritual awakening were one and the same. She talked
> about her reasons for joining her residential religious com-
> munity: "At that time . . . it was the Vietnam War and I
> just felt the political situation in the country was so hope-
> less that there was nothing you could do politically. Part
> of my reason for going was the only thing you could do
> was to try and work on yourself . . . and I wanted to live
> in a spiritual community that as a group, could somehow
> change the country." She stayed for fifteen years and left,
> after becoming very disillusioned with the leaders, whose
> lifestyles were not consistent with their Buddhist teachings.
> She described the changes in her attitude: "Now, am I
> committed to a religious group and willing to live in a
> communal situation? No. Am I willing to have no material
> possessions? No. Am I worried about retirement? Yes. It's
> not like I've become a conservative or something, or even
> that I would go get a job in a corporation." But she wants

nothing more to do with group living. "I did it for fifteen years and basically it was a failure. I'm very disillusioned with group situations."

Some parents, no longer committed, still expressed some nostalgia about the period. "It was wonderful—I'm glad I did it, and I'm glad I'm alive and healthy." One described herself as an ex-hippie saying, "I still, in a lot of ways, feel like the person I was then, but I have to live in a different world and environment now." She felt guilty when she considered her upper-middle-class lifestyle. "Now I seem to care [about material things] too much, which isn't really good. I see myself turning into my mother in a lot of ways and I don't like that." Her feelings reflected a larger group of parents who still had some identification with the counterculture but much diluted or conflicted. Another mother said, "I went to all of the antiwar demonstrations. I went to all the love-ins. I went to all the concerts. I did all that then. So I'm part of that generation, but I'm just not as involved. . . . I'll leave that up to the kids."

Some of the teens who grew up in the HiLower or LoLo groups of families had also become very involved with drugs. One had been a heavy acid user; after a bad trip he stopped using but continued to sell it. Several others reported smoking "a lot" of pot, but there were also teens who had made the conscious decision not to start smoking. Some teens had unhappy memories of their early years related to drugs and alcohol. One remembered being left in the car with other children while his mother and her friends went bar hopping. "I guess he felt like I was abandoning him a lot—I was all he had, and I moved around a lot," commented his mother.

Sometimes, teens made an effort to be positive about their parents' countercultural involvements even though they had not appropriated any of their parents' ideals and had not excused the pain the parents may have caused them. Jason talked about his family's economic struggles: "I think my parents made the decision to follow their ideals rather than do what would have made them wealthy. It has some negative material consequences, and the sadness in my life is that I am way too aware of these material consequences." He was not sure he would be happier than his parents as an adult, but he was confident he would be richer. For some teens, then, the memories and personal losses they experienced made them unlikely to say they had a positive attitude toward their parents' family lifestyles.

For the most part, however, these teens had surprisingly positive attitudes toward their parents' lifestyles—often much more positive than in their own reports. The son of Wendy, who had lived in a religious community for 15 years, respected his mother's decision to live a "nonmaterialistic lifestyle." He appreciated growing up with the realization that "there was something more out there besides a nine-to-five job and financial security." The son who remembered being left in the car also talked at length about how much he had been positively influenced by his mother's spirituality.

But like the teens in the HiHi group, they also had more conventional ideas about how they would like their children to be raised: with more financial security, in a two-parent home, and with more father involvement. "I want to live in a house and not an apartment," Evie explained. "My parents will never own a house. And I want a house where I can have a yard with a dog—that's my thing."

COUNTERCULTURAL IDENTITY AND FAMILY LIFE

A countercultural generational identity at midlife is higher among parents who, in their previous years of family life, tried practices that were intended to be countercultural, challenged implicit cultural conventions, and tried to reflect their values in how they lived out family life with their children. Sex-egalitarian values for raising children, for example, involved reallocating domestic tasks, picking special toys, developing nongendered stories for children, and so forth (Weisner and Wilson-Mitchell 1990; Weisner et al. 1994). Pronaturalism—a concern for the environment and for a free (i.e., "natural") expressiveness—is another example (Weisner et al. 1983). Living out a very modest life with respect to material possessions, including a kind of voluntary poverty, is another area of life with direct translation of countercultural values of antimaterialism into family practice (Weisner 1982). Political activism incorporating family members into activist groups, causes, marches, and so on, is yet another example. The HiHi and HiLower parents both had relatively high countercultural values and ideals in their youth. But parents who attempted to translate those values into family practices were more likely to have retained their countercultural identity at midlife, as their children moved through adolescence.

Those who actively tried to put their countercultural goals into practice in child rearing in 1980 were more likely to be in the HiHi group of parents in 1994. In 1980, 47% of the HiHi families had been high innovators in actual family practice, compared to 24% of the entire sample and 18% of the HiLower parents. Most HiLower parents were classified early in the study as having countercultural values as well as some practices, but the Lower parents showed only modest or inconsistent *incorporation* of them into practice in family life as their children grew up.

FAMILY LIFESTYLE AND GENERATIONAL IDENTITY

Parents who started out with a high commitment to the counterculture and who are still identified with it (HiHi) lived in varied family styles. What distinguishes their family patterns over time is their commitment to sustaining their family circumstances, whether as single mothers, as social contract couples, in some sort of collective living situation, or in legal marriage. Parents with a sustained high countercultural identity were single mothers by choice for most of their child's life (40%) or in a stable married-couple family (33%), with 13% each either in communes or in unstable, changing family situations. The single mothers in the HiHi group were more likely to have stayed single for most of the child's life, rather than divorcing, remarrying, or living with mates for years at a time and then leaving. Of these other paths, changing partners over time is the most common.

In contrast, 73% of the HiLower parents who started off high but *declined* in their generational identity have been in two-parent family situations for most of the child's life. However, most of these are re-marriages or unmarried couple situations that have been changing over time. Those who never had a particularly strong generational identity—the LoLo and LoOther groups—are predominantly single mothers whose status is due to circumstance—divorce, separation— more than to ideological commitment. Sixty percent were in unstable, changing family circumstances.

Since the HiHi and HiLower groups began the study similarly high in generational identity, the longitudinal data suggest that it is the *family* experiences, especially instability and troubles in parents' family lives, that lead to the changes in identity over the years more than the other way around. Clearly generational identity *at* midlife and family experiences *leading up to* midlife are interconnected, so our design does not allow strong causal inferences. Nonetheless, successfully achieving a sustained, meaningful, congruent family life using values, goals, and practices from the countercultural era seems to assist in maintaining that positive generational identity over time. Parents who started out with countercultural orientations who were not able to achieve this kind of family adaptive resilience more often have abandoned that identity, blame it for their problems, deny it ever was important to them, or find it a false self.

CONTINUITY IN COUNTERCULTURAL VALUES: PARENTS' GENERATIONAL IDENTITY AND ADOLESCENT DEVELOPMENT

Two of the central concerns of our countercultural parents at midlife were: the adaptive competence of the teenage children, and parents' success at transmitting their countercultural values to their teens. This is also the single most common question we are asked about the sixties parents and their "children of the children of the sixties": So, how did the kids turn out?

Parents hoped that the positive values from their past would live on in their children, but also recognized how different their children's world today is, and, in many cases, how much their family life now did not match their plans of eighteen years ago. Listening to parents one might conclude, and worry as they do, that things have changed so much in their lives, and in the world around their children, that little continuity is likely at this particular point in midlife—a point when teens complete high school and many begin their move out of their parents' home. The extent of change and turmoil, drug use, and economic hardship experienced by a subset of our parents and teens might also lead to concern about the teens' future, for these are real risks. Was there continuity between parents and teens in values and ideals, and what were the levels of competence and achievement as the teens complete high school?

To answer this question, we turn to analyses performed on the full Family Lifestyles Project sample of parents and teens. We include interview materials from the forty-two nonconventional families we studied intensively, in order to complement the quantitative findings with family stories that exemplify the qualitative patterns in the families.

VALUE ORIENTATIONS

The countercultural parents in our study had teenagers who tended to share their parents' values. Further, parents with a sustained values commitment and generational identity over the eighteen years of our study had children who were more similar in values than parents whose generational identity had declined.

For example, table 1 shows our data on eight values dimensions, comparably measured over an eighteen-year period. All eight correla-

TABLE 1. Correlations of Mother Values and Teen Values across Time ($N = 200$)

	Time of Survey				
Value Domain[a]	Mother, Trimester and 3-Year	Mother, 3-Year and 6-Year	Mother, 6-Year and 18-Year	Mother, Trimester, and Teen, 18-Year	Mother and Teen, 18-Year
Achievement	.11	.55**	.19**	−.08	.15*
Authority	.48**	.71**	.63**	.33**	.40**
Humanism	.09	.48**	.42**	.33**	.40**
Materialism	.19**	.40**	.49**	.14*	.21**
Scientific Knowing	.24**	.52**	.50**	.30**	.20**
Pronatural	.44**	.69**	.60**	.32**	.30**
Future Orientation	.29**	.66**	.26**	.08	.19**
Sex Egalitarian	.52**	.62**	.50**	.32**	.45**
Canonical Correlation[b]	.71**	.78**	.72**	.63**	.54**

[a] Values assessed with eight questionnaire items each; scale ranges, 1–8.
[b] Canonical correlation computed between two sets of eight value domains.
* $p \leq .05$; ** $p \leq .01$.

tions between mothers and their teens are statistically significant, more than between mothers and their own values orientations when they were pregnant eighteen years earlier. The canonical correlations are particularly striking and show a substantial common variance across all eight values (Weisner and Garnier 1992, 1995).

Nevertheless, the teens and parents vary in the strength of their commitments to these eight values. Values and cultural goals were transmitted—but also transformed. In our sample, values are selectively transformed by new generational cohort effects, by parent or teen gender, and adolescent rebellion against parents. For example, most parents in conventional as well as countercultural lifestyles turn out to be less materialistic than their adolescent children. Differences in materialism show a generational, cohort influence, as well as a counter-cultural influence. Teens and parents alike were responding to the economic changes of the 1980s and 1990s. Times are tougher, there are fewer jobs than job seekers, and wages are flat or declining. These current economic conditions were clearly influencing teens' (and parents') cultural goals and values. Our field notes and interviews with teens and parents were filled with concerns about jobs and long-term financial security. Many voluntarily poor countercultural parents regretted their nonmaterialistic pasts, feeling that it is too late for them to enter the economic mainstream.

Teens worried about a declining economic future.—Teens with worries about their own future were also worried about their parents' ability to support themselves in their old age. As one teen commented regarding his family's economic circumstances, "I think they might have some problems. . . . I get a little worried. I feel like I'm the parent."

Differences in gender-egalitarian values show a gender effect as well as a countercultural effect. The teenage girls and their mothers in the study were more committed to gender egalitarianism than boys and fathers—this is true for both conventional and nonconventional families. The countercultural parents (mothers and fathers alike) also were more feminist and egalitarian than parents in our comparison sample. But mothers and daughters are more feminist and egalitarian in values *within* the countercultural sample as well. This holds for parents with sustained (HiHi) as well as declining generational identity. The character of feminist beliefs among most of our countercultural teens and parents at midlife is predominantly liberal and humanistic, rather than a more radical feminist orientation (Stein 1995).

Another important feature of intergenerational transmission of cultural values is that adolescents would resist or oppose their parents' beliefs about accepting normative societal authority. Teens who grew up in our conventional comparison sample were *less* likely than their parents to say that they accepted such authorities as politicians, advice books, and experts. Teens in countercultural families with sustained countercultural identity (HiHi) were *more* likely to say that they *accepted* such authority than teens in other groups, even though the HiHi group *parents* were most likely to counter authority. Boys and girls alike showed this pattern. Parents with declining generational identity were in the middle on this measure, as were their teens. Our interview data with teens support the interpretation that teens tended to do the opposite of what their parents sometimes said regarding such matters as following or resisting authority—in part simply because it was opposite. Teens in our sample did resist, rebel, and reject (although selectively) society's norms as had their parents. But they also rebelled against their parents' authority—whichever direction their parents tended to lean toward, they sometimes just leaned the other way.

Social and political attitudes of teens.—The teens in our sample, like their parents, were clearly more liberal in political and social attitudes than their peers. We asked the teens in our study to respond to the Freshman Questionnaire, which has been used to monitor the values and attitudes of college freshmen since 1966 (Astin et al. 1993). Most of the differences between the countercultural and the national sample were in the area of *political attitudes* and *values orientations* and *not* in such domains as aspirations, self-perception of abilities, or favorite activities.

The teens in our sample were substantially more left of the political center than the national Astin sample (table 2). Only 4% of the teens from our countercultural families said they were "right of center," compared to 23% of the national sample. Fifty-nine percent of teens from higher-values commitment families (HiHi) identified themselves as liberal or far left in their political views (adding together the first two rows in table 2), compared to 47% from HiLower or LoLo families, 44% of the conventionally married comparison sample, and 27% of the Astin national-sample freshmen.

Teens in our sample also had significantly stronger humanistic, nonviolent, and egalitarian views than the national sample teens. They were more likely to be in favor of the legalization of marijuana, more likely to feel that the federal government is not doing enough to stop

TABLE 2. Comparison of Political Views of Family Lifestyle Project Adolescents, with a National Sample of College Freshmen[a]

Political View	Conventional Comparison Sample (%) (n = 43)	Nonconventional, Higher Commitment (%) (n = 98)	Nonconventional, Lower Commitment (%) (n = 53)	National sample of freshmen[a] (%)
Far left	0.0	8.5	8.0	2.5
Liberal	35.9	51.1	38.0	24.7
Middle-of-the-road	38.5	36.2	50.0	49.9
Conservative	23.1	4.3	2.0	21.4
Far right	2.6	0.0	2.0	1.5

[a] Student information responses of 220,757 first-time, full-time freshmen attending two- and four-year colleges and universities are described in Astin et al. (1993). Numbers indicate percentage identifying themselves as holding a particular political view.

pollution, and more likely to disagree with the statement that married women should remain in the home (table 3).

Our findings were that, compared to a comparable national sample (Astin et al. 1993), the teens from our countercultural families were much more liberal than their U.S. peers and shared their parents' liberal social values. Countercultural parents seem to have successfully transferred many of their ideals to their children. Furthermore, the parents with a sustained generational identity (HiHi) more often had teens with values similar to their own than did those parents with declining identities (HiLower). For one mother, the similarities between her generation and her son's were at once amusing and a bit discouraging. "I notice there's a segment of today's kids who are wandering off to Grateful Dead concerts, smoking a lot of pot," she said, laughing. "And I think 'Oh don't do that'; I mean I know it's a lot of fun, but it's so unoriginal for one thing."

In spite of the clear success of most countercultural parents to have carried their goals and ideals into their children's lives, many parents did not see these signs of relative continuity. Paradoxically, many parents believed that their teens were *unlike* them, were much more conservative than they were, and were part of a current teen generation very different from them. They struggled to come to terms at midlife with their goals of creating some continuity between their own and their children's ideals.

Parents often focused on the many changes they perceived in the cultural and economic circumstances of their teens' birth cohort compared to theirs and the effect of these changes on the discontinuity parents perceived in values and beliefs between them and their children. Sharon talked about her son, Evan, for example. "Evan's generation has it tough—there's not as much hope and the world is more depressing now. A lot of kids in this generation feel really angry about a lot of things; that's kind of depressing. And frankly there's nothing very wonderful or special about them. Our generation . . . everything was open to us and everything was exciting and I don't see that for them. The music was wonderful. Look at the music today, there's nothing coming out today. I think it's much more difficult."

Parents also focused on relatively small differences in values between family members, which loom very large *within* the family but not from the perspective of national samples. Many of our parents thought their own generational identity weakened and countercultural

TABLE 3. Comparison of Responses by Family Lifestyle Project Adolescents, with the National Sample of College Freshmen

Questionnaire Item	Conventional Comparison Sample (%) (n = 43)	Nonconventional, Higher Commitment (%) (n = 98)	Nonconventional, Lower Commitment (%) (n = 53)	National sample of freshmen[a] (%)
Agree strongly or somewhat:				
The federal government is not doing enough to promote disarmament.	69.8	84.4	82.4	64.3
The federal government is not doing enough to control environmental pollution.	83.7	95.9	92.1	84.4
The death penalty should be abolished.	14.8	38.6	23.1	22.1
If two people really like each other, it's all right for them to have sex even if they've known each other for only a very short time.	48.8	67.8	67.9	44.8
The activities of married women are best confined to the home and family.	39.5	10.3	13.5	24.2
Marijuana should be legalized.	28.6	62.3	54.6	28.2
Objectives considered to be essential or very important:				
One should help others who are in difficulty.	53.5	65.3	73.5	63.6
One should participate in an organization like the Peace Corps or Vista.	9.3	22.9	18.9	25.6
One should develop a meaningful philosophy of life.	55.9	66.4	75.5	44.6

[a] Student information responses of 220,757 first-time, full-time freshmen attending two- and four-year colleges and universities are described in Astin et al. (1993).

values commitments declined, of course. But this is a judgment relative to their own pasts or their perception of relative changes with their own past friends and peers. In contrast, we have already seen how relatively liberal, or feminist, or concerned with the environment the nonconventional families actually are overall, compared to the Astin sample or our own comparison sample.

Those families with declining generational identity and values (Hi-Lower) were definitely more likely to blame their teens' problems on the counterculture itself as well as in part on themselves and their family situations. Annie commented on the lack of stability in her son Noah's life, emphasizing that Noah's generation is coming from a more unstable lifestyle than she came from. "I was almost going to say 'dysfunctional,' but we all come from that, so that's really not the right word." Her own family or origin, for example, had been much more stable than what she had to offer her own son, in her view.

PROTECTIVE EFFECTS OF A SUSTAINED GENERATIONAL IDENTITY AND VALUES COMMITMENT

Schooling.—Significantly more teens living in nonconventional families with a strong commitment to their lifestyle and values (HiHi) remained in high school and graduated compared to either teens in nonconventional families with a lower lifestyle commitment (Hi-Lower), or teens in the conventional comparison sample. Stronger commitment to nonconventional lifestyle values also significantly correlated with higher grade point averages and SAT scores. This finding holds after we control for parental socioeconomic status and the child's IQ at age 6.

Parental values seemed to help protect adolescents from substance use and related school problems. In our sample, many of the usual troubles of adolescents and their families lead to noncompletion of high school in about 8% of teens (e.g, heavy drug use, family stresses, a history of school trouble). A sustained generational identity offered both some family stability and, we believe, some parental ability to provide their children with meaningful cultural and personal interpretations regarding family problems. Parents in more troubled, changing family situations without sustained generational identity, had teens who were more likely to stop out or to drop out fully. Furthermore, children who stopped out of school were more likely to go back and complete high school if they grew up in families with more stability and stronger generational identity. Adolescents in stronger commitment families reported in our interviews and in questionnaires that their parents were more positively involved with their children, more accepting of individuation, more child centered and less rejecting, and more likely to value and encourage verbal interaction than parents in families with lower or declining values commitment (Garnier et al. 1995). (Academic data summarized in Weisner and Garnier 1992; Garnier, Stein, and Jacobs 1995; Garnier and Weisner 1994; Weisner and Garnier 1994.)

Drug use.—Countercultural parents were often heavy drug users, and their adolescents were heavier drug users than their age cohort when compared to national survey data and our comparison sample. The magnitude of differences was substantial: National Institute of Drug Abuse (NIDA) national survey data reported that 18% of boys and 16% of girls use hard drugs; our adolescents reported use two to three times higher. The National Institute of Drug Abuse reported 24% of boys and 18% of girls as using cannabis; about 50% of our teens reported use (see Johnston et al. 1993).

Our parents worried about teen drug use. The nature of drug use has changed, many said; they often felt that their own use had been a major mistake. They often recalled that because their mates were now or had been users, family life had been ruined. They hoped never to repeat this mistake. At midlife, many of the parents in our study altered their beliefs regarding the significance of drug use and feared its influence because it threatened the future of their children.

Our data suggested that daughters in our nonconventional sample are relatively heavier users than daughters in the NIDA survey data and that the negative effects of drug use affected girls more in our countercultural sample. Associated with girls' drug use were more dropouts, pregnancy, leaving home before graduation from high school, and more troubled interpersonal relationships than reported for boys and their parents.

Parents with greater continuity in their generational identity were less likely to have teens who were heavy drug users compared to families with declining identity and commitment. The effect of continuity in values and countercultural generational identity persisted after controlling for family stability, parents' prior and current drug use, and SES. Again, parents' explanations and the meanings they gave their teens regarding drug use seem to have provided some protective effect. (Data summarized from Garnier and Stein [1994], and Garnier and Weisner [1992, 1995]).

CONCLUSION

An interesting paradox marks European-American parents' talk about their midlife course and countercultural generational influence. The counterculture emphasized the collective in many of its values and social practices. Communes, group decision making, resource sharing, open family life, and a "spirit of community" were shared values of the "new tribes." Yet when many countercultural parents talked about their own identity and what had led them to live their lives in certain ways, they, like most Americans, were reluctant to say, "I was a product, at least in part, of a social movement; it was the subculture of the time that shaped my present identity." They were reluctant to lose the personal agency and choice that Americans suppose directs their cultural careers. They implicitly at least, utilized an individualistic, self-affirming, autonomous definition of what produced their life course. They either spoke of the self as personally constructed by individual choice rather than social forces, or they critiqued the counterculture for having *denied* them the ability to be agents of their destiny. Parents most often described their generational identity at midlife as influenced by and influencing their internal, private self, a self with agency, goals, values, and feelings of worth (Modell 1996). Parents did, however, consider at least one social group—their *family*—a powerful social force shaping identity. Family losses, change, and instability as well as successes were often mentioned. In the implicit view of our informants, social and political movements (prior or current) are less salient for self and identity than either personal experience or family.

Parents experiencing sad and sometimes tragic life events were more likely to blame the counterculture directly for their suffering, whereas those with more satisfying lives attributed their satisfaction to their *own* agency, albeit perhaps aided by the cultural movements of the 1960s. Happier countercultural parents more often described their cultural career as a series of personal achievements and decisions, perhaps loosely informed by their earlier experiences. In this respect, the parents in our study were thinking about the self and about identity much as all Americans do. Countercultural parents' goals and values and family practices were different than other Americans' in many ways, but these parents' model of the individual and egocentric self was similar to the conventional American model (Markus and Kitayama 1994).

Our results point to the importance of family life in the formation and expression of generational identity at midlife. A sustained, consistent generational identity can make the difference between a positive or negative life experience between youth and midlife and can have protective effects for teens and parents alike. By focusing on family influence and personal identity over time, we are certainly not in any way suggesting that the culture-historical world around the families—its economy, cultural representations of aging and gender and class, the American concern with school achievement, and certain cultural definitions of "success" in adolescence—did not matter to parents' views of their generational identity. Rather, we look at the family and personal levels of identity to bring out the *meanings* of the wider culture-historical world. Exclusively economic or demographic models sometimes miss or omit family and personal meanings entirely.

Similarly, some versions of cultural discourse theories and cultural constructionist theories do not take account of agentic actors, with both a social and a private self, with cultural as well as personal goals, actively responding to cultural constraints and opportunities. The parents and teens in our samples were not overly constricted or overdetermined by cultural categories ("the sixties," "midlife").

The countercultural generation is but one of many American generational units engaging in its adaptive project. Our results cry out for comparisons to other American subcultures, ethnic groups, and parents and children reaching their adolescent and midlife transitions in other populations around the world. Our focus on this particular group of countercultural families is intended to contribute to comparative developmental study such as in this volume, and should not be prematurely generalized to other American subcultures.

We have emphasized the successes as well as failures, in the parents' eyes, of countercultural experimentation with family life. Families sometimes lost a positive generational identity or despaired that their idealistic goals from the sixties were not met in society or in their own family experience. Although individuals may have despaired at midlife in some cases, we should not lose sight of the wider achievement of the countercultural movement. Their family experiments were examples of cultural evolution at work: parents trying out new practices, new family forms, in the service of their cultural and personal goals. Some practices survived, some did not.

This view fits, we believe, with many of the classic longitudinal developmental studies that take culture and cohort into account. Life course analysis of this kind moves back and forth between the individual's desires and planful strategizing to achieve goals, and the regulatory, normative influence of the cultural community (Elder 1987, 186; LeVine 1979; LeVine et al. 1994). Many of the ideas and practices of the counterculture have diffused into the wider society, so that many Americans actually no longer recall that there was a time when these were rare, stigmatizing, and difficult paths to take: single parenthood by choice, unmarried couples raising children, gender-egalitarian child rearing, environmental concerns brought into the home and community, returning to at-home births and experimenting with nonconventional birthing practices and less medicalization, the practice of non-Western religion and new spiritual movements, healthier and safer foods and diets. In the 1970s, only the counterculture and other "deviant and minority groups" advocated those things. Other experiments tried at the time have not diffused because they were too hard to put into practice, had significant social or personal costs, or did not fit with other American goals: communal living, "open" family relationships, isolation from family and community, excessive drug use, voluntary poverty (as opposed to frugal living), and others.

Perhaps midlife, among its other meanings in our culture, is the time when parents are able to recall and assess the results of their successful and sometimes flawed experiments as youths, as they see their own adolescent children facing some of the same adaptive projects. Midlife for countercultural parents was and is a negotiated agreement between self, family, and society (past and present), not the playing out of some invariant institutional-normative imperative. Indeed, American family norms themselves were revised by the nonconventional family lifestyle members in our study. In similar fashion, midlife for parents and teens is in part an agreement worked out, revised, and made visible in family interactions and values.

REFERENCES

Astin, A. A, W. S. Korn, and E. R. Riggs. 1993. *The American Freshman: National Norms for Fall 1993.* Los Angeles: UCLA Higher Education Research Institute.

Baltes, P., and O. G. Brim. 1980. *Life-Span Development and Behavior,* vol. 3. New York: Academic Press.

Bellah, R., et al. 1985. *Habits of the Heart.* New York: Harper & Row.

Berger, B. 1981. *The Survival of a Counterculture: Ideological Work and Everyday Life among Rural Communards.* Berkeley and Los Angeles: University of California Press.

Chisholm, J. S. 1983. *Navajo Infancy: An Ethological Study of Child Development.* Hawthorne, New York: Aldine.

———. 1992. "Putting People in Biology: Toward a Synthesis of Biological and

Psychological Anthropology." In *New Directions in Psychological Anthropology,* edited by T. Schwartz, G. M. White, and C. A. Lutz, 125–49. New York: Cambridge University Press.

DeMartini, J. R. 1983. "Social Movement Participation: Political Socialization, Generational Consciousness, and Lasting Effects." *Youth and Society* 15:195–223.

Easterlin, R. A. 1980. *Birth and Fortune: The Impact of Numbers on Personal Welfare.* New York: Basic Books.

Eiduson, B. T, J. Cohen, and J. Alexander. 1973. "Alternatives in Child Rearing in the 1970s." *American Journal of Orthopsychiatry* 43:721–31.

Eiduson, B. T, M. Kornfein, I. L. Zimmerman, and T. S. Weisner.1982. "Comparative Socialization Practices in Alternative Family Settings." In *Nontraditional Families,* edited by M. Lamb. New York: Plenum Press. (Reprinted in *Childhood Socialization,* edited by G. Handel, 73–101 [New York: Aldine, 1988].)

Eiduson, B. T, and T. S. Weisner. 1978. "Alternative Family Styles: Effects on Young Children." In *Mother/Child Father/Child Relationships,* edited by J. H. Stevens, Jr., and M. Mathews, 197–221. Washington, D.C.: National Association for the Education of Young Children.

Elder, Glen. 1985. "Household, Kinship, and the Life Course: Perspectives on Black Families and Children." In *Beginnings: The Social and Affective Development of Black Children,* edited by Margaret B. Spencer, Geraldine K. Brokins, and Walter R. Allen, 29–43. Hillsdale, N.J.: Erlbaum Associates.

Elder, G. 1974. *Children of the Great Depression: Social Change in Life Experience.* Chicago: University of Chicago Press.

———. 1987. "Families and Lives: Some Developments in Life-course Studies." *Journal of Family History* 1 (1–3): 179–99.

———. 1991. "Family Transitions, Stress, and Health." In *Family Transitions,* edited by P. Cowan and E. M. Hetherington. Hillsdale, N.J.: Erlbaum Associates.

Elder, G., A. Caspi, and T. van Nguyen. 1986. "Resourceful and Vulnerable Children: Family Influence in Hard Times." In *Development as Action in Context: Problem Behavior and Normal Youth Development,* edited by R. K. Silbereisen, K. Eyfurth, and G. Rudinger, 167–86. Berlin: Springer Verlag.

Erasmus, C. J. 1977. *In Search of the Common Good.* New York:Free Press.

Fendrich, J. M., and K. L. Lovoy. 1988. "Back to the Future: Adult Political Behavior of Former Student Activists." *American Sociological Review* 53:780–84.

Flacks, R. 1988. *Making History: The American Left and the American Mind.* New York: Columbia University Press.

Gallimore, R., T. S. Weisner, S. Kaufman, and L. Bernheimer. 1989. "The Social Construction of Ecocultural Niches: Family Accommodation of Developmentally Delayed Children." *American Journal of Mental Retardation* 94 (3): 216–30.

Garnier, H., and J. A. Stein. 1994. "Long-Term Impact of Maternal Drug Use and

Family Nonconventionality on Adolescent Academic Performance." Paper presented at the meeting of Society for Research on Adolescence, San Diego, February.

Garnier, H., J. A. Stein, and J. Jacobs. 1995. "Longitudinal Model of Family Nonconventionality, Adolescent Achievement and Drug Use on Completion of High School." Paper presented at the meeting of the American Educational Research Association, San Francisco, April.

Garnier, H., and T. S. Weisner. 1992. "Countercultural Drug Use Then and Now: A 16-Year Longitudinal Study of Children Growing Up in Drug-Using Families." Paper presented at the meeting of the American Educational Research Association, San Francisco, April.

———. 1994. "Long-Term Effects of Nonconventional Family Life-Styles on 12th Grade School Achievement." Paper presented at the meeting of the American Educational Research Association, New Orleans, April.

———. 1995. "Countercultural and Nonconventional Family Lifestyles, Family Values, and Adolescent Substance Use." Paper presented at the meeting of the Society for Research in Child Development, Indianapolis, April.

Gitlin, T. 1993. *The Sixties: Years of Hope, Days of Rage.* New York: Bantam.

Gitlin, T., and M. Kazin. 1988. "Second Thoughts." *Tikkun* 3 (1): 49–52.

Goldschmidt, W. 1990. *The Human Career: The Self in the Symbolic World.* Cambridge, Mass.: Blackwell.

Gottlieb, A. 1987. *Do You Believe in Magic? The Second Coming of the Sixties Generation.* New York: Times Books.

Jennings, M. K. 1987. "Residues of a Movement: The Aging of the American Protest Generation." *American Political Science Review* 81:367–82.

Johnston, L., P. O'Malley, and J. Bachman. 1993. *The "Monitoring the Future" Study, 1975–92,* vol. 1. Rockville, Md.: National Institute on Drug Abuse.

Keniston, K. 1968. *Young Radicals: Notes on Committed Youth.* New York: Harcourt, Brace, & World.

———. 1971. *Youth and Dissent.* New York: Harcourt, Brace.

Law, L. 1990. *Flashing on the Sixties: A Tribal Documentary.* Produced and directed by Lisa Law. Pacific Arts Video (PAV5044). Videocassette.

LeVine, R. 1977. "Child Rearing as Cultural Adaptation." In *Culture and Infancy,* edited by P. Leiderman, S. Tulkin, and A. Rosenfeld, 15–27. New York: Academic Press.

LeVine, R. A., S. Dixon, S. LeVine, A. Richman, P. H. Leiderman, C. H. Keefer, and T. B. Brazelton. 1994. *Child Care and Culture: Lessons from Africa.* New York: Cambridge University Press.

LeVine, S. 1979. *Mothers and Wives: Gusii Women of East Africa.* Chicago: University of Chicago Press.

Mannheim, K. 1972. "The Problem of Generations." In *The New Pilgrims: Youth Protest in Transition,* edited by P. G. Altbach and R. S. Laufer. New York: David McKay.

Markus, H., and Kitayama, S. 1994. "A Collective Fear of the Collective: Implications for Selves and Theories of Selves." *Personality and Social Psychology Bulletin* 20 (5): 568–79.

Marwell, G., and D. Aiken. 1987. "The Persistence of Political Attitudes among 1960s Civil Rights Activists." *Public Opinion Quarterly* 51:359–75.

Miller, T. 1991. *The Hippies and American Values.* Knoxville: University of Tennessee Press.

Modell, J. 1996. "The Uneasy Engagement of Human Development and Ethnography." In *Ethnography and Human Development: Context and Meaning in Social Inquiry,* edited by R. Jessor, A. Colby, and R. A. Shweder, 479–504. Chicago: University of Chicago Press.

Nassi, A. J. 1981. "Survivors of the Sixties: Comparative Psychosocial and Political Development of Former Berkeley Student Activists." *American Psychologist* 36: 753–61.

Nesselroade, J. R., and A. Eye, eds. 1985. *Individual Development and Social Change: Explanatory Analysis.* Orlando, Fla.: Academic Press.

Newman, K. 1988. *Falling from Grace: The Experience of Downward Mobility in the American Middle Class.* New York: Free Press.

Partridge, W. L. 1973. *The Hippie Ghetto: The Natural History of a Subculture.* New York: Hold, Rinehart & Winston.

Reich, C. 1970. *The Greening of America.* New York: Random House.

Rochford, E. B., Jr. 1985. *Hare Krishna in America.* New Brunswick, N.J.: Rutgers University Press.

Roszak, T. 1969. *The Making of a Counter-Culture: Reflections on the Technocratic Society and Its Youthful Opposition.* New York: Doubleday.

Schlegel, A. 1995. "A Cross-Cultural Approach to Adolescence." *Ethos* 23 (1): 15–23.

Schlegel, A., and Herbert Barry III. 1991. *Adolescence: An Anthropological Inquiry.* Free Press: New York.

Stein, R. 1995. "Feminism and Countercultural Values." Paper presented at the meeting of the American Anthropological Association, Washington, D.C., November.

Super, C. M., and S. Harkness, eds. 1980. *Anthropological Perspectives on Child Development.* New Directions for Child Development no. 8. San Francisco: Jossey-Bass.

———. 1986. "The Developmental Niche: A Conceptualization at the Interface of Child and Culture." *International Journal of Behavior Development* 9:1–25.

Tipton, S. 1982. *Getting Saved from the Sixties: Moral Meaning in Conversion and Cultural Change.* Berkeley and Los Angeles: University of California Press.

Weisner, T. S. 1982. "As We Choose: Family Life Styles, Social Class, and Compliance." In *Culture and Ecology: Eclectic Perspectives,* edited by J. G. Kennedy and R. Edgerton, 121–41. Special Publication no. 15. Washington, D.C.: American Anthropological Association.

————. 1984. "Ecocultural Niches of Middle Childhood: A Cross-Cultural Perspective." In *Development during Middle Childhood: The Years from Six to Twelve,* edited by W. A. Collins, 335–69. Washington, D.C.: National Academy of Sciences Press.

————. 1986a. "Implementing New Relationship Styles in Conventional and Nonconventional American Families." In *Relationships and Development,* edited by W. Hartup and Z. Rubin, 185–206. Hillsdale, N.J.: LEA Press.

————. 1986b. "Parents and Children in American Creedal Communes." Paper presented to the Symposium on Issues in the Scientific Study of Religions: Devotions of Self-Maintenance in Contemporary America, sponsored by the American Association for the Advancement of Science, Philadelphia, May.

————. 1993. "Siblings in Cultural Place: Ethnographic and Ecocultural Perspectives on Siblings of Developmentally Delayed Children." In *Siblings of Individuals with Mental Retardation, Physical Disabilities, and Chronic Illness,* edited by Z. Stoneman and P. Berman, 51–83. Baltimore: Brooks.

————. 1996. "The 5-7 Transition as an Ecocultural Project." In *Reason and Responsibility: The Passage through Childhood,* edited by A. Sameroff and M. Haith, 295–326. Chicago: University of Chicago Press.

Weisner, T. S., M. Bausano, and M. Kornfein. 1983. "Putting Family Ideals into Practice: Pronaturalism in Conventional and Nonconventional California Families." *Ethos* 11 (4): 278–304.

Weisner, T. S., and B. Eiduson. 1986. "Children of the '60s as Parents." *Psychology Today* 20 (1): 60–66.

Weisner, T. S., and H. Garnier. 1992. "Nonconventional Family Lifestyles and School Achievement: A 12-Year Longitudinal Study." *American Educational Research Journal* 29 (3): 605–32.

————. 1994. "Long-Term Effects of Nonconventional Family Lifestyles on 12th Grade School Achievement." Paper presented at the meeting of the American Educational Research Association, New Orleans, April.

————. 1995. "Family Values and Nonconventional Family Lifestyles: An 18-Year Longitudinal Study at Adolescence." Paper presented at the meeting of the Society for Research in Adolescence, Indianapolis, March.

Weisner, T. S., H. Garnier, and J. Loucky. 1994. "Domestic Tasks, Gender Egalitarian Values and Children's Gender Typing in Conventional and Nonconventional Families." *Sex Roles* 30 (1, 2): 23–54.

Weisner, T. S., and J. Wilson-Mitchell. 1990. "Nonconventional Family Lifestyles and Sex Typing in Six-Year-Olds." *Child Development* 61 (6): 1915–33.

Weiss, R. S. 1990. *Staying the Course: The Emotional and Social Lives of Men Who Do Well at Work.* New York: Free Press.

Werner, E. E., and R. S. Smith. 1977. *Kauai's Children Come of Age.* Honolulu: University of Hawaii Press.

Whalen, J., and R. Flacks. 1989 *Beyond the Barricades: The Sixties Generation Grows Up.* Philadelphia: Temple University Press.

Whiting, B., and C. Edwards. 1988. *Children of Different Worlds: The Formation of Social Behavior.* Cambridge, Mass.: Harvard University Press.

Whiting, J., and B. Whiting. 1975. *Children of Six Cultures: A Psychocultural Analysis.* Cambridge, Mass.: Harvard University Press.

Will, G. 1995. "The Last Word." *Newsweek,* August 21.

Yinger, J. M. 1982. *Countercultures: The Promise and the Peril of a World Turned Upside Down.* New York: Free Press.

Zablocki, B. 1980. *Alienation and Charisma. A Study of Contemporary American Communes.* New York: Free Press.

Place and Race: Midlife Experience in Harlem

Katherine Newman

Developmentalists interested in the subjective experience of midlife in the United States are often drawn to the study of middle-class Americans who have, on the whole, experienced "canonical" careers and now contemplate the pleasures and strains of retirement. How do they maintain their identities when the defining features of corporate employment slip through their fingers? Under what conditions do they remain psychologically resilient in the face of declining physical strength? What adaptations do they undergo as their children leave home and their roles as parents begin to recede, perhaps just in time to contend with the need to care for elderly parents who are now dependent upon them? These are the questions that confront many researchers hoping to understand what midlife means in American society.

Yet just as earlier researchers sought to broaden our understanding of childhood and adolescence by moving beyond the white middle class to the experience of minorities passing through the life course, it is important to expand the study of midlife in America to incorporate the expectations and experiences of African-Americans and other ethnic groups who may differ in the problems they face at midlife. A mosaic approach, represented in this book through its examination of midlife in different national cultures, needs to be applied internally, to the study of midlife in America. Only when the study of midlife is expanded to include minority communities will we have a full appreciation for the complexity of this life stage.

This paper is based upon a pilot study of African-Americans in middle age funded by a grant from the MacArthur Foundation Network on Successful Midlife Development to the Social Science Research Council. I wish to thank Bert Brim for his support of the Social Science Research Council seminar group and my colleagues in the seminar—Larry Aber, Jeanne Brooks-Gunn, David Featherman, Frank Furstenberg, Diane Hughes, Frank Kessel, Orlando Rodriguez, and Mary Waters—for the insights they have contributed that have found their way into this paper. I am particularly grateful to John Jackson, doctoral candidate in the Anthropology Department at Columbia University, for the work he contributed in the form of life history interviews with all of the informants discussed in this paper.

As an initial step along this path, this essay explores the experiences of men and women in their forties and fifties who live in poor neighborhoods of Harlem in New York City. They came to participate in this study because children in their households—their own or those of other close family members—were already part of my on-going study of youths in low-wage service-sector jobs in the inner city.[1] These parents, aunts, and uncles are all long-time residents of Harlem and for the most part are among the working poor themselves. They work as building superintendents in slum neighborhoods, home attendants for the elderly, housekeepers for wealthy families, and transit workers who clean the subways at night.

Most have experienced bouts of unemployment; some have been through precipitous slides in their standard of living, moving, for example, from the well-paid military to the low-wage service sector. Their economic lives are punctuated by insecurity, but they remain doggedly attached to the labor force, believing that working for a living is a necessary aspect of human dignity. They have tried to transmit the same values, both by word and by example, to their own children, with varying degrees of success. Indeed, as I explain below, they have had to contend with the fact that their upstanding morality must compete for their children's attention with the mean streets that surround them. Much of their midlife experience, then, consists of intervening between their children or grandchildren and the forces of destruction loose in the ghetto.

The meaning of these experiences, the ways in which they "add up" to a sense of satisfaction or disappointment, cannot be fully understood in a presentist mode. Middle age, unlike previous life stages, builds up against a backdrop of earlier experiences.[2] It is an important consolidation of a trajectory whose curves may have been hard to discern earlier in life. It is part of a long process of arrival that culminates in old age, but begins, I would argue, in the middle of life, when youth is clearly in the past and old age is visible on the distant horizon. Given this, it is particularly important to recognize the influence of place, period, and in this case, race, in organizing prior life experience. For the social, political, and economic context within which this generation of midlife Harlem dwellers reached their mature years differs quite dramatically from the context of their childhood years. Indeed, there is relatively little continuity between their communities of origin and their communities of midlife "destination," and the differences cast a long shadow over the meaning of middle age.

Some of the discontinuity is quite positive in its impact. Men and women who grew up in the South before the Civil Rights movement have aged into a climate of race relations that, whatever its faults may be, they see as a distinct improvement over the police state they experienced in their youth. But other forms of social change have been negative to the point of near debilitation. Northern urban neighborhoods that were, in the 1950s and 1960s, home to a stable, employed, and basically safe black community have become devastated wastelands that are dangerous places to live.[3] Ghetto dwellers confront middle age in places where going outside after dusk is risky, where advancing age renders them physically vulnerable. African-Americans in Harlem reach this life stage with both forms of discontinuity—the encouraging and the terrifying—in the background. If we are to understand how this social history colors their assessment of their mature years, we must understand the trajectory of their lives as they moved through distinctive historical periods and geographical locales.

THE JIM CROW SOUTH

The great migration of African-Americans out of the rural South began in the period between the two world wars, but gathered steam in the 1940s and 50s, the era when the oldest of my informants were children (see Lehmann 1993). Nearly 5 million Americans left the agricultural areas of the South for the greater opportunities of the industrial north during this period—the largest internal migration in U.S. history. There is a tendency in much of the historical literature on this movement to focus upon what the migrants found when they arrived in the north. Contemporary history begins, it would seem, with life in New York or Chicago.

But if we are to understand what this migration experience means today, in particular, the ways in which it shapes perceptions of an urban midlife in the 1990s, we must back up and understand life as it was lived in small towns in the South. For this migrant generation, some small town in a rural area was "home," the place to which they returned every summer, the place where their grandparents, aunts, and uncles remained.[4] Life was a seasonal affair in these agricultural communities. Sharecroppers who worked the land and settled up with the landlord every year supplemented their income with jobs in the local mills processing peanuts, tobacco, or some other crop. Women took in washing and did other kinds of domestic work to add to the family coffers. Older children took their place in this wage labor and sharecropping economy, working in the fields when they were not in school. Younger children took care of the littlest ones in the house, often for many hours while the able-bodied adults were out working.

Alvia Ford—an African-American woman now in her early fifties— grew up outside a small town in Alabama, one of ten children in a sharecropper household. Her grandparents, aunts, uncles, and cousins all lived in the same community and had done so for generations. She rode a bus many miles to school every day, something she enjoyed as much for the company as for the education. But poverty put a stop to her schooling: "We were dirt poor. There wasn't enough money to buy clothes. So, in the seventh grade, I got left back for a year. I didn't have shoes and clothes to wear to school, so I just missed the seventh grade."

Men and women who come from communities like Alvia's remember living without running water and running low on food; they always recall the sense most sharecroppers had that it was impossible to get ahead. Factory work was the only local alternative for making ends meet. Poorly paid and deadly dull, agricultural mills were nonetheless essential elements of the rural economy. Barbara James, a fifty-year-old black woman from a small town in Georgia, remembered how limited the opportunities were for her family:

> There wasn't any factories, and like I said, in the two towns where my grandparents growed up in and where I growed up in, there wasn't nothing else left for you to do. I mean, you had maybe one or two supermarkets. So . . . that was it. And there wasn't any kind of [manufacturers] there, just peanuts and cotton and stuff like that. That was all the kind of work you had to do, so that's mostly what everybody did in those days. They [were sharecroppers]. If they wasn't farming for they self, they were farming for the white man. And it's still the same [in my town]. . . . With my father, he worked at the peanut mill for so long, I don't even know what year he left there. He decided to go twenty-four miles away and he ended up getting a job at the Marine base and worked there until he retired. My brothers, they worked in the peanut mill.

As far as Alvia and Barbara recall, the best a family could hope for was to just get by. Nothing better than that, nothing approaching prosperity, was ever likely to happen in small-town Alabama or Georgia.

Being black and poor in a southern community was hardly remarkable. Everyone around Barbara had the same standard of living. What stands out in her mind about growing up in her hometown was the fact that there was absolutely nothing to do there—no entertainment, no excitement, endless sameness. Like Alvia, Barbara had all her kin in town where they had lived for as long as anyone knew. But that was half the problem: she already knew everyone there and realized that she was not likely to see anything new as she got older.

> [There's] nothing really they do there, except visit, you know? You can go from house to house and meet peoples and things like that, but that's about it. There's nothing there to do. There's no movies. You would have fun on Friday and Saturday night because they would have a "juke joint," a cafe and a DJ where they play music. You can go there and dance a half hour and you can do the same on Saturday night, but the place have to close at twelve o'clock, so that's it. After Saturday night there's no more fun, so you sit out in the yard and that's it.

Barbara's hometown was really two communities: one white and one black, with little contact between the families on either side of the dividing line. On the black side of town, the community was so small that she knew every house in the area:

> Nobody goes by the names of the streets. Where my mother lived at, they called it "the bottom." It's in town, but they called it "the bottom." Its not a big town, its just like a little neighborhood. All black on one side. You have houses over on the other side which is where the white live at, where they church is at and everything. But [my neighborhood] was a little block of black people, that's all.
>
> You don't have very many street lights . . . and there's like houses sitting on both sides of the street. It's like a Western town. You seen the Westerns, right? You seen the hitching posts where they tie horses. Well, that's the way my whole town was for so many years. They just tore the last hitching post down ten years ago. No kind of business . . . nobody wants to move there. So this town has been like this since I was a little kid and it's never going to change.

Small-town life was slow and familiar, qualities that came to have some meaning for Alvia and Barbara as they got older and moved north to the hustle and noise of the big city. But for young people who knew—through magazines, radio, and eventually television—that there was a big world beyond Alabama and Georgia, small towns began to feel like deadweights around their shoulders. For African-Americans, of course, living in a small, segregated community was a schizophrenic experience. Close knit ties among friends and kin were paralleled by open hostility and constant, belittling barbs from whites across the tracks. As Barbara tells it, racial hatred enveloped every aspect of daily life:

> The whites was real nasty. . . . They never referred to the black mens as "mens." It was always "boy." That's the way [whites] treated [blacks] and we were used to it. I would have loved to go to school with white kids, but I didn't. It wasn't allowed when I was going. The black had they own school, the white had they own school, they own bus. They still had their signs up—Whites Only. You couldn't sit in restaurants, you couldn't go in and eat. Certain bathrooms you couldn't go in. If you working in the white peoples' house you couldn't go in the front door, you had to go in the back door or the side door. If you rode in the car with them, you had to ride in the back seat. That's the way it was.

Jimmy Hardin—at fifty-six a little bit older than Alvia or Barbara—was actually born in New York. But like most people of their generation, the ties to the South were strong. He spent every summer of his youth in two communities in the South, one in Georgia and one in North Carolina, where his grandparents lived. For Jimmy, the experience of living down south was a running confrontation with racial hatred. Where Barbara and Alvia had been raised to live with the indignities of southern bigotry, Jimmy's northern upbringing led him to resist demands for deference:

> One time I was going to school, so I got on the . . . school bus, and basically when you get down south they have a sign up there, "Niggers to the rear." I'm telling you "Niggers to the rear!" You know? So this is a school bus, we're always clowning around, so I was talking to a guy, then accidentally got on the bus and turned my behind and sat

down on the wrong spot. There was a white man sitting next to me. He [said] "Nigger are you crazy? Get back there, get back there!" There was a panic in there, you know? I said, "Oh shit, this may be lynch time," cause the way he just swelled up, you know, "Nigger!"

I was not supposed to stand on corners, you know? But I started hanging out. Them cops come down, they come down, they move [you] off the corner. It's not like it up here, you know. Cops will pass [young people] by five or six times [here in New York] but they just leave them standing. But down south, you can't be congregating on corners. Them crackers are mean. I never got in no serious trouble down in the South, maybe just said something with them crackers, you know, or refusing to buck when they want me to buck.

Ultimately, Jimmy's relatives had to "hustle [him] out of the South" because they were afraid he would get into serious trouble with the police or endanger their safety. The years of exposure to the open racism of the Deep South left an indelible impression on Jimmy, setting a benchmark from which he evaluated race relations in the north in his youth and in his mature years.

The combination of racism and extremely limited economic opportunity in the South prompted many African-American youths to enlist in the armed forces—then, as now, a major route of upward mobility and freedom from the suffocation of small-town life. Barbara and Alvia saw most of their brothers and other boys of their generation off to the army, becoming frontline soldiers in Vietnam or the part of the Cold War military in Europe.

When I was growing up, [all there was] was the cotton fields and stuff like that for my brothers. The two oldest ones . . . never really got good jobs until they left home. My oldest brother, he left when he was about eighteen. The next oldest one, he joined the marines when he was fighting in Vietnam. So . . . all of them have been in the services except for two. I think that's what you mostly got their training . . . and they [now] doing the jobs that they doing because they all, you know, went into the army. That's all that was left for the boys down there, otherwise they stayed and worked on the farms. Most of them, they chose to go into the army.

When today's generation of midlife Harlem residents examine their lives in middle age, they do so against a background of profound change. They were liberated from a degree of racial oppression that is hard for many of today's youth to imagine. They were able to seek out opportunities that would have been unthinkable for their own parents in middle age. The men who joined the army were able to see the world—a chance that no one in their families had ever had before—and learn trades that were utterly closed to them in the rural South. Most of all, Harlem's middle-aged migrants were able to escape to the city that fired the imagination of the nation's African-Americans.

HARLEM IN THE POSTWAR YEARS

Barbara and Alvia were among the first in their family to move to New York, joining cousins already living in Harlem. Domestic jobs were relatively easy to find, and although they did not pay well by urban standards, the wages were well beyond anything they had earned in agricultural factories or domestic work in the South. To hear them tell it, however, almost any wage would have made the move worth it. The excitement of living in a big city—with its twenty-four-hour street life, its music, its crowds—made Harlem a mecca for young blacks.

Harlem was a crowded, raucous community in the 1940s and 1950s when my older informants came to town. But it was not wholly unrecognizable to rural folk because so many southerners had come north in a chain migration pattern, settling in particular districts or on particular blocks that were dominated by friends and kin from their hometowns in South Carolina, Georgia, and the other southern states.[5] Social structures were dense in Harlem neighborhoods because the ties binding neighbors reached back into small towns where ascending relatives still lived and where young kids would be sent back in the summertime. Hence, when today's midlife adults were teenagers and young adults, they came to a big city that felt more like a cluster of close knit neighborhoods. Everyone looked out for one another; everyone knew their neighbors' children. Community was more than an abstract concept: it was a concrete experience of block parties, holiday rituals, churchgoing friends, and elders who kept a close watch on the streets.

Jane Easton, now fifty years old, is of the same generation as Barbara and Alvia. But like Jimmy Hardin, she was born in Harlem and grew up in the heart of the community. She remembers the tight-knit quality of her neighborhood, the neighborhood into which southerners like Barbara moved in the 1950s:

> It was a nice neighborhood then, you know? You could leave the door open. Everybody knew everybody. . . . My grandmother used to go to work. She'd open the door to her friend's house and she'd say, "Go on Rosalie [Go on in]." You could run from one person's house to another and you didn't have to ring the bell 'cause the door would be open. We had fun when we were kids, running around. The neighborhood was safe. Everybody would come downstairs and you'd play, running in the fire hydrant and stuff like that. You could go to the store for your mother and stuff. You had the watermelon man coming [around] . . . and he yelled, "Watermelons!"
>
> You knew everybody. You knew the lady that ran the grocery store. . . . My grandmother's family . . . owned the cleaners. You knew the man that owned the supermarket and the meat market. They knew you personally, you know . . . "Oh, you're Miss ——'s granddaughter." It was a real family thing.

Jimmy Hardin remembers the same kind of atmosphere:

> You could go outside your apartment and go down to the store and leave your door open. You'd have the next door neighbor living next to you, if you needed something from her icebox. At that time there wasn't all these frigidaires; you'd go in there and take something.

Jane and Jimmy agree that Harlem was not only a safe place to raise a family in those days, it was a community filled with disciplined adults who expected their children to adhere to strict standards of behavior. This is not to suggest that everyone in the community was an angel; but those who misbehaved were regarded as less than respectable, failing to hold to community standards that were widely embraced. "You had a home, and everybody's home looked nice and presentable. You ate dinner at a certain time. You had to be in the house at a certain time. You couldn't eat at nobody's house unless you called up and asked." Jimmy Hardin described how social order was maintained on his block through a network of adults who monitored the behavior of their own children and the children of their friends and kin closely.[6] Young people could not misbehave without their parents finding out about it:

> When I was growing up, they had a lot of people [on the stoops], just stationed themselves waiting in front of the buildings and they'd talk about you. You know, "Oh, you ain't going to be no good when you grow up, you ain't doing nothing. . . ," you know? Other people encouraged you to go to school, try to do the right thing. "Don't mess with that boy, you're going to get in trouble with that boy." . . .
>
> You had a strong environment. People couldn't come in the neighborhood and do [bad] things, 'cause these older people would get together, you know, and tell them, "You can't do that round here" or something like that.

The backbone of the community was a stable and employed adult population. Some people in Jane's family were small-business owners like her grandmother. But most had regular jobs working in factories or for middle-class and wealthy white families in the richer parts of the city. The truly fortunate among them had government jobs:

> Some of the adults used to sew, some cleaned houses. My grandmother had people [who came to her shop] to iron. . . . A lot of people worked in the post office then. Some were teachers, and at that time we used to have a lot of people come from . . . City College to take the kids to different places, to see different things.

Typically mothers and fathers both worked, leaving older relatives and the oldest of the children at home to watch over the young ones after school. Kids were routinely shipped off to their relatives in the South— as Jimmy Hardin was every summer—when school was out. Family life was organized around the tasks of the breadwinners, the backbone of the whole enterprise. And kids learned early about the importance of contributing. As Jane continues,

> When I was growing up, all the people that I knew was encouraged to do something else other than just sit around, you know. At least they got a job. Kids now . . . I was starting shining shoes when I was about nine, ten

years old. Sell Sunday newspapers, you know, at the week-
ends.

THE END OF ORDER

From Jane Easton's perspective, this orderly, disciplined character
has long since disappeared. Her neighborhood has become a dangerous
place to live, with drug dealers and loose guns infesting the streets like
a plague of locusts. Children can no longer run free on the sidewalks
and only a fool would leave his door open. She notes, "A young person
will shoot you out of your shoes if you cough wrong. They killing they
own selves now. See, we didn't have all that . . . drug dealing. It wasn't
like this, the money, the drugs."

Jimmy confronts the same conditions in his Harlem neighborhood.
Since he works as a building superintendent, he has to face the grim
consequences of the local drug economy every day.

> [In the old days] it was nice to get outside the house and
> go out in the street. Now it's almost like a threat to go
> outside. You don't know what direction any harm's com-
> ing from. You might think [everything is okay] then go
> outside and these guys shooting at each other across the
> street. I was walking down the street one time and I started
> smelling gunpowder, and they started shooting out there.

Violence has become so commonplace that middle-aged residents of
Harlem and their children plan their movements around it. They know
which buildings to avoid walking near, which streets are safe to cross,
whom they can trust and to whom they must be give a wide berth.
Intimate knowledge of the neighborhood, born of many years in residence, is also important as a survival strategy. The older adults have
often known the drug dealers on the corner since childhood; they trade
upon these long-standing acquaintances as a source of safety, figuring
that they have much more to fear from strangers than locals. As James
Langford, a forty-year-old African-American man who is raising seven
children in Harlem, explained:

> I know these people, you know, and I know what they do.
> They may sell this or that, but they don't look for trouble
> [with me]. They live down the block. . . . They know my
> family from when we were growing up. . . . They speak to
> my wife and my kids, but they basically don't bother us

or make trouble. . . . But they may bring in other people
that may cause trouble.

Navigation strategies and the capacity to trade on personal acquaintance do not always work. They are, however, the only "ecological" adaptations available to Harlem's poor if they are to survive the pathologies they face in public spaces.

African-Americans in the inner city confront the fact that their economic circumstances condemn them to living in a place where these dangers are ever-present. Many, particularly those in midlife, long for the opportunity to leave the problems of the ghetto behind, to get on with their work lives and their family responsibilities safe from the relentless pressure of crime. But this requires resources that are out of their grasp and not likely to materialize in the future. Hence, law-abiding, hard-working, mature citizens of Harlem end up locked inside their own houses, unable to enjoy the freedoms that most working people in suburban communities take for granted.

If Harlem had always presented these obstacles, midlife adults who grew up there or moved to the community in their youth might have grown to equate life in the inner city with this kind of social disorganization. However, for today's generation of midlife adults, Harlem represents a place that has undergone a profound transformation—for the worse. It was not always a dangerous and difficult place to live. Indeed, it was regarded as exciting but safe, diverse but ordered. What has happened in the last twenty years, however, has been that Harlem has seen a near total loss of the job base that used to sustain it and a consequent rise in the myriad social problems that confront midlife adults in the form of street dangers. Midlife has become a life stage of vulnerability, a condition that did not obtain for previous generations, but one that most assuredly worries middle-aged men and women today.

This is not to suggest that everyone in the ghetto is involved in crime or in harassing their neighbors. On the contrary, the majority of people who live in high poverty areas of Harlem are the working poor, as are their teenage and young-adult children. In central Harlem, for example, where poverty rates are nearly 40% and official unemployment is now 18%, more than two-thirds of all households have at least one worker in them (City of New York 1990). Nonetheless, the working poor do not earn enough to live in problem-free neighborhoods. Inner-city minorities, in particular, are likely to reach middle age in the midst of communities where they feel under siege, even though most of the people they know personally are working and trying to manage their way around the bad apples.

The fact that living among conditions of crime and unemployment was not always necessary registers profoundly among midlife adults examining what they have accomplished in their lives. They speak with dignity of their participation in the working mainstream, even if this has meant a poorly paid job. But they cannot be proud of the kind of place where they have to live when that place is home to crack dealers who commit random acts of terror. Relegated to these circumstances, they feel the weight of the community's problems as inescapable and draining. Why they have to put up with this deterioration, why it happened in the first place, what is wrong with their people or their society that this should be their fate—all of these questions recur again and again, the refrains of midlife in a place where race and the changing economy has laid the groundwork for a ghetto experience of midlife vulnerability.

Along with danger comes the recognition that the inner city, or the segregated suburb, is a place that has been ignored and rejected by white society. Services and amenities commonplace in middle-class communities are utterly absent. Shattered windows are left broken. Graffiti fills the walls, street signs, bus stops, and schoolyards, and no one seems bothered enough to clean it. Streets are dirty and the pavement is broken. Police, often depicted in the popular press as unwelcome in poor, minority neighborhoods, are more often the target of complaint because they seem absent, unconcerned, or corrupt.[7]

While often tagged an urban problem, the morass of difficulties described above long ago engulfed the segregated suburbs outside of New York. Al Sampson, a forty-year-old African-American man, grew up on Long Island in the 1950s and 1960s, coming in and out of Harlem to visit his relatives and friends. As he reached high school, however, whites began to move farther out on the island, and African-Americans, anxious to leave inner-city apartments for private houses, started arriving in large numbers.

> When I was growing up here . . . in the beginning it was fifty/fifty [white and black]. By the time I graduated, it was probably 90 percent black and 5 percent . . . Latins and maybe 2 percent white and then whatever [left over]. They tried to mainline all the blacks into certain areas on

Long Island, and they wouldn't want to give them social
services.

Segregation deepened, adjacent white communities drew their tax dollars inward, and the relentless degradation of Al's neighborhood began.
Today, his community is rundown and depressed:

> The main street is the worst thing. I've never been in a
> place where the main street doesn't even have one garbage
> can on the street, not one. My landlord owns a liquor store,
> has a garbage can outside the store, that's chained to the
> pole. This old plastic garbage can, and the guys still con
> tinue to throw their wine bottles [on the ground]. I live
> right next door to the building. They throw everything
> right outside on the ground. . . .
>
> The real problem [here] is the drugs. . . . There's a lot
> of crack houses. As far as robbery and all that, there's no
> one really to rob. There are very few stores, very few, and
> the homeowners don't really own anything. It's just the
> drugs, right out there, wide open, on the street. I'm talking
> about right across the street from the firehouse, where . . .
> police officers change shifts.
>
> [In other places] fire departments hold social functions
> and things like that, but here, nothing. . . . The police . . .
> can't stop the drug dealing that's going on right across the
> street [from the fire station]. They're always at the train
> station . . . but right across the street, in front of my house
> . . . they can't stop [the drugs].

Depressed conditions breed trouble on the streets. Although Al
knows how to take care of himself on the streets, he has found that a
wise man steers clear of trouble and stays indoors:

> It's sort of a . . . a locked-in situation. Stay upstairs in my
> apartment and I don't bother anybody. I come out once
> in a while, but I don't get involved, you know? I mean, I
> know a lot of the people that are involved [in drugs], I
> speak to them. But I got more important things to do, like
> looking for work.

The best way for Al—a robust man, six feet tall—to protect himself
is to stay close to the people that he knows, to confine himself to the

bosom of his family and other close friends he can trust. While affluent Americans may greet midlife as a time of expansion, a time free of the confining obligations of child rearing and open for outward movement, the poor who live in ghettos experience midlife as a period of vulnerability, a time when one's best bet is to pull inward and seek the safety of the known.

This strategy may speak to Al's safety, but it does not do much for his self-esteem. For the neighborhood he lives in reflects back on his station in life and makes him feel that he is a person of minimal standing. No one who has a choice visits his neighborhood; it is an undesirable place to live. Anyone who has to live there is, by this definition, an outcast, a failure. He feels helpless to change the situation, except to focus on extracting himself from it. But because that is much easier said than done, the character of the place in which he lives takes a toll on the character he believes himself to be.

Of course, middle-aged minorities living in similar circumstances do not always react this way. Barbara James, who works as a housekeeper for wealthy families on the East Side of Manhattan, comes home to her walk-up apartment in Harlem and confines herself until she has to go back to work:

> I come in from work on Friday and that's it. I don't go back out again 'til maybe on Sunday. I go to church then, and that's right [around the block]. When service is over, I come back in my house and I don't go back out no more until Monday morning.

Yet, where Al sees his neighborhood reflected in his life, Barbara defines the threatening element as deviant and distinguishes herself sharply from it. She describes herself as decent, hard-working, churchgoing, and surrounded by an enemy element bound on ruining her environment. She does not internalize the problems she experiences, she distances them. Their divergent reactions are easily understood as reflections of the economic differences that separate Barbara from Al. Barbara works full-time and defines herself as part of the mainstream world, albeit not a well-paid member. Dignity comes from the fact that she is dependent on no one and works to support herself and her daughters. There are real cultural and class differences between her and the crack dealers she is so angry with.

Al, like many black men in midlife, has had a much rockier employment history.[8] After a long period of time in the service, where he was able to live overseas, earn good money, and enjoy a respectable status, he was discharged in his mid-thirties, only to find that there were no decent jobs available to him. He returned to Long Island and re-connected with his friends from the old neighborhood, hoping to activate a network that would help in job hunting, but he discovered that his friends had never been able to find good jobs. In the time he had been in the service, they had taken entry-level jobs in local warehouses or factories. Some had prospered, but most had spent those ten years cycling in and out of low-wage jobs. The best they could do to help an old friend was to clear the way for a job that offered a fraction of his military wage.

> I got out of the Air Force . . . and [went] looking for a job. I took a job [in a warehouse] and a lot of guys who were there, I went to school with, or they went to school with somebody I knew or one of my brothers. . . . All the people who worked in the front office were white and all the people who did all the dirty work, maintenance, worked in the warehouses and things like that, were all black. Now all these guys that did all the physical labor, of course, they got paid less. It was really bad news. . . . One of the warehouse managers considered us as being 'porch monkeys,' words from his mouth.

It is hard for Al to accept this fate after having had a steady, respectable career for a decade. Returning home after so many years, only to find that his age-mates had "gone nowhere" during the ten years he had been gone, only added to the sense that there was no future. Since the end of the warehouse job, he has had only sporadic employment. To-day, he is unemployed and depressed about his prospects.

It comes as little surprise that, given this history, he looks upon his physical surroundings and sees in the community's depression a mirror of his own troubles. His financial circumstances lock him in to a bad neighborhood, force him to be dependent upon the charity of family and friends, and make him feel like a failure. Unfortunately, circum-stances like these are all too common among African-Americans, par-ticularly among middle-aged men. For they have taken the brunt of the economic slowdown that has shuttered the factories where they once worked; they have seen their occupational prospects wither.

For men in midlife, this reality is particularly harsh. They cannot hide behind youth or fool themselves into thinking that something much better is around the corner. Like others in middle age, they assess their accomplishments and, if they have suffered an occupational history of intermittent work or low-wage jobs, they come up short of the kind of biography they consider respectable. As Al put it,

> I'm forty years old, I'm unemployed, and even with all the experience and the different jobs I've had, for some reason I still find it difficult to move ahead in life. . . . All I can do really is menial tasks and then, if you have all this knowledge, they tell you that you're overqualified to do some of these menial tasks. So, like I say, it's really been rough for me.

When Al looks around his community, he sees the broken glass and the dead-end inhabitants of the streets and feels trapped by his inability to move out. The physical and social surroundings symbolize his economic impotence. Barbara, who must contend with similar social problems in her neighborhood, has a different vantage point. She has an identity that lifts her above her surroundings.

RACE AND FATE

The relationship between place and identity presses upon Barbara and Al not only because they have to contend with the consequences of living in an unsafe neighborhood, but because segregation and poverty have insured that African-Americans are—unlike other racial groups—faced with such a fate in such large numbers. As members of a stigmatized community, they feel compelled (both by themselves and by an abstract mainstream) to answer for this condition, to explain why "their people" are in such abiding trouble.[9] And when you live in a community with so much failure in evidence, it becomes a challenge to be answered, even by those who are solid and steady.

Midlife Americans who are white rarely face this query, even though millions of them are also poor or unemployed.[10] White Americans have no cultural identity as a group for which they have to answer. For minorities, however, reflection upon midlife achievements and failures is rarely an individual matter, at least not wholly so. As Ellis Cose (1993) and others have noted,[11] even those African-Americans who are successful in life are often "charged" with having abandoned their troubled counterparts in the ghetto or with the necessity to be a role model for unfortunate members of their racial group. They are implicitly asked to account for the plight of the urban underclass. African-

Americans who live in inner-city communities are no less "responsible" (in an abstract sense) for explaining how these troubles came to be. The answers to these questions impinge upon their own experience of midlife because a subtext of racial failure lurks below the surface. Why did I do well in life (when so many of my people have not)? Why have I seen so much trouble in my life (just like the millions of other African-Americans who are similarly situated)? As Barbara put it:

> People can't get a good job, can't get a better place to live, nothing in life seem to go right. You got more people counting on failure than they do on anything, because it's like a every day thing to them. If they put it as a struggle, so they failing everyday at trying to do better, trying to get a better life. Me, I say I'm OK. Long as I'm alive . . . I ain't going to say I got good health, I don't know that, but I'm alive and my kids are OK and I'm OK.

My informants are steeped in the culture of inequality, a fractured experience of promise and betrayal, a constant test of personal dignity, a fundamentally hierarchical experience in which their "people" are almost always on the bottom. They are not, however, alone in this rat race for material and social prestige. Their fellows citizens are also entrenched in a struggle for well-being, one that has increasingly threatened the standard of living of millions of middle-class whites who have, in previous decades, had little to fear in terms of economic security. American society as a whole is preoccupied with an ongoing conversation over the moral dimensions of inequality.

On one side of this debate lie conservative believers in a natural order of stratification, modern-day social Darwinists who embrace the notion that those who are deserving will prosper (see Newman 1988). On the other side are liberals who believe that forces larger than any given individual can overwhelm even the deserving and that whole categories of people—especially African-Americans—start so far behind the starting line that no credence can be given to the idea of "fair competition." The former view places primacy of effort on the shoulders of the individual or the family; the latter gives greater emphasis in achieving fairness to interventions either of government or of charity.

These cultural arguments are routine fare on broadcast talk shows such as those hosted by Rush Limbaugh and Sally Jessy Raphael. They figure prominently in tabloid stories of celebrity tragedy,[12] they are the deep structure of crime stories. The subtext is inescapable in virtually any discussion that attempts to answer the question: How did this group come to be where it is in the social pecking order? For my informants, explanations about the condition of their neighborhood or the behavior of their children can never be merely a matter of personal opinion. It is part and parcel of a larger debate over the link between race and fate.

But the answers given by any individual—in this case middle-aged African-Americans living in high poverty communities—are never so straightforward as the two polar opposites given above. Nor are individual views ever so internally consistent as my dichotomous account would suggest. Moreover, informants are aware that their views on the subject are part of a debate, and they attempt to refute other points of view as much as state their own in the course of explaining how race matters (or does not).

The dominant perspective among working poor African-Americans is that individuals are indeed responsible for their fate and that membership in a stigmatized racial group is no excuse for poor personal performance as a parent or a young adult. Indeed, those who damage their children through neglect or poor oversight are held fully accountable. Barbara James is certainly of this opinion. She believes that her community has seen a collapse in responsibility, with young people having children before they are ready and with drugs engulfing young men. And among this latter group, many of whom she knew as children, she holds parents responsible for poor supervision and guidance. The contrast between Barbara's strict upbringing and the troubled families in her midst could not be more stark:

> The kids that I watched grow up in this neighborhood, they are the young boys, they're the ones that's out there [dealing drugs] now. A lot of them out there, they don't have fathers and they mothers don't care, so long as they bring the money home. They don't care. When I came up, things wasn't like that. My father, he wasn't anyone to play with. We had to go to church every Sunday morning, we had to go to Sunday school. . . . When Sunday morning come, you all think up a lie, you say "We can't go to church today, Dad, we don't have nothing to wear." So he'd tell us, "You ain't got nothing to wear, then you can't go out at night." So a bunch of kids go running through the house

finding something to put on! . . . He was real strict; so was my mother. A whole lot different than what it is today.

Barbara James herself has raised her kids the old-fashioned way, and she believes that this is why they never succumbed to the temptations of the streets, as so many of their age-mates did. However, she lives in a community where many families have taken a different pathway. She "cuts them no slack" for these mistakes and attributes the connection between race and fate to the willful neglect of people in her own community.[13]

Al Sampson has a slightly different view. He shares Barbara's disgust for the failures of many parents he knows to raise their kids right:

> There's too much babying today. . . . [Parents] are pampering everybody. . . . Nowadays, parents are just giving in too much . . . there's no . . . its a simple word that I'm trying to think of . . . more discipline, more discipline man. . . . I know a lot of parents out there and I know [them] from the age that I grew up in . . . and they're out there still getting high. . . . Nobody is really pushing the kids. . . . No respect, no respect for their elders.

However, Al also sees a larger system of racial stratification and bigotry that has placed African-Americans at a consistent disadvantage from the beginning:

> The color of your skin, your neighborhood and where you're from. That's how most people judge you. The way it should be is individually, but when they first look at, say an [employment] application, that's the first thing they're going to judge you by, the very first thing.
>
> [Race] matters a lot, it does. Because, you know, every time you look in the mirror you see the color of your skin and you see what black people have gone through. Really. There's no doubt in my mind [that race matters a lot].

Al's general observations are grounded in many particular experiences where he has been singled out for abusive treatment simply because he is African-American. He can recount endless examples such as these:

> A couple of weeks after [the 1993 mass murders on the Long Island Railroad], we were on the train. . . . Something must have happened on one of the lines further down.

Now, you hardly ever see the cops on a train. But they're coming on there like the big gestapo. . . . They come on, they're going to stand me down. I said "You better keep on walking, 'cause I know you know I'm not the person you're looking for." The conductor's right there with them, but everybody black on the train is who they're stopping.

I used to work for a family-run business and a lot of times I used to have to go to do personal work at their homes. You find a lot of times, especially if it's an all-white town and you're a black guy, you're driving through there, people lock their doors in their cars. I'm talking about in the middle of traffic, you'll see them locking their doors. The police will routinely run you. . . you know, stop you. One time . . . I was stopped for running a red light, which I know the light wasn't red. The cop . . . continued to give me a lecture about things with my car. . . . Then two or three other cars came by and one of the officers in one of the other cars says, I swear to God, "You having any problems here?" I mean, I'm one guy, in a car, by myself. But I'm in a white neighborhood. It always happens like that.

He is keenly aware that where jobs, housing, and the general standard of living are concerned, blacks are shoved to the bottom, their individual qualifications disregarded. Al would add, as do many of his middle-aged counterparts in the inner city, that African-Americans are further hampered by competition with new immigrant groups, principally with Latinos who have flocked to New York City from the Dominican Republic in recent years (and with Puerto Ricans in the past).

IMMIGRANT COMPETITORS

Native-born, inner-city blacks often point to the rising number of immigrants in New York City as a contributory cause of the economic inequality which their communities face. Whether the influx of immigrants depresses wages for Americans in the nation's ghetto is a matter of controversy among labor economists, but it is a closed case among the people I have studied.[14] Most African-Americans believe that immigrants are willing to work for wages that no American—of any color—would accept, effectively undercutting African-Americans in a struggle for a piece of the pie (at the bottom of the social order). Others argue that the government was generous to immigrants, providing them with financial benefits (access to welfare, health clinics, and social services) that somehow they do not deserve. African-Americans I speak with sometimes suggest that the government, and the mainstream white world it represents, is more concerned about taking care of these new-comers than it is with improving the economic prospects of native-born blacks. Finally, because both groups suffer from poverty, they are often geographically contiguous, living in low-rent neighborhoods that border one another, throwing the competition between them into high relief. As Al put the matter:

> The only real work out there [on Long Island] . . . is the factories. Most of those factory jobs now are being held by, I hate to say it, but people of Hispanic or Latino [de-scent]. . . . When I first came back [from the Air Force], I went to a job interview and the foreman was a black guy, and he told me that they really don't like hiring people from where I'm from.
>
> [The government] let too many people in. You know that it is a law that when they let the Russian immigrants in or anybody, any immigrants . . . automatically, we have to take care of them. Automatically. They're set up, they're getting social services. That's how they get set up in these small businesses, while a black man, just let him try to get a small business loan. Drives you crazy. I'm serious. . . . You can't tell me that all these Columbians and Hondu-rans and all these people here are legals. I remember when you was going home you had to go way, way up town . . . to Spanish Harlem to find Puerto Ricans. Man, now the Dominicans are moving damn near all the way down to 125th Street [the heart of Harlem] . . .
>
> I get on the subway . . . [to come] up here when these kids are coming out of school. Listen and see what lan-guage they speak. I've got nothing against them, but if you let it get too far . . . then you can't control it.

Jane Easton, who is ten years older than Al but a longtime resident of Harlem, sees the same kind of competition for housing, for services, and for jobs, and she resents the attention given to immigrant Latinos. From her perspective, much of the recent slide of African-Americans in New York is attributable to their presence:

Dominicans come here and they just take. They have good
ones that work hard, but they have so many that just slide
and pass. Doing nothing, taking up space, taking up jobs,
and different things that somebody else might want, you
know? That's why you have all this . . . we had homeless
before, but not like this. Look at it!

Old people that worked all they lives hard, and they
don't even have enough money when they get . . . pension
. . . to pay rent. . . . That's not right. And here [Domini-
cans] come in, 'Give me a welfare check.' 'Here go you,
have twenty or thirty kids.' . . . An old person that's been
here all their life and they can't even get a little room . . .
that's safe. And here [the immigrants] come and just have
babies.

I heard this lady . . . talking to her granddaughter, she
was so hurt, you know. She said, "I go now to the welfare
. . . and they treat me like a piece of dirt." She said, "I
worked all my life to get what I got, and then when times
get hard . . . and they talk to me like I'm nothing. They
[immigrants] come . . . having babies and they get anything." Your own kind, blacks [working in the welfare of-
fices] are talking to blacks like they're nothing, you know?
That's what makes [blacks] want to jump across that desk
and beat the daylights out of one another, you know?

However, inside the stacked deck—consisting of one part white ani-
mosity toward blacks and one part competition from immigrants—
Al and Jane believe that people must still take responsibility for their
own actions. It is a "cop-out" in Al's judgment to lay the blame for
one's fate at the door of racism, even though this is the unavoidable
environment within which African-Americans must function.

You have to realize, any situation that you're in today, it
ain't because of [being] a black man. I mean, some of it,
you know, it is, but if you want more out of life, you've
got to work a lot more harder than what you did. Ain't
nobody going to give you anything. You got to get out of
here and get it.

For Al the two polar positions discussed earlier are blended into
one. There is a "system" of structured inequality that does indeed make

it much harder for African-Americans to claim their fair share. Yet, even though these forces are arrayed against him, it is up to him—the acting subject—to make his way in the world, even to redouble his efforts. In this, he accepts the basic burden of the conservative position, that individuals must take responsibility for their own fate, even though he knows that such a burden differs dramatically for blacks than for others.

None of the people who participated in this study argued the more radical view that all the ills of the black community can be chalked up to racial injustice, with no provision for personal fault. Indeed, they characteristically frowned upon local political figures—like Al Sharpton or Louis Farrakan—who consider racism the most compelling diagnosis of the problems of the inner city. The variation lies along the continuum between Barbara and Al with some middle-aged ghetto dwellers seeing a larger hand for racial prejudice in the predicament of the community than others. But all of them accepted the mainstream cultural prescription that places individual agency and responsibility at the heart of explanations for the fate of individuals.

This confluence with mainstream culture, however, is little comfort for those upstanding middle-aged citizens of Harlem who nonetheless look around their neighborhood and see the boarded up buildings, the drug dealers menacing people on the street, and the many troubled families in their midst. For the emphasis on individual responsibility merely points back to the direction of the community and the metamorphosis that its older members have witnessed over time. They realize that many families, including most of their own, lead admirable, responsible, and stable lives, that they monitor the behavior of their children, instill a work ethic, and take care of their friends and relatives. But it falls to them to explain why so many people in their midst have dropped off the mainstream wagon, why there is so much trouble in their community.

Success as the Absence of Failure

Popular accounts of middle age recount the psychological experience of recognizing the finite character of human life and of "taking stock": measuring one's accomplishments against some imagined plan for adult life. It is unclear how widespread this experience is, to what extent it happens absent the prodding of a researcher. In an open-ended elicitation of life stages, for example, the African-American informants in this project never mentioned "middle age" as a period in the life cycle, preferring instead a long period of undifferentiated adulthood, ending in a clearly defined segment called "old age," "going back to childhood," and a variety of other descriptors for the declining period at the end of life.

Older African-Americans clearly know that people age biologically, and they have definitive ideas about the normative behavior and responsibilities entailed in earlier stages of life. However, midlife is a missing category. They recognize that other social groups utilize the term, and therefore they have a distant recognition of its meaning for others. Bit it is not a cognitive category with any emic significance.

It is possible that this lacunae reflects the fact that midlife is part of a middle-class culture that these working poor men and women do not participate in. They are, for example, not free of responsibilities for dependent children even though they are in their fifties. Most have, at a minimum, adolescent children of their own still at home. Some are primary caregivers for grandchildren whom they are raising. None can foresee a time when they will have sufficient resources to retire on their own steam: Only those who have had a career as public-sector employees have pensions or retirement funds, and they are in the decided minority. Indeed, they often worry about how they will fare in old age since their comfort depends to a great extent on the resources (time and money) that their children will be able to make available to them. The question of just how widespread (or class or race bound) the concept of midlife is deserves much greater emphasis than this suggestive account.[15] Suffice it to say, for the moment, that it is not a prominent feature of the life cycle landscape for African-Americans in Harlem.

However, although my informants never offered the term (or any of its equivalents) in elicitation, their life histories are filled with lengthy discussions of the success stories and failures in their lives in these, their mature years. Their frame of reference, however, contrasts sharply with the cultural imagery of the suburban, white middle class where questions of success are concerned (see, esp., Newman 1993). For when the more privileged assess their lives, their referents involve occupational prestige and financial comfort: a successful person is one who has become a professional and whose children are following along a similar path. They are people who own nice homes and live in comfortable communities. African-Americans in the inner city are not unaware of this kind of benchmarking, but they do not engage in it very much. This is not to suggest, for a moment, that they do not think about

financial stability or career mobility. In fact, most face degrees of instability that force them to pour a great deal of psychological energy into
worries over finances and job security.

But they also face trials that are much graver, particularly where
their children are concerned. Living in neighborhoods that are often
dangerous, where drugs seem to be the only growth industry, where
schools are often little more than warehouses, they look upon success
as the absence of major failure. A middle-aged parent is to be congratu-
lated if she or he has managed to raise a family where the children are
not in trouble. Parents of sons worry constantly about the threatening
nature of the streets, about the lure of the underground economy,
about violent confrontations with police. From the age at which they
are old enough to navigate the streets on their own, when parents can
no longer expect to rein them in, sons are at risk. Daughters pose other
kinds of problems. Parents are less worried about their physical safety
and more worried that they will be vulnerable to exploitative relationships, and above all that they will get pregnant young and thus lose
educational and employment opportunities. Great value is placed upon
having children, but mature mothers realize as well that giving birth
too young will cause their daughters a great deal of hardship.

In families where these problems have been bypassed, where parents
have worked hard to keep their children free of influences they consider
pernicious, seeing kids through to adulthood intact is a significant
achievement. As Art Sands explained:

> The thing over here is M-O-N-E-Y, you know what I
> mean? Prestige, money. . . . But my mother raised thirteen
> kids. . . . She died of a stroke, and there was many nights
> she'd be in the house crying and you'd know things would
> bother her. But she raised us. I mean, none of my brothers
> and sisters has spent any time in jail or ever been in any
> really serious trouble.

Barbara James makes the same kind of point in talking about her
daughters, one of whom works in a fast food restaurant and the other
of whom is in high school. She "knocks on wood" that they have es-
caped a fate that many of their friends and neighbors have succumbed
to: "[I'm proud that] my girls haven't got pregnant yet. I never really
had any trouble out of them, they really been great. . . . I always say,
'You can always come back home when you can't go nowhere else.' "

Alvia Ford, who works as a nursing home attendant, has not been so lucky. Her oldest son died young in the course of a conflict between competing drug kings. She buried him before he reached twenty-five. Her firstborn child, a twenty-eight-year-old daughter, is a crack addict who has cycled in and out of treatment programs to no avail. If Alvia buys her daughter clothes, she sells them for crack. Any money that Alvia keeps in the house is ripe for stealing. And now the daughter is sick:

> I learned how to pray a lot, and I [kept my] Bible [near]. I told [my daughter] she'd be better off dead . . . and you're not supposed to say that to your child. But . . . that girl has hurt me so bad. And now she is an HIV carrier. They said to her, you could live forever as an HIV carrier, but if you don't keep yourself clean [free of drugs] it will turn into AIDS.

Alvia has had to confront these problems alone, with no help from the state agencies she has turned to for drug counseling and protection:

> I asked this cop, I told him, please pick her up, take her to jail. He said, 'I just can't pick her up for nothing.' 'Possession of drugs,' I said. 'Pick her up for possession of drugs. Once you take her downtown, then I can come and tell the judge she's a danger to herself, and he can put her away.' But he can't never catch up with her.
>
> After [my son] was dead for a while, I got happy again because I had my two daughters. But this daughter here is not far off [from dying] unless I can get help for her and soon. I don't know of any organizations, unless I took off from work and take her. But she got to be off the street.

For poor people in middle age, who know that life is finite and old age a period of vulnerability, troubled children can spell personal disaster. They add to a persistent anxiety that they face about their futures when they have no margin for error, no means to save for the time when they can no longer take care of themselves.

Alvia has been through a great deal of grief and hardship on account of her children. But she is also dependent upon them in the long run, for she will not have the resources to take care of herself as she moves from midlife to old age. She is going to have to rely on her kin when she can no longer work, and she must worry, in ways that few middle-class people do, about whether her children will be able and willing to take care of her:

> I'm telling people that I'm banking on my baby daughter . . . to be here for me in case, when I get old and I get sick, I have somebody to wait on me. I'm hoping and praying that [my oldest daughter] going to hear this voice and it's going to turn her around. But I don't think so.

Jimmy Hardin also feels anxiety about the future, for he knows that he operates close to the margins and that there is no one else who will look out for him if he ever finds that he cannot look out for himself:

> You got to get up every morning and try to go to work and do something. Once you lay down, that's it. If you're not able to work, you're totally destroyed if you don't have no one to rely on. . . . When everybody's trying to hold you down, you got to try to get up. . . . You . . . [can] rock back on your heels and . . . go down, like a person when they get hit. . . . That's how bad you can be doing sometimes. You don't have a dime in your pocket, and like the whole damn world is closing up on you, and you can be sick all inside with fear, hurt, scared of what's going to happen. Then some little spark comes in, and you say, 'Man, get a hold of yourself.' That's really fear, when you have nothing, and you can't look to any place to get anything.

The kind of problems Alvia's children have had with drugs and guns make them an extreme example of the difficulties poor parents face in their middle-age years. However, Alvia's friends and neighbors know that they too could wind up with problem children because they are so often exposed to people who might lead them astray. Being a good parent, a vigilant parent, is no guarantee that one's children will turn out on the right side of life. Yet it is an imperative that Harlem's midlife parents feel keenly: their diligence, their monitoring, is crucial in increasing the odds that their children will turn out to be honorable people.

David and Lila Williams have been married twenty years and have seven children, the first of whom was born when Lila was seventeen. David works full-time for the New York Transit Authority on the night shift. Lila's job is to make sure her kids stay in school, go to work, and keep out of trouble. The parents agree that they must be vigilant in order to make sure their kids come through adolescence in Harlem in one piece. John explains:

> I don't want [my kids] to spend too much time out there on the street . . . you know, rubbing shoulders with certain people. Because some of them, they don't have really the best intentions. Sometimes the bad will rub off on the good instead of the good rubbing off on the bad. So I try to tell [my kids] if you want to go out, try not to be in front of the building where you've just got nothing to do. . . . It's better to go to the park, play some ball, run round the track, go ride a bike, do something, you know?
>
> Fellows that come to the house, I know their parents. The other guys that come [around], the other friends, I don't let them in my house. I just don't let anybody come in my house.
>
> [We] try to keep a record of what happens to them, how many times they're missing for a class. I call the school regularly. We were just at my daughter's school two weeks ago. I think that's a big concern, trying to make sure that they do what they're supposed to do at school.

Lila adds:

> [The biggest problems we faced when the kids were little] were watching their health, watching when they grew up. The area we lived in was . . . getting bad. So we couldn't let them go outside and play in the street. We had to, you know, take them where they needed to go. When they became teenagers, the biggest problem was just the people they were out with. The people that came to the house, the people they hung out with in school, they had a great influence on them. . . . When I found out that [my kids] were getting a negative influence [from certain friends] you had to make sure they cut those out. And once we did that . . . there was a change in attitude of the children.

It would be comforting to these parents to believe that these strategies always pay off. Yet virtually everyone in the community can name families where the parents did everything possible to prevent their kids from "going bad," only to find they were fighting a loosing battle. Carol Estes talks about her neighbors, a hard-working couple with kids who are in deep trouble despite their best efforts:

> [My friend] used to work at American Express. . . . Her husband works in the flea market on [the main thorough-fare in Harlem]. They pull together very hard to make things [work]. They don't bother people about things, and if you ever need a favor from her, you can just ask. . . . They have three children, and you can't blame them for what the children are doing. Their oldest son, I think he dropped out of eleventh grade. Their baby son, he got back in school because he got left back [a grade] last year. . . . Their middle son is messing with drugs, selling drugs, and he has got the baby son running behind him.

In a period of economic instability, even members of the solid middle class worry about the fate of their children. Opportunities appear to be closing down, the competition for a piece of the pie is fierce, and no one (save those with inherited wealth) can be absolutely sure that their efforts to foster their children's well-being will be successful. But they have many carrots to dangle in front of their kids. Families living in the poverty-stricken neighborhoods of central Harlem face more than the average rate of risk that their children will be dragged down by drugs and gangs. They can make few real promises about their children's futures. Given the pervasiveness of these problems, midlife parents can never be sure that their best efforts will be enough. Jane Eaton, who has a son in his early twenties and a nephew of the same age to raise, described this uncertainty well:

> It's hard 'cause they have so much distractions out there, you know? 'Cause they see . . . it's this big temptation. They see, like, there's a lot of money to be made in selling drugs. But it's also very dangerous. If you got a 'I don't care kid', well . . . I'm happy that my kids are sort of scared of the street. I'm telling them, 'Those guys will get you in jail.' But you have a lot of . . . that fast money.

Harlem families in poor areas have no cocoon of protection that guarantees that such a tragic fate will never befall them. Hence, those who have managed, by good fortune and hard work, to see their families through the storms of adolescence and early adulthood without confronting these problems thank their blessings and define themselves as success stories.

CONCLUSION

It would be a mistake to try to understand the experience of middle age in a working poor African-American community like Harlem if one were to simply take the present on its own terms. Instead, I have tried to show that the particular problems that beset midlife men and women in this inner-city setting are "products" of a historical transformation that they have experienced in the course of their own lives. Harlem has gone from being a segregated working- and middle-class community in the 1940s and 1950s to a place where poverty is widespread and the social problems it engenders difficult to escape. This does not mean everyone in Harlem is poor or that an urban underclass has engulfed all of its residents. In fact, the "bad apples" are relatively few, but they cause major problems for the upstanding people who do not earn enough money to get away from them.

For people in midlife, this evolution has been a source of dismay. They remember rather vividly a different way of life, a disciplined existence of churchgoing neighbors, vigilant parents, and open doors. It is a transformation that has had an effect on many of them in the form of unemployment, deteriorating housing, and increasing danger on the streets. Now that most are parents, with children in their teenage years and early twenties, they confront the need to protect them from dangers that they did not have to contend with in their own youth. Moreover, they must come to grips with the fact that a sizable minority of their fellow Harlem dwellers have been unable to do the same. The children of these "failed" parents now menace the rest of the community.

Yet this generation of midlife adults also knows another kind of history, a history of place and race that is more positive. Having come up from the Jim Crow South, they have lived to see the Civil Rights era open doors that were tightly shut in their youth. They have moved from places where they could not walk the streets or board buses or attend schools of their choosing busted open with legal sledgehammers. Jane Easton is not sanguine about the current state of African-American ghettos, but she would never trade the present racial situation for that of the 1950s:

You have a lot of different jobs available to you now, to minorities, that they didn't have before. You can practically be anything you want to be now. A long time ago, you couldn't. Who would have thought you would see a black mayor?"[16] You got a lot of black mayors, you got all kinds of jobs. I mean, who would have even thought, besides shining somebody's shoes or dealing up the office. Now you have the education. We haven't hit . . . president, but we're sure knocking on the door.

Jane is not suggesting that equality is a reality or that prosperity is a common condition in her community. On the contrary, she realizes that for most people life is very tough. She speaks of businesses moving across the border, of the impact of the North American Free Trade Agreement (NAFTA) on jobs, and the pressure on American wages that is driving so many working people below the poverty line. But she also knows many people her own age whose futures might have been nothing more than working in the peanut mills for lousy wages. Her vantage point of the present begins with this kind of past.

The generation of midlife Harlem dwellers represented in this chapter do not necessarily see eye-to-eye with their own children on these issues. Having never witnessed the Jim Crow South, their kids can only know this past as a history, not a lived reality. They have a different set of benchmarks, in which race appears to be hardening as a line of division. Nationalist movements in the ghettos, backlash movements in the white suburbs—these are the political realities that the younger generation has grown up with. And, one imagines, this divergent historical reality will shape the middle-age experience of new generations differently. This merely points back to the underlying thesis of this chapter: place (a combination of period and locale) and race matter a great deal in shaping images and experiences of middle age. I would argue that this is true, perhaps to an even greater degree, of midlife than of other points in the life cycle. To the extent that middle age involves a kind of assessment, a meditation upon where one has been and where one may be able to go in the last phase of life, midlife calls forth generational memories, cultural grids through which an individual's life trajectory, and the transformations of his or her community, are evaluated (see Newman 1996a).

Notes

1. Participants in this project are the older relatives of young people working in fast food restaurants in central Harlem. Some two hundred of them—African-Americans, Dominicans, and Puerto Ricans—participated in my two-year study of low wage workers in 1993–95 (see Newman 1996b).

2. This is undoubtedly true of old age, too, but I would not argue it for other, earlier, stages.

3. Recent accounts suggest that the urban north is not alone in the trend toward increasing crime and drug traffic. In particular, the southern communities from whence my informants hail are also becoming more dangerous places to live. (See "In Selma, Everything and Nothing Changed" *New York Times,* 2 August 1994, p. 11.)

4. See Carol Stack (1996) for a description of persistent attachment to southern communities among blacks who were born in the north but have returned to the South in record numbers.

5. Black gay men in Harlem follow similar patterns of block settlement (Hawkeswood 1995).

6. Jimmy's memories parallel Elijah Anderson's (1990) research on the transformation of his inner-city neighborhood in Philadelphia. See also James Coleman (1988, 107) for a theoretical discussion of monitoring as an aspect of social capital.

7. The Mollen Commission, formed in 1993 to investigate police corruption in New York City, discovered that the Thirtieth Precinct (which covers much of the area where my informants live) has been mired in kickback schemes involving local drug dealers, harassment, and a variety of other forms of corruption. Many years of citizen complaints about the police had gone unheaded until this commission took an official look.

8. In general, black men have done poorly in the labor market compared to black women, in part because of educational differences, but also because women have been able to work in domains that were closed to men (e.g., domestic service), while the jobs that traditionally attract men have been evaporating with each wave of plant shutdowns.

9. One might be tempted to attribute this "burden to explain" to the research encounter. These interviews were all conducted by an African-American doctoral student with far more years of education than these informants. However, the same pressure to account for the fate of fellow members of one's racial group is documented in the literature on the African-American middle class. See Ellis Cose (1993) for more on this.

10. Charles Murray (1990), the conservative critic of the welfare system, has recently written popular articles warning that a white underclass is forming out of the increasing population of white women who are having out-of-wedlock births. It is conceivable that the old category of "white trash" may be resurrected here with many of the same consequences for nonpoor whites. At the moment, however, we are a long way from expecting whites in general to account for the deviant behavior of some member of their racial group.

11. See Feagin and Sikes (1994) in addition to Cose for further discussion of

the psychological burdens of middle-class African-Americans charged with either abandoning their race brethren or explaining to others how the masses.of blacks came to be poor.

12. The most prominent example in 1994 was the O. J. Simpson murder trial, a veritable litmus test of racial ideology that saw most whites believing he was guilty (giving no special dispensation for his upbringing in a poor black neighborhood) and a majority of blacks believing both in his innocence and the unfair nature of the judicial process (giving weight to Simpson's race in both aspects).

13. We shall see in the next section that many of my informants who still have young children at home do indeed spend a great deal of time and energy monitoring their behavior and their movements outside the home. Nonetheless, Barbara argues that there are far too few "old-fashioned" families of this kind.

14. Some economists have argued that there is no evidence for immigrant/native-born competition in the job market. Others have taken the opposite viewpoint and have said that in those areas where immigrants live, wage depression among the native born is widespread. See Borjas et al. (1992).

15. In a companion pilot study of middle-aged Latinos in New York City—conducted during the same 1993–95 time period—it became clear that there is no real Spanish equivalent for the term "middle age." The term had no meaning in Spanish, whether Puerto Rican, Mexican, or Dominican translators were used. Similarly, open-ended elicitation of life stages never yielded a single example of middle age as a "subdivision" of adulthood, much less a distinctive period in the life cycle.

16. She refers here to David Dinkins, then mayor of New York City.

REFERENCES

Anderson, E. 1990. *Streetwise.* Chicago: University of Chicago Press.

Borjas, George, Richard Freeman, and Lawrence Katz. 1992. "On the Labor Market Effects of Immigration and Trade." In *Immigration and the Workforce,* edited by G. Borjas and R. Freeman, 213–44. Chicago: University of Chicago Press.

City of New York, Department of Urban Planning. 1993. *Socio-Economic Profiles: A Portrait of New York City's Community Districts from the 1980 and 1990 Censuses of Population and Housing.* New York: Department of Urban Planning.

Coleman, James. 1988. "Social Capital in the Creation of Human Capital." *American Journal of Sociology,* suppl. 94:S95–S120.

Cose, Ellis. 1993. *Rage of the Privileged Class.* New York: HarperCollins.

Feagin, J., and M. Sikes. 1994. *Living with Racism: The Black Middle-Class Experience.* Boston: Beacon Press.

Hawkeswood, William. 1995. *One of the Children: Black Gay Men in Harlem.* Berkeley and Los Angeles: University of California Press.

Lehmann, Nicholas. 1993. *The Promised Land.* New York: Knopf.

Newman, Katherine. 1988. *Falling from Grace: The Experience of Downward Mobility in the American Middle Class.* New York: Free Press.

———. 1993. *Declining Fortunes: The Withering of the American Dream.* New York: Basic Books.

———. 1996a. "Ethnography, Biography and Cultural History: Generational Paradigms in Human Development." In *Ethnography and Human Development,* edited by Richard Jessor, Anne Colby, and Richard Shweder, 371–94. Chicago: University of Chicago Press.

———. 1996b. "Working Poor: Low Wage Employment in the Lives of Harlem Youth." In *Transitions through Adolescence,* edited by Julia Graber et al. Hillsdale, N.J.: Erlbaum Associates.

Stack, Carol. 1996. *Call to Home: African-Americans Reclaim the Rural South.* New York: Basic Books.

Lucinda P. Bernheimer, Department of Psychiatry, University of California, Los Angeles

Margaret Morganroth Gullette, Independent Scholar, 68 Pembroke Street, Newton, Massachusetts 02158

Sudhir Kakar, Psychoanalyst and Independent Scholar, C-22, Gitanjali Enclave, New Delhi, 110017 India

Robert A. LeVine, Graduate School of Education, Harvard University

Sarah LeVine, Graduate School of Education, Harvard University

Margaret Lock, Department of Humanities and Social Studies in Medicine, McGill University

Usha Menon, Department of Psychology, Sociology and Anthropology, Drexel University

Katherine Newman, Kennedy School of Government, Harvard University

Bradd Shore, Department of Anthropology, Emory University

Richard A. Shweder, Committee on Human Development, University of Chicago

Thomas S. Weisner, Departments of Psychiatry and Anthropology, University of California, Los Angeles